Franklin, OOPS, Mud & Cupcake

For Harland and Lenore,

Hope you enjoy

our River Adventures!

Michael

Kathleen

OTHER BOOKS BY MICHAEL D. PITT

Three Seasons in the Wind: 950 Kilometres by Canoe down Northern Canada's Thelon River.

Second Edition. Hornby House Publications. 2000.
(co-authored with Kathleen Pitt)

Beyond the End of the Road:
A Winter of Contentment North of the Arctic Circle.

Agio Publishing House. 2009.

Franklin, OOPS, Mud & Cupcake

CANOEING THE COPPERMINE, SEAL, ANDERSON & SNOWDRIFT RIVERS IN NORTHERN CANADA

MICHAEL D. PITT

Agio

PUBLISHING HOUSE

Agio
PUBLISHING HOUSE

151 Howe Street, Victoria BC Canada V8V 4K5

Cover and book design by Marsha Batchelor.
Editorial insight and advice by Tracey D. Hooper
and Bruce Batchelor. All photographs by the author
and Kathleen T. Pitt. Janice Power provided technical assistance for some Coppermine River images.
Route and location maps prepared by Nola Johnston
Graphic Design & Illustration.

*For rights information and bulk orders, please
contact:* info@agiopublishing.com *or go to*
www.agiopublishing.com

Franklin, Oops, Mud & Cupcake
ISBN 978-1-927755-12-9 (trade paperback)
ISBN 978-1-927755-13-6 (ebook)

Printed on acid-free paper that includes no fibre from
endangered forests. Agio Publishing House is a socially
responsible company, measuring success on a
triple-bottom-line basis.

10   9   8   7   6   5   4   3   2   1

DEDICATION

To Kathleen, my companion in life and adventure.
People often tell me how lucky I am to have a wife
who shares my passion for "roughing it" in northern Canada.
I usually smile, and simply nod my head in agreement.
"That's right," I say. "I sometimes think that Kathleen enjoys paddling
down wilderness rivers even more than I do. I am one very lucky guy."

TABLE OF CONTENTS

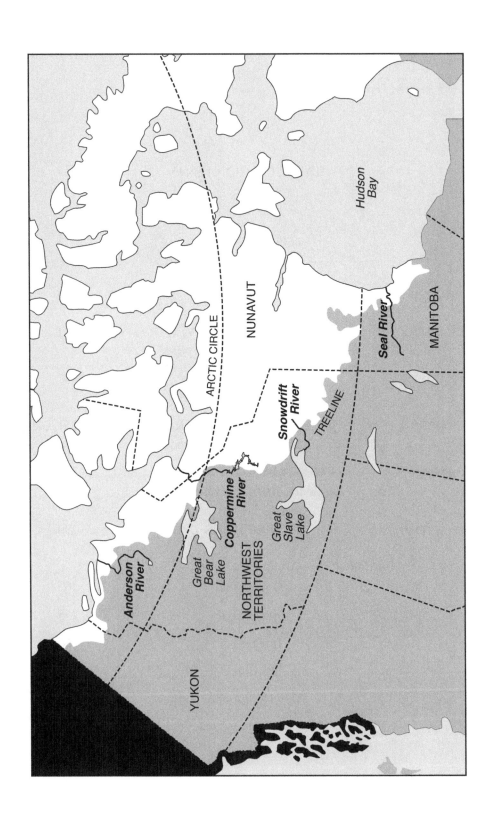

INTRODUCTION

T his book details four extended canoe trips in northern Canada. For me, the Coppermine, Seal, Anderson and Snowdrift Rivers offered true wilderness experiences because no towns or villages existed along any of their banks. And, despite obvious similarities among all paddling expeditions, each of these four adventures offered distinct memories and surprises, most of which were enjoyable but some of which were decidedly uncomfortable. I should warn you, however, that no one died on any of these canoe trips. No one broke any bones. No one even got sick. This book is not about danger lurking around every bend or harrowing escapes from near-death situations. No. This book is simply about what it's like to be on four glorious rivers.

In 1995, Kathleen and I joined one other couple to descend 645 km down the Coppermine River. Well, "descend" might not actually be the most appropriate word to describe this trip, which began by flying in a Twin Otter approximately 230 km north of Yellowknife to Winter Lake, very near the site of abandoned Fort Enterprise, where Sir John Franklin overwintered in 1820/21.

The primary problem with this starting point, from a canoeing perspective, was that the Coppermine River system could be reached only by crossing over the height of land. From our first camp at Winter Lake, we spent 11 days dragging, portaging, tracking, lining and occasionally paddling our canoes 110 km to reach the Coppermine River system at Point Lake. From there, we travelled another 16 days to reach the village of Coppermine (now Kugluktuk) on the Arctic coast, at 67°50' N. Our trip began in the mostly treeless country between Winter and Point Lakes, passed through dense spruce forests surrounding Redrock and Rocknest Lakes, and ended in the mountains and rolling hills of the tundra, also known as the Barren Grounds.

Of all the northern rivers Kathleen and I have paddled, the Coppermine, by far, was the most physically demanding. This river also tested the limits of our paddling skills with numerous and often very difficult rapids.

In 1997, Kathleen and I ventured out alone down the Seal River in northern Manitoba. Of the four major rivers in northern Manitoba, only the Seal remained completely undeveloped. We chartered a Beaver float plane from Lynn Lake to fly into Shethanei Lake, just downriver from the small Chipewyan community of Tadoule. From there, we paddled 280 km down the Seal River to its mouth on the western shore of Hudson Bay, approximately 70 km north of the town of Churchill.

Until early 1997, Kathleen and I didn't know anything about Manitoba rivers but became intrigued by the Seal River based on what we read in a four-page brochure produced by Manitoba Natural Resources for the Canadian Heritage Rivers System (CHRS):

> *The Seal begins its course ringed by magnificent sand-crowned*
> *eskers. Its velocity accelerates dramatically into the rapids*
> *and gorges which surround Great Island. Beyond the island,*
> *the river leaves the boreal forest and enters a sparsely-treed,*
> *transitional sub-Arctic environment of tundra and heath,*
> *christened by the native peoples as the "Land of Little Sticks."*
> *Finally, the Seal flows through barren Arctic tundra, huge*
> *boulder fields and complex rapids, spilling into a beautiful*
> *estuary where its fresh waters mix with the salt of Hudson Bay.*

Now that sounded very interesting. There also existed the exciting possibility of seeing polar bears. Churchill is famous for polar bear watching, particularly in October and November, when the bears congregate in town waiting for the ice to re-form on Hudson Bay. Before then, during the summer months, the bears wander up and down the coast. We would almost certainly encounter these true predators.

In 1999, Kathleen and I paddled down the Anderson River. Twenty-seven days and 557 km from Colville Lake to Wood Bay/Liverpool Bay on the Arctic coast, at 69°42' N. A trip of constant daylight. A trip that took us from the boreal forest out onto the open tundra.

Kathleen and I began this journey not by flying into the headwaters from a northern community but simply by paddling away on June 20 from our isolated one-room cabin where we had been overwintering since January 31.

Our 141 days in that cabin at the north end of Colville Lake are chronicled in my 2009 book, *Beyond the End of the Road: A Winter of Contentment North of the Arctic Circle*. If you have ever fantasized about living simply on the frozen shores of a quiet northern lake, I think you would enjoy our story.

Anyway, back to the Anderson River. Kathleen and I canoed away from the cabin immediately after breakup, on the spring flood, and spent a great deal of time scouting and running high water through narrow, twisting canyons. Along the way, we encountered grizzly bears and cold temperatures. We often struggled against strong headwinds, and sometimes wondered and fretted if we would ever reach the Arctic coast.

In 2001, Kathleen and I ventured out alone again to paddle 26 days and 330 km down the Snowdrift River, from Lynx Lake to Austin Lake. We intended to start this trip at the exact location where we began our Thelon River adventure in 1993 (chronicled in Kathleen's and my book, *Three Seasons in the Wind: 950 Kilometres by Canoe Down Northern Canada's Thelon River*). Instead of travelling east toward Hudson Bay, however, we planned to paddle west toward Great Slave Lake. We would start at the same spot on Lynx Lake but would end up in completely different watersheds. The Thelon River leads to Hudson Bay and the Atlantic Ocean. The Snowdrift River leads to Great Slave Lake, the Mackenzie River and then beyond to the Arctic Ocean.

According to a six-page summary prepared by Ed Struzik as part of the series of Northwest Territories River Profiles:

> *For someone looking for a bit of everything in a northern river, [the Snowdrift] is the river for you. Beginning in the tundra ecosystem, the Snowdrift flows through the tundra/ treeline transition zone into the thick of a mixed forest system. There are lake(s), fast portions of river, and many extremely picturesque waterfalls. Although it is relatively close to Yellowknife, it is rarely travelled.*

So there's a brief summary of the kinds of adventures each of these four rivers provided. Before beginning the river accounts, however, I will devote a chapter to tell you a bit about how Kathleen and I prefer to paddle wilderness rivers. I'm not saying that our way of river running is the best way. I'm just saying that's how we like to paddle. It's the best way for us.

CHAPTER 1

RIVER RUNNING

ONE COUPLE VERSUS A GROUP

Kathleen and I very much prefer to paddle on our own, an approach that is considered wrong, even foolhardy by most "experts" and wilderness paddling books. The general recommendation is that all wilderness canoe trips should include at least three tandem boats. If one boat is lost or damaged by capsize or broaching on a rock, then the remaining two boats can each accommodate one of the unfortunate paddlers. Also, three tandem boats with six people provides a critical mass for camp chores and the flexibility to spell off a tired or sick paddler. All of this makes good sense.

I should say though, that Kathleen and I never capsize on wilderness canoe trips. Never. I'm a firm believer that you should never capsize on wilderness rivers. Despite this confidence bordering on hubris, people still ask us, "Well, what if you do capsize?"

I tell them again that we don't capsize. Ever. Kathleen and I are experienced. We know our skills. We work well as a team. We are always reading the river, anticipating what hazards might be waiting for us downstream. And, if the truth be told, as I am about to tell you, more boats and more people sometimes just inject bravado and peer pressure into the paddling expedition.

Imagine that six people are standing on shore, looking at the rapid, and deciding whether or not to run. One pair of paddlers is definitely worried and apprehensive. They would rather portage. The other four paddlers start saying things like, "I can run this. You should be able to run it too. Come on. We don't even need to scout the entire rapid. Let's just go. What are you worried about?"

So all six people climb back into their canoes and turn down into the noisy, rocky maelstrom of white and foam. The worried pair of paddlers becomes hesitant. Their strokes become tentative. Hesitation and tentative strokes often produce very bad results in a rapid. The frightened paddlers make it halfway down before broaching on a midstream rock. Their Kevlar canoe wraps, shudders for a second or two, and then shatters into pieces. Gear and now-panicked canoeists float away at the mercy of the unforgiving current. Maybe all of the gear and both canoeists are saved. That is certainly the best-case scenario.

So, one of the tandem boats has been lost. The remaining two boats now have three paddlers and approximately 50% more gear. This is not a good option. On all of our wilderness canoe trips, our boat is full, pretty much from the beginning to the very end of the trip. Kathleen and I really don't have room for more people and more gear in our canoe.

In this example, the recommended group size of three canoes and six people caused the problem. The capsized couple, on their own, would almost certainly have portaged the rapid. No one has ever capsized on the portage trail. There would have been no shattered canoe. There would have been no potentially missing gear or food. There would have been no frightened paddlers.

PREPARATION AND
AVOIDING PROBLEMS IS THE BEST APPROACH

Kathleen and I feel quite safe on our own. We never run any rapid unless both of us agree to run. We often scout where others might not. We are alone on the river, so we must not capsize. Ever. Kathleen and I actually feel secure in our aloneness, not threatened. We are free to paddle when we want. We are free to camp where and when we want. We are free to take unplanned rest days and hikes when we want. We are free to stop to botanize and birdwatch when we want. We are free to be ourselves.

I should also point out that larger groups do not even guarantee rescue of capsized paddlers and gear. I have read and heard of many fatalities that have occurred among larger groups. A mid-river capsize on a large, Arctic river can initiate fatal hypothermia before help arrives. A foot entrapment can cause drowning before help arrives. Large groups can improve safety and security, but they provide no such guarantee. Wilderness canoeing emancipates the paddler from regulations and rules. Travel in groups if you wish. Paddle alone if you prefer. It's your choice no matter what anyone says.

I am not, however, recommending that anyone should just go out, buy a canoe, charter a float plane, and head off down any of the rivers in this book. Such a recommendation on my part would be irresponsible. Appropriate wilderness and paddling skills are absolutely essential before heading out. I began backpacking into wilderness areas at the age of 12. Wilderness travel has remained a nearly constant aspect of my life since then. Kathleen and I took up canoeing in 1986 and immediately joined the Beaver Canoe Club in Burnaby, British Columbia. This was the best decision of our paddling lives. The club provided basic instructions in canoeing and paddling safety. The club also provided companions and guides for year-round canoeing throughout southwestern British Columbia. Nearly every Sunday for four years, we paddled with the club to develop and hone our whitewater skills and confidence.

I'm not suggesting that Kathleen and I are elite paddlers. We are not. But in our prime, we were very competent. We have good forward strokes and excellent balance in the canoe. We have a strong forward and backward ferry. We can hit eddies nearly at will, along river banks as well as behind rocks in mid-channel. We can side slip confidently into slower water while descending rock gardens. I have a strong high brace. Kathleen has a strong low brace. Both of us have effective stationary and sculling draw and pry strokes. We lean the canoe instinctively when crossing eddy lines. We communicate very well and have nearly identical approaches to running the river. These skills took a long time to develop and have allowed us to enjoy the rivers described in this book. If you don't know what these strokes are, or if you are not skilled with these strokes, then I recommend that you don't attempt to paddle wilderness rivers on your own.

The first wilderness canoe trip that Kathleen and I took was with two other couples from our Beaver Canoe Club, on the South Nahanni River in August of 1990. Most paddlers have heard of the Nahanni River and are aware of the whitewater challenges in the Rock Gardens below the Moose Ponds, where we began our trip. This headwaters section of the Nahanni River is approximately 50 km of nearly continuous Class II–Class IV rapids, depending on water levels. Our flights into the Moose Ponds from Blackstone Landing on the Liard River were delayed two days due to heavy rains. Canoeists coming off the river reported that Kraus Hot Springs was under water. The Liard River itself was choked with logs and debris pell-melling down the river. Our group of three canoes likely faced higher than normal water levels and more difficult rapids than usual in the Rock Gardens. We ran them all without incident, and, except for the first rapid, without scouting. I mention this to give you an idea of our paddling skills so that you might better judge whether you should attempt the rivers in this book.

IRC SCALE FOR RATING RAPIDS

You will notice throughout this book that I often refer to the class of a rapid. For those of you who aren't familiar with this classification, I offer the following from Madsen and Wilson's *Rivers of the Yukon*.

INTERNATIONAL RIVER CLASSIFICATION SCALE

Class I: Moving water with a few riffles and small waves. Few or no obstructions.

Class II: Easy rapids with waves up to one metre (three feet). Channels are wide and obvious without scouting. Some manoeuvring is necessary.

Class III: Rapids with high, irregular waves that could swamp an open canoe. Narrow passages often require scouting and complex manoeuvring.

Class IV: Long, difficult rapids with constricted passages that often require precise manoeuvring in turbulent water. Scouting from shore is often necessary, and conditions make rescue difficult. Generally impossible for open canoes. Boaters in closed canoes and kayaks should be able to Eskimo roll.

Class V: Extremely difficult, long and violent rapids with complicated routes that should be scouted from shore. There is a significant hazard to life in the event of mishap. It is essential to be able to Eskimo roll.

Class VI: Difficulties of Class V carried to the extreme of navigability. Nearly impossible and very dangerous—(only) for experts who have taken all possible rescue precautions. Serious risk to life.

In my experience, virtually all serious canoeists can learn to paddle Class II rapids with confidence after only a few weekends of practice. It is also my experience that only a very small percentage of serious canoeists ever become confident and proficient in Class III rapids.

SPRAY DECK

Note that Class III rapids "have high, irregular waves that could swamp an open canoe." Kathleen and I always paddle wilderness rivers with a spray deck on our canoe, which means that we are not truly an open canoe.

We use a spray deck for a variety of reasons. Most importantly, the spray deck keeps our gear dry when it rains. The spray deck also seems to reduce wind resistance. And, the spray deck certainly can deflect large waves that might otherwise swamp an open canoe. I should say, though, that our spray deck does not ever influence our decision about whether or not to run the rapid. We run the rapid because we think we can, based on our paddling skills without the spray deck. I strongly believe that it is a potentially serious mistake for people to run rapids that they normally would portage just because they have a spray deck. A spray deck does not substitute for, nor does it augment, paddling skills.

Commercial spray decks for canoes generally come with the spray skirt permanently attached to the deck. Perhaps it is only canoeing mythology, but we had heard that capsized canoeists had occasionally drowned because they became entangled in the spray skirt. So Kathleen made our nylon spray deck and spray skirt as two separate pieces. After fitting the deck to the canoe, Kathleen cut out cockpits for the bow and stern paddlers. She then sewed a sleeve on each cockpit, leaving a small gap in each sleeve. We then inserted a poly butyl pipe into the sleeve, with the two ends held together with a plastic connector. Kathleen then made the two spray skirts with a sleeve at the bottom to enclose elastic that fitted snugly over the poly butyl coaming. Another sleeve at the top of the spray skirt contained a drawstring to hold the spray skirt tightly to our chest. This design would prevent water from pouring into the cockpit, and would also allow the spray skirt to easily come loose from the coaming in case of a capsize. We would never become entrapped, and we could wear the skirt or not, depending on river and weather conditions.

We attached the spray deck with stainless steel snaps to the underside of the wooden gunwales of our 16-foot (4.9 m) canoe, a model known as the Explorer, made by Mad River. We paddle the Explorer because we believe it is an excellent all-purpose boat. It has good secondary stability, and is slightly rockered, bow and stern, for manoeuvring in rapids. Yet it tracks well on lake water, even under windy conditions. The Explorer weighs 72 lb. (32.7 kg), and is light enough and short enough for me to portage on my own. Longer and heavier canoes are too unwieldy for me. I am not particularly strong at 5 ft. 6 in. (1.67 m) and 140 lb. (65.5 kg). Both Kathleen and I, however, do have stamina and determination. *[Note: Canoes are still marketed in imperial units, which is why I presented the length and weight of our Explorer canoe in feet and pounds, with metres and kilograms in parentheses, respectively. Similarly, I'm an old guy, and still think of my height and weight in feet and pounds, respectively.]*

ROYALEX VERSUS KEVLAR VERSUS FIBREGLASS VERSUS WOOD AND CANVAS

Our Explorer is made of a type of plastic known by the trade name of Royalex. The canoe hull has two layers of Royalex enclosing a foam core, plus an outer layer of vinyl on each side. This canoe hull can be fairly easily repaired in the field but is very resistant to damage. Early in our canoeing career, Kathleen and I saw a Royalex canoe wrap around a rock, with its bow and stern nearly touching. The group pulled the canoe free, towed it to shore, and jumped up and down a few times on the jackknifed hull until it popped back into shape. The paddlers then got back in and happily canoed downstream. At that moment, we decided that a Royalex canoe was the canoe for us.

Royalex canoes, though, are not as rigid as canoes made of fibreglass or Kevlar. Royalex canoes tend to flex, which means that they are slower than fibreglass or Kevlar canoes of similar designs. That doesn't bother me, though, as I am not in any particular hurry on a wilderness canoe trip. Kathleen and I once gave a slide show on our Thelon River trip to an audience in which sat the owner of Western Canoeing & Kayaking, maker of the iconic Clipper Tripper canoe. After the presentation, he said, "You know, you can do these northern trips in my fibreglass canoes. They are a lot lighter than Royalex."

I told him about the time I saw that wrapped Royalex canoe paddle away after being pulled off the rock. I also told him about the time I saw a Kevlar canoe burst into a zillion pieces as it wrapped around a post in a very slow-moving current in the Fraser River delta. "That's why I paddle a plastic boat, Marlin. Because a person might wrap around a rock."

"Well," he asked, "how often have you ever wrapped around a rock?"

"Never," I said.

He looked smug, as though he had proven his point. And maybe he had. Even so, I like to paddle a Royalex canoe. *[Note: In April 2014, Royalex went out of production. It could be that there will be no more Royalex canoes, which would make many wilderness river paddlers very unhappy. The good news is that Esquif Canoes, in Quebec, announced almost immediately that they were developing a material called T-Formex that will be "10 percent lighter and 20 times more abrasion resistant than Royalex." Very good news indeed!]*

You might be wondering about those classic canoes made of wood and canvas. Such canoes are certainly beautiful. Such beauty comes with a price, though. Wood and canvas canoes are heavy, particularly when wet. Wood and canvas canoes require a keel to protect the canvas, which means such canoes require deeper water and are more difficult to manoeuvre in rock gardens. I have never seen anyone paddling a wilderness river in a wood and canvas canoe. I'm not saying it doesn't happen. I'm just saying I have never seen it. A wood and canvas canoe would certainly not be my choice.

NAVIGATING WITH TOPOGRAPHIC MAPS AND COMPASS

I also like to travel with topographic maps and compass. I love looking at the maps. I enjoy working with a compass. I don't need, or even want, a GPS. The compass doesn't need batteries. The compass doesn't need satellites. For me, topographic maps and compass seem to signify wilderness trips. By reading the map, I always know where I am within 100 m or so. Well, I know where I am almost all of the time. Okay, I know where I am most of the time.

And in reality, in most situations, I don't need to know exactly where I am. Besides, how can I get lost on a river? The river goes downhill. The river has banks on both sides. The river has tributaries spilling in from the sides. I can locate tributaries on the topographic maps. The river has canyons and rapids and calm sections and waterfalls. I can locate these features on the topographic maps. I can't get lost on the river. Well, it doesn't seem likely that I can get lost on the river. Yes, I know what you're saying, there was that time on the Thelon River in 1993 when Kathleen and I had misplaced ourselves for three to four hours. Even so, topographic maps and a compass will always be my familiar, comfortable, navigational tools.

PLANNING OUR RIVER TRIPS

Before each trip, I estimate the distance to be travelled on each paddling day by using the "three times forefinger-drag method." Let me illustrate. Suppose that I am using 1:50,000 maps. Gridded squares on these Canadian topographic maps are all 1 km × 1 km. I place my right forefinger at the starting point and drag it along the map, usually next to the shoreline, to get my best estimate, 1 km at a time, for the day's journey. I estimate when I have dragged 1 km by looking at the gridded squares as my finger passes through. The first bit of shoreline might go through 20 percent of the length of a square. The second bit might go through 50 percent of the length of the next square. The third bit might go through the full length of two squares or more. When I drag a little way into this third bit, I count *one*. I do this very quickly. I can count off 20 km in less than 30 seconds. I don't explicitly measure anything. I do this for the entire tentative itinerary, writing down the daily distances as I go along. I then hide this piece of paper and repeat the process after I have forgotten the recorded distances. It usually takes only a few minutes for me to forget. I then repeat the process a third time, and assume that the average of the three numbers is my best estimate of the distance.

The gridded squares on 1:250,000 topographic maps measure 10 km × 10 km. For these larger squares, I use the same "three times forefinger-drag method" but estimate distances in 5-km chunks.

I prepare this tentative itinerary to determine approximately how long the trip will take. I don't necessarily expect to be exactly where the tentative itinerary suggests on any particular day. While on the trip, however, I frequently refer to the tentative itinerary to make sure that I am making reasonable progress. Falling too far behind the tentative itinerary suggests that longer days, or fewer rest days, might be necessary.

For your information, I have listed these distances and tentative itineraries, in both kilometres and miles, for each of the four rivers, at the end of their respective chapters. I think that you will enjoy these stories more by referring to this information.

For all those readers who prefer imperial units of measure, I have provided some kilometre and mile equivalencies in Appendix 1. For your information, 1 km equals 0.62 miles. For a quick and easy ballpark estimate, you can simply divide the number of kilometres (km) in half (and then add little bit more).

Finally, I commonly refer to distances in metres. It's OK if you just read "yards" when you see metres. Although a metre is actually a little more than 3 inches longer than a yard, my references to metres were always just visual estimates. When I say, for example, "I saw a sow grizzly and her cub heading directly toward the tarp, only 100 m away," I didn't actually measure the distance. So it's fine if you just read 100 yards. In fact, 100 yards might very well have been more accurate than 100 m anyway.

EMERGENCY COMMUNICATION

Accidents and medical emergencies can certainly occur on wilderness canoe trips. As members of the Beaver Canoe Club, Kathleen and I were able to borrow the club's Emergency Position-Indicating Radio Beacon (EPIRB) for all of our northern canoeing adventures. In an emergency, we could simply push the button to send out a signal, and rescue would soon be on its way. Or so the theory goes. There is, however, no voice communication with an EPIRB; it only provides a signal that help is needed. So, if one of us had suffered a burst appendix, or a broken leg, we could push the button and hope for the best. We would not have known, however, if help was actually on the way.

Many articles have been written on the usefulness or appropriateness of an EPIRB on wilderness canoe trips. Many of these articles recommend against EPIRBs. Current literature stresses the importance of satellite phones. Indeed, many outfitters require their clients to carry satellite phones. Kathleen and I paddled these isolated northern rivers without taking any communication device (apart from the aforementioned EPIRB). Is that approach prudent? Likely not. Is that approach wrong? Not if that's how we feel comfortable travelling. I paddled these four rivers to escape. I would not have truly escaped while clinging to an umbilical cord. That's just how I felt.

Without doubt, satellite phones can be extremely useful in situations of a burst appendix or a broken leg. They are next to useless for a paddler with a foot entrapment, whose head has been pulled under water by the current. In such a situation, the paddler's life expectancy equals the amount of time they can hold their breath. Satellite phones are totally useless when they are submerged in a pack beneath a log-jam after a capsize. Satellite phones increase safety and security, but they guarantee neither. Caution, good judgement, skill and experience provide the greatest degree of safety and security.

All that being said, I have recently heard of three cases where wilderness canoeists suffered heart attacks. Two of these people survived because their group carried a satellite phone, which they used to arrange for emergency evacuation. As I become older, and increasingly aware of my own vulnerability, I am more inclined to take a satellite phone on future wilderness canoe trips. I seem to have misplaced the bravado and sense of invincibility of my younger days.

FIRST AID AND OTHER REPAIRS

Heart attacks, burst appendices and broken legs do not happen very often.

Minor accidents and less significant medical issues are much more likely. Kathleen and I always take a first aid kit with the following items:

CONTENTS OF WILDERNESS AND CANOEING FIRST AID KIT

SUPPLIES

Adhesive wound closures (1/8 × 3 inches)
Alcohol wipes (6)
Bandages (assorted)
Cavit (temporary tooth filling)
Compresses (12, non-adherent, 4 × 3 inches)
First aid manual
Gauze cleansing pads
Lighter/matches
Medical tape
Moleskin
Pressure bandage (2)
Q-tips (100)
Scissors
Tensor bandage (1)
Triangular bandage (1)
Tweezers

EXTERNAL MEDICINES

Bactroban (antibiotic ointment)
Dermovate (cortisone to aid healing)
Fucidin (antibiotic ointment; prescription)
Nerisone (anti-inflammatory; prescription)
Second Skin (5)
Stop Itch (bites, minor burns, cuts, rashes, sunburn)
Sting Stop (bee stings)

DRUGS

Aspirin
Acetaminophen (pain reliever)

Novo-Nidazole/Metron/Dazole (Giardia; prescription)
Novotrimel/Trimeth/Sulfamethx (infection antibiotic; prescription)
Seldane (antihistamine)
Throat lozenges

We have never used most of these supplies. The worst accident we've ever had is when I spilled very hot tea on my bare thigh, after which I applied Second Skin. I removed the Second Skin after two days because the burn wasn't healing by being all covered up. Exposed to the air, the wound dried out and healed very quickly. Perhaps the Second Skin wasn't necessary or even useful. I'm not actually a medical doctor, so I don't really know.

We also take a repair kit that contains many items: Cold Cure, a two-part epoxy for glueing broken things back together; stir sticks, mixing cups and spreading brush; fibreglass or Kevlar cloth for repairing a damaged canoe; spare shoelaces, clips, screws, D-rings, plastic connectors and buckles; small crescent wrench and screwdriver with multiple bits; duct tape; ripstop nylon; needle and thread; replacement cap for fuel bottle; Therm-a-Rest valve kit; glues such as Goop, Vinyl-Tec or contact cement; 3-in-One oil for the white-gas stove pump gasket; and extra mosquito netting for the tent. The list goes on and on. I try to anticipate what might break and what I would need for repair. You should do the same.

STOVES, BUGS AND FOOD

Kathleen and I always take a Coleman white-gas backpacking stove for (1) those days when we are too tired or rushed to cook our supper over a camp-fire, or (2) Barren Ground rivers, such as the Coppermine and Snowdrift, that have long sections with no firewood. We actually take a second stove in case our primary stove fails.

Mosquitoes and black flies pose the greatest threats to human comfort on northern Canada canoe trips, particularly trips out on the tundra. Kathleen and I protect ourselves primarily by wearing open-weave bug jackets that we saturate with a product that contains 95% or 100% DEET. In our experience, nothing works like DEET. We have tried alternatives. Compared to "insect-proof shirts," our open-weave light-mesh jackets, with hood, makes it more comfortable to work hard for long periods in sometimes hot conditions. Depending on how much one is sweating or working in the rain, one bottle is usually enough for the saturated bug jacket to be effective for about two weeks. A little more DEET applied to hands and face makes for a relatively bug-free environment. We have never felt overly tormented by bugs and have never taken a mesh tent for cooking and eating in. If the bugs are particularly bad, we simply retreat to our sleeping tent after supper. In the tent, we drink tea, study our topographic maps, and read historical journals or plant books. The mosquitoes and black flies remain outside the tent, where they belong.

We try to live as simply as possible on our canoe trips, and that includes meals. As you will discover in this book, Kathleen and I generally have tea and bannock for breakfast, soup for lunch, and one-pot meals for supper. We also both enjoy one bag of gorp (raisins, nuts and liquorice all sorts) per day.

For those of you who might not know, bannock is a thin, flat bread that originated in Scotland, and was traditionally made with oatmeal or barley meal. Kathleen prepares our bannock mixture from scratch. She sets our largest mixing bowl on the table, and adds four cups of flour, two tablespoons of baking powder, one teaspoon of salt, four tablespoons of dry milk powder and two tablespoons of sugar. Next she cuts in one cup of shortening and mixes thoroughly. Kathleen then measures out a cup-and-a-quarter of the bannock mixture into each of five individual freezer bags, and ties them off with twist ties. Repeating this process five more times gives us thirty bannocks. On the river, we simply squeeze out the contents of a freezer bag into a skillet, and cook the bannock to a golden brown. This hot, fresh bread, smothered in butter and jam, provides a very satisfying morning meal.

I admire the truly exquisite suppers that people often prepare on their wilderness canoe trips. That is not our style, however. Evening meals with three or four courses, followed by dessert, just seem like too much work to Kathleen and me. We generally cook and dehydrate all our suppers at home, and then package them in a Ziploc bag. At the beginning of each day on the river, we put the evening meal in a Tupperware container filled with water. Our supper rehydrates while we paddle. We then need only to heat it up over an open fire or the small, white-gas stove. Quick and easy. Thirty minutes, including preparation and clean up, and it's all done. Is this the best way? It is for us, particularly if the evening is windy, or rainy, or particularly buggy, or at the end of a long or difficult day. Would we enjoy a more elaborate meal? Very possibly, particularly if someone else prepared it. Would we enjoy a cappuccino? Very likely, especially if someone else made it and packed all the necessary equipment.

For the occasional treat we bring along a fruitcake, which packs and keeps very well. We also take one litre (34 ounces) of brandy and allow ourselves one small cup per week. We usually finish the trip with brandy left over. I'm not in favour of getting tipsy on wilderness canoe trips, not even in camp.

So, that's how Kathleen and I travel on wilderness canoe trips. With that background out of the way, it's time to travel to northern Canada, step into the canoe, and paddle down four fantastic rivers.

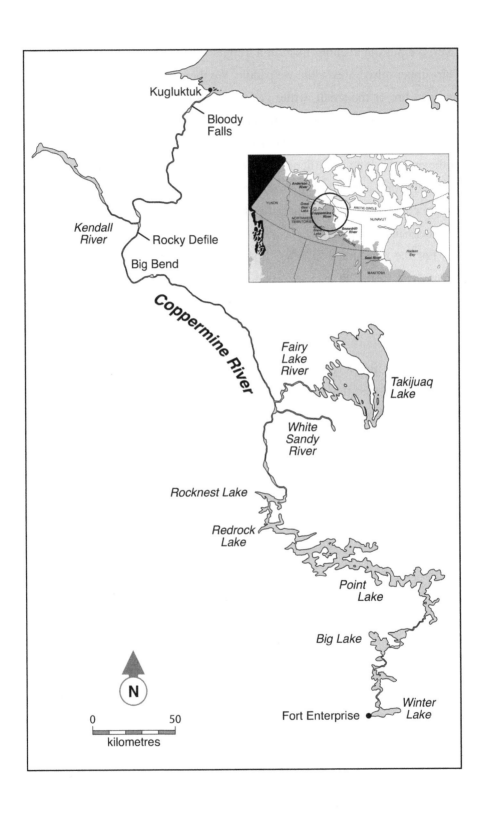

Kugluktuk

Bloody
Falls

*Kendall
River*

Rocky Defile

Big Bend

Coppermine River

*Fairy
Lake
River*

*Takijuaq
Lake*

*White
Sandy
River*

Rocknest Lake

*Redrock
Lake*

*Point
Lake*

Big Lake

N

0   50

kilometres

Fort Enterprise

*Winter
Lake*

CHAPTER 2

THE COPPERMINE RIVER

Overland from Fort Enterprise

In the spring of 1993, Carey Robson called to ask if Kathleen and I would be interested in paddling the Coppermine River with him and his wife Janice Power. Carey and Janice were members of our Beaver Canoe Club in Burnaby, British Columbia. Carey was arguably the most prominent member of the club. He was President of the Recreational Canoeing Association of British Columbia, and was also the perennial Training Director of our canoe club. He was, in fact, the most skilled paddler I knew. Carey had taught Kathleen and me much of what we knew about canoeing, and we were flattered that he would want us to join him and Janice on their Coppermine River trip.

Carey had also invited us on the South Nahanni River trip in 1990. He therefore knew and trusted our paddling skills. Carey also preferred to travel with couples. Not just any two people in a tandem canoe, but true couples.

He preferred to paddle with couples who had experience paddling together. People like Kathleen and me. When Kathleen and I wake up in our tent in the morning, we both know our respective tasks. We know where the pots and pans are. We know who starts breakfast. We know who takes down the tent. We know who does the dishes. We know what items, and in what order, go in each of our three large Duluth-style canvas packs. We know where each of these packs goes in the canoe. We are efficient. Carey highly values efficiency. Carey's trips are always highly organized and efficient. He expects people to be ready to paddle at a specific time every morning. He does not countenance delays. People new to paddling with each other just can't perform up to Carey's expectations. For those people who are not prepared to meet those expectations, paddling with Carey can be challenging.

When Carey called in the spring of 1993, however, Kathleen and I were already committed to our Thelon River trip. "We can't go on the Coppermine, Carey. We've already made plans to go on the Thelon River."

I thought that would be the end of it. Carey would go with someone else, and we wouldn't have to actually decide whether or not to join an "efficient" trip down the Coppermine River. But no, that was not the end of it. Carey didn't go on the Coppermine in 1993 but called again in the spring of 1994.

"So do you want to go on the Coppermine next year, Mike?"

"I don't know, Carey. After our Thelon trip, Kathleen and I kind of prefer to paddle by ourselves."

"Well, think about it. It will be a great trip. I plan to start at Winter Lake, near Fort Enterprise, where Sir John Franklin overwintered in 1820. Then, like Franklin, we would go overland to the Coppermine River and paddle down to the Arctic coast. It will be a great trip."

For many years—I don't know how many, perhaps 10 or 15—Carey had been fascinated with the Coppermine River, particularly in relation to Sir John Franklin. Maps of the Coppermine River adorned Carey's basement walls. Carey was driven to paddle the Coppermine River. Carey was destined to paddle the Coppermine River. He wanted us to join him.

"I don't know if Kathleen would like the overland part very much, Carey."

In fact, I was pretty sure that Kathleen wouldn't like going overland from Fort Enterprise to the Coppermine River. In 1988, Kathleen and I saw a presentation of people dragging 140 km up the Rat River, in the Northwest Territories, to get over the height of land to reach the Bell and Porcupine Rivers in the Yukon. They spent a lot of time struggling in deep water and clambering through dense, riverside brush.

"That's an interesting trip, Kathleen," I said afterwards. "Maybe we should do that someday."

"I'm not going up the Rat," she replied.

Kathleen didn't even think about it. She was very definite. Every once in a while I would suggest the Rat River trip again, just to get Kathleen's reaction, which never changed.

"I'm not going up the Rat."

So if Kathleen wouldn't go up the Rat, then why would she go overland to the Coppermine? I didn't see it happening.

"I'll talk to Kathleen, Carey, but I don't think she would want to go."

The next Sunday, at the end of a Beaver Canoe Club day trip, while waiting for the shuttle, Janice asked Kathleen to accompany her and Carey on the Coppermine River trip. The pressure was mounting. Other than Kathleen and me, I don't think there were many other paddlers who would want to, or could, join Carey and Janice on their Coppermine River adventure. It was a long trip of about 30 days, not counting getting there and back. Most people wouldn't have that much available time. The trip also required overland travel. Most people wouldn't want to go overland with a canoe. The Coppermine also featured many difficult rapids. It was an expensive trip that necessitated flying into Winter Lake, as well as flying back to Yellowknife. And it would require a calm, patient personality to spend 30, often strenuous, "efficient" days with Carey.

Let me illustrate. Every summer, the Beaver Canoe Club headed into the interior of British Columbia for Rivers Week, where we paddled four or five rivers with varying degrees of difficulty—a fantastic week that provided an opportunity for people to improve their paddling skills. Carey, as the best and most experienced paddler, was always and logically in charge. On this one particular evening, as we sat around the campfire enjoying snacks and happy hour, the discussion turned to tomorrow morning's departure. The paddling day was going to be short. Only a few hours down the Coldwater River to reach the town of Merritt and tomorrow's camp on the Nicola River.

"No need to get up early," someone said. "We don't need to leave at nine. We could sleep in, and head out at say ten, or even eleven."

All eyes turned to Carey. "No. We leave at nine."

Grumbling and moaning ensued, followed by more discussion, most of it leaning towards a later departure. Carey remained firm. "We leave at nine."

Finally, someone, whom I'll call Gary, because that was his name, asked, "Why do we have to leave at nine just because you say so?"

Uh-oh. This should be good. In his defence, Gary was new to the club. He didn't know any better. Carey looked at Gary and simply replied, "Because I can paddle class four rapids and you can't."

Now that might seem like an illogical response to you. Just because Carey was a better paddler, did that mean he got to decide when we left camp in the morning? Well, it sort of did. I repeat: Carey was the best paddler. Carey easily performed canoe-over-canoe rescues when people capsized. Most everyone felt more secure with Carey on the river. Carey assumed responsibility for people's safety on Beaver Canoe Club trips. Carey had earned the right to be in charge, and to make decisions for the group.

Still, the discussion continued. Not mutinous, but certainly persistent. Finally, someone suggested a vote. Carey indicated that a vote was not needed. "Why not?" I asked. "A vote can't hurt." I was a veteran member of the club. I could afford a little impertinence.

So we voted on whether to leave at nine or ten. I don't know how many people were there. Maybe 25. Maybe even 40. I'm an early riser. So, along with Carey, I voted to leave at nine. There were several abstentions. It seemed, though, without actually counting, that everyone else who voted indicated a preference to leave at ten.

We left at nine.

That's how I remember the famous Coldwater River vote. I think you see my point. Travelling with Carey on the Coppermine River might require acknowledging his position as the presumed trip leader. Not necessarily an easy task for strong-willed people whose opinions might differ from Carey's point of view.

OK. I hear what you're saying. "But, Mike. You've already been on the South Nahanni River with Carey. And that must have worked out fine if he's asking you to go on another trip."

You're absolutely right. The Nahanni trip did work out great. No problems at all. We loved it. In 1990, however, Kathleen and I had never been on a wilderness canoe trip before. Since 1990, we had developed much more confidence in our own opinions and paddling skills. Things were different now. Kathleen and I were much more likely to prefer our own approach to paddling wilderness rivers.

Anyway, Kathleen probably wouldn't want to go on the Coppermine River. She wouldn't go up the Rat, after all. But I was wrong. The next day, on Monday, Kathleen and I went to the University of British Columbia library on our lunch break to review the topographic maps. Kathleen said her plan "was to show that this trip couldn't be done without a lot of work and struggle." The topographic maps featured countless small lakes and streams haphazardly spread along any potential route to the Coppermine River. Well, maybe not literally countless. Too many for me, though, to want to count. After studying the maps for maybe 20 minutes, Kathleen looked up and said, "It's not possible to get to the Coppermine River from Winter Lake. Let's do it."

I never understood why Kathleen wanted to go overland to the Coppermine River once she decided that it wasn't possible. After all, she absolutely refused to go up the Rat River, even when the route was obvious and very possible. Didn't make sense to me. But there it was.

So, I called Carey that night to tell him that we were "in." In some sense, Kathleen and I had now come full circle. It was Carey and Janice, after all, who had invited Kathleen and me on the South Nahanni River, an experience that gave us the confidence to paddle the Thelon River by ourselves. Carey

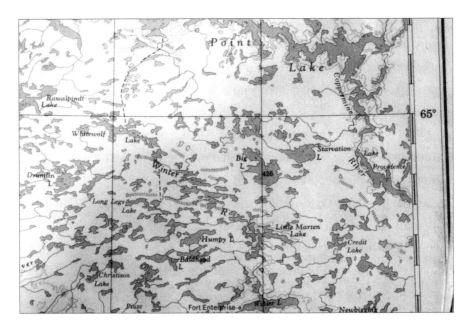

*Kathleen said, "It's not possible to get from
Winter Lake to the Coppermine River. Let's do it!"*

and Janice had also introduced us to bannock, a breakfast tradition on all our wilderness canoe trips. How could we not accept their invitation? How could we not join Carey and Janice as they chased their dream of paddling down the Coppermine River?

Yes, we welcomed the opportunity to join Carey and Janice when they ventured overland from Fort Enterprise—a trip that Kathleen and I would not likely do on our own. Travelling with Carey and Janice, though, would make a strong foursome. They had excellent paddling and wilderness skills, and we highly valued their judgement and experience.

The following Inuit creation legend describes the origins of the Coppermine River:

> *It is said that a long time ago an Inuk, who was named
> Upaum, was being chased by a brown bear. As he ran north,
> he bent down and drew a line with his finger in the earth.
> Immediately a great stream of water gushed along the line,*

growing into a huge river. This great river flowing north became the Coppermine.

The previous quote is how Kathleen and I begin our Coppermine River slide shows, many of which we have given to people in hospitals and long-term care facilities. On one such afternoon, after the quote, an elderly, indignant lady in the back of the room shouted out, "If you're going to lie to us, then we're not going to listen." Apparently her "truth" did not include Inuit creation legends.

This little anecdote regarding "lies and truth" might sometimes also apply to my description of the Coppermine River trip. Carey and I both kept diaries, but I have used only my diary for this story. I have no doubt that Carey's version would differ in minor, and even some major, aspects. For example, at the end of the trip I had tallied four trackings totalling 1.7 km, 13 drags upriver totalling 5.8 km and 15 portages totalling 9.6 km. Carey's numbers differed markedly. Such is the challenge of recording what seems obvious. Different people have different interpretations. Nevertheless, what I present here is, to the best of my knowledge, entirely accurate without any embellishment or revisionist thinking.

In addition to its historical use and significance to the Dene and Inuit peoples, the Coppermine River was very important in early European exploration of northern Canada. Samuel Hearne, led by the famous Chipewyan hunter, Matonabbee, reached the Coppermine River in 1771, in search of the copper that native peoples had been bringing to Fort Prince of Wales on Hudson Bay. Indeed, the river and town of Coppermine derive their names from this source of copper. In 1996, the community of Coppermine changed its name to Kugluktuk. I have read two versions of the meaning of Kugluktuk: either "place of moving water," or "place where the river drops," in reference to Bloody Falls.

Sir John Franklin, in 1821, was the next European to travel down the Coppermine River. Sent by the Royal Navy, Franklin's task was to map the

Arctic coast from the mouth of the Coppermine River to Hudson Bay, as part of the British quest to discover the Northwest Passage.

Joining Franklin on the expedition were men whose names are now associated with early European exploration, including Sir John Richardson, Robert Hood and Sir George Back. As you might know, Sir John Franklin achieved a great deal of notoriety for his 1845 voyage to seek the Northwest Passage—a voyage on which he and all of his 128 men lost their lives. Franklin's Coppermine River trip was nearly equally disastrous. Of the 20 men in the Franklin party who travelled to the Arctic coast in 1821, nine voyageurs died due to fatigue and starvation, Robert Hood was murdered by Michel Teroahaute, and Teroahaute himself was then executed by Richardson.

Although this history is intriguing, Kathleen and I looked forward to paddling the Coppermine River primarily because of its isolation, and the fact that it ran north to the Arctic Ocean. It seemed a perfect adventure to renew our fascination with, and love for, Canada's northern landscape.

So, I sent away for the necessary topographic maps, and using the "three times forefinger-drag method" I developed and submitted a tentative trip itinerary to Carey.

We would begin by flying to Winter Lake on July 28, intending to reach the town of Coppermine on August 28. Kathleen and I would have preferred to start a couple of weeks earlier to maximize the amount of daylight on our trip. It is fair to say, though, that Carey and Janice hate bugs. Perhaps they even detest bugs. Accordingly, Carey and Janice preferred to begin the trip as late as possible, hoping that an early frost would provide some bug-free days later in the trip. We were happy to defer to their wishes.

In July of 1995, Kathleen and I loaded the van, drove away from our home in North Vancouver, and headed north to Yellowknife. We pulled into the campground there on July 27, and joined Carey and Janice for beer, wine and potato chips. Our last night in civilization, and we indulged ourselves with junk food and alcohol. The next morning, July 28, we loaded our gear and canoes on a chartered Twin Otter to fly north from Yellowknife. Below us, the expanse of tundra and lakes rekindled the peace and contentment that

Kathleen and I felt on our 37-day trip down the Thelon River two summers before.

We approached the site of abandoned Fort Enterprise, just below the outlet of Winter Lake, in only 90 minutes—much easier than Franklin's gruelling portage and drag of 16 days. Sir John Franklin reached this location at the end of summer in 1820—too late to reach the Arctic coast before winter. His native guide Akaitcho suggested that he stay here and use the large stand of trees to build cabins for the winter before continuing down the Coppermine River the following summer.

We intended to land at the northwest bay where the Snare River drains Winter Lake. Instead though, because of the rocky shore, the pilot put down at an island opposite the Winter River, 6 km up Winter Lake. The wind was calm in the lee of the island, but waves on the lake indicated a brisk breeze. We loaded the canoes, quickly ate a sandwich, donned our PFDs, stepped into the canoes, and paddled around the point. *[Note: PFD stands for personal floatation device, commonly called a life jacket.]*

Kathleen and I immediately renewed our acquaintance with the northwest wind, which we came to know so intimately on the Thelon River. Straining to put as much power as possible into our strokes, we paddled slowly toward shore, 1.5 km distant. The wind had obviously welcomed our return, and had apparently been waiting for Kathleen and me since 1993.

We reached shore, set up camp, and ventured onto the tundra to visit our plant friends: Crowberry, Cloudberry, Labrador Tea, Prickly Saxifrage, Lapland Lousewort. Only moments later, swarms of mosquitoes forced us to retreat back to our windy, sandy beach. An hour later, the wind increased, the sky filled with masses of black clouds hurtling over the northwest horizon, and we retreated even farther—into our tent.

Kathleen and I lay next to each other, in silence. It was as though we had never left the Thelon River. The tundra's unpredictable weather extremes are so predictable. Our beach felt like home, but we were somewhat anxious about the arduous 110 km over the height of land to reach Point Lake.

During a short walk across the tundra after supper, Carey and Janice seemed discouraged by the harsh extremes of wind, rain and bugs.

"What made you want to paddle the Coppermine, Carey?" Janice asked.

"I'm beginning to wonder," he said.

We rose the next morning at 5:30, to a temperature of only 5°. After our first tundra bannock in two years, we paddled west down Winter Lake, into a slight breeze, towards the site of abandoned Fort Enterprise. Near the outlet, we spotted two herds of caribou, nearly 200 animals, swimming toward shore, where they exited, one after the other, just like in nature films. While walking down the Snare River, we spotted more caribou, swimming the river between rapids, and then disappearing into a spruce and bog maze of centuries-old caribou trails.

[Note: I have reported temperatures in degrees Celsius. To obtain a reasonable estimate of Fahrenheit, you can multiply the Celsius temperature by 2, and then add 30. For example, 5°C would equal approximately 40°F. The actual conversion is to multiply Celsius by 9/5, and then add 32, meaning that 5°C actually equals 41°F. Pretty close, don't you think? For your convenience I have provided some Celsius and Fahrenheit equivalencies in Appendix 2.]

Using site descriptions in diaries from the Franklin party, plus aerial photographs taken by an archeological investigation in the 1970s, we found the cairn marking the spot of Fort Enterprise in about two hours. Nothing remains of the three buildings that comprised the fort, as the Franklin survivors, after they returned from the Arctic coast, burned most of the fort for cooking fuel, and to keep warm. Carey had finally realized his quest of many years to stand at the site of Fort Enterprise. He was obviously pleased and satisfied.

"The trip's objective has been achieved," he declared. "Time to get to Coppermine."

I told you Carey was focused. The efficient, highly organized expedition had begun.

Back at the northwest bay where we had left the canoes, we gathered firewood from the abundant spruce, and ran before the wind, covering 5.5 km in 55 minutes.

In the tent at 8:00 p.m.; 10° with cold winds bringing one squall after another across the northern horizon. Kathleen and I again studied our route to the Coronation Gulf on the Arctic Ocean. From Winter Lake, we planned to go upriver to Lastfire Lake, which was named by Sir John Franklin on his 1821 expedition. Lastfire Lake would likely be one of the last places that our group could count on finding firewood until near the outlet of Point Lake, nearly 200 km away.

From Lastfire Lake we would continue up the Winter River through Little Marten Lake, to Big Lake, over the height of land to Starvation Lake, and then down the Starvation River to Point Lake. We anticipated this 110-km leg of the trip would take six days. We then planned about one week for the 165 km through Point Lake, Redrock Lake and Rocknest Lake. After Rocknest Lake, the strong current of the Coppermine River would carry us the final 370 km to Coppermine (Kugluktuk) on the Arctic coast.

You probably know from looking at the tentative itinerary, that I had scheduled tomorrow as a fishing and hiking day. Well, our group decided not to take this rest day. Today was already pretty restful, and all four of us were eager to get going. The topographic map showed 12 symbols for rapids spread evenly along the 1 km of the Winter River leading up to Lastfire Lake. This suggested that the rapids would likely be more or less continuous.

July 30. We woke to a 6° morning, with a brisk wind, and set off precisely at 9:00 a.m. for the Winter River, which we reached in about an hour. Following a short hike to a ridge to view Lastfire Lake, Carey and I elected to track our canoes up the Winter River. Or should I say, Carey elected to track our canoes up the Winter River. I would have gladly portaged, as I had never tracked before, but was willing to give it a try. Tracking was certainly preferable to paddling, as the rapids were too swift and rocky to canoe up.

Tracking, by the way, is when two people (or sometimes one person) stand on the shore, holding the bow and stern lines (technically known as

Canoeing up the Winter River to Lastfire Lake.

"painters"). Carey took the bow painter and began pulling upstream, ensuring that the bow remained pointed in toward the shore. Ideally, the bow would be right up against the shore to ensure that it did not swing outward into the current. If the bow did swing outward, the canoe would become broadside to the current and would likely broach on one of the many boulders that choked the Winter River. That would be bad.

I took the stern painter to help guide the canoe around rocks. I also needed to make sure that I didn't pull so hard on the painter that the stern would swing to shore, causing the bow to swing out. This tandem tracking required good teamwork, particularly because some of the rapids to Lastfire Lake were Class II+, maybe even a low Class III.

We successfully tracked Carey's canoe to Lastfire Lake in two hours, and returned for my canoe. Well, it wasn't all tracking. Sometimes we stood in the water or on boulders to pull and guide the canoe upstream. Janice and Kathleen, who had been watching from the shore and taking pictures of the adventure, suggested that we eat lunch, and rest before beginning the second half of our somewhat gruelling task. But Carey and I were feeling good. We were ready to complete the job, and we sauntered back downriver with only a sausage to replenish our energy.

Tracking was actually kind of fun. I was enjoying the challenge, and welcomed this new skill to my canoeing repertoire. Things were going even better this time than on the first trip up the Winter River. We were 15 minutes ahead of that initial trip, and in good spirits, when we reached the last major rapid before Lastfire Lake.

Perhaps Carey and I had become complacent—confident and pleased with our work. After all, there was just one major rapid to go. Whatever the reason, though, a diagonal wave in that last major rapid suddenly grabbed the bow and began to pull the canoe under. As paddlers know, virtually all capsizes occur to the upstream side of the canoe, and this would be no exception.

To avoid immediate capsize, Carey had no choice. He let go of the bow painter and yelled, "Hang on, Mike!" The bow swung out, my canoe wallowed, turned broadside and overturned. I braced against the jolt that was sure to come when the canoe reached the end of my stern painter, and managed to keep my feet to belay the boat into an eddy.

Both of our boats had homemade spray decks, which keeps the gear dry during rain and also prevents (or so we hope) the canoe from taking on too much water when running rapids. As it turns out, a third benefit of the spray deck is that it keeps the gear in the boat when the canoe overturns. Glancing downstream, I didn't see any gear floating away. This could only be good.

Carey ran to my assistance and rolled the canoe right side up. He then did most of the work of unsnapping the spray deck bit by bit to unload the gear. We then dumped the water and reloaded the canoe. Carey seemed very apologetic. It wasn't his fault, though. Things happen. And, in fact, nothing was lost. Not even our tea cups and water bottles, which had been floating loose in the canoe. I should mention that we never tie gear into the canoe, which would just add additional time and effort to unload and reload on portages. And, as I've said, the spray deck kept all gear in the capsized canoe.

Kathleen had been away from the river, standing on a ridge taking pictures, when she had heard Carey yell out, "Hang on, Mike." She saw him bolt downstream, out of sight. She ran toward the river, not knowing what had happened, and fearing the worst. She was relieved, a few minutes later, when she again saw Carey and me with the canoe upright, making our way slowly back upstream.

Our spray deck had been badly damaged, and all the canoe packs and liners were filled with water. Kathleen and I always place our gear in double garbage bags, even though the gear is already in an ostensibly waterproof liner. Our caution proved useful, as everything was mostly dry. Unfortunately, the garbage bag in a day pack had a small hole, and all my books were wet. Oh well, they will dry out.

I have learned since this trip that the bow is generally quite vulnerable to being pulled under the water when tracking. It is often recommended that an under-the-keel bridle be looped around the bow. This approach gives much greater control than simply pulling on a painter at the end of the bow. I have recently seen videos of this technique, and am very impressed. It would be interesting to try it sometime.

In the tent that night, Kathleen cried because of the anxiety of the day. She felt particularly guilty just standing around on shore watching me work so hard. She wanted very much to help.

Despite the capsize, I'm glad that we tracked the canoes rather than portaging everything to Lastfire Lake. Janice was suffering from fibromyalgia, a disorder in which a person has long-term, body-wide pain and tenderness in the joints, muscles, tendons and other soft tissues. Fibromyalgia has also been linked to fatigue, sleep problems, headaches, depression and anxiety. Janice said that she can carry no more than a 25-pound (11 kg) pack. Portaging would have been slow. I think Carey's concern for Janice might have been his primary reason for suggesting that we track up the Winter River rather than portage to Lastfire Lake. I would have done the same for Kathleen. You had to give Janice a heck of a lot of credit for even attempting this trip.

July 31. We broke camp quickly, and headed upriver toward Little Marten Lake. A gentler gradient allowed us to make faster progress because Carey and I were each able to track our own canoe. Soon, though, the rocky shore forced us into the water. As I dragged upriver, I often had to balance from one rock to the next to avoid plunging into waist-deep water. Every once in a while I would stop to look upstream, only to see the rocky current disappearing around the bend.

We tracked and dragged up five rapids today, ranging in distance from 200 to 600 m. Kathleen eventually jumped in to help me. Bruises covered her legs that night, from her thighs to her ankles. She said that she mentioned to Janice in the morning, "that I feel useless just watching Carey and Michael do all the work." Apparently Janice said, "Don't worry about it. They're guys. They love it."

And you know what, people? Janice was right. I was loving the physical challenge. I had never done anything quite like this before. I was having a good time.

We enjoyed seeing Dog Rib Rock throughout the day, a prominent landmark for native peoples, and a feature that the Franklin survivors used to find Fort Enterprise on their return from the Arctic Ocean in 1821. We set up today's camp near the upper end of the Winter River flowing out of Little Marten Lake. Climbing onto the bank to assess a potential campsite, we saw a herd of 75 caribou standing on the ridge only about 100 m away.

We were pretty darn tired, and likely still five days from Point Lake. Although we did have some moments today when we could actually paddle upstream, even that was hard work. In the tent that evening, Kathleen read in Farley Mowat's book *Tundra* about the exposed, wet, miserable conditions suffered by Samuel Hearne during his trek across the tundra in 1770–1771:

> *On the 3rd of July the weather was again very bad, but we*
> *made shift to walk ten or eleven miles, until we were obliged*
> *to put up because of not being able to see, due to the drifting*
> *snow. By putting up, no more is to be understood than we*
> *got to leeward of a great stone, or into the crevices of rocks,*

where we smoked our pipes or went to sleep until the weather
permitted us to proceed.

Compared to Hearne's conditions, our situation was much better. We had nothing to complain about.

August 1. Up at 6:30 a.m. Weather still cold at 6°. Away at 9:30 a.m., hoping to make good distance today. Based on my reading of the topographic map, I expected that we would have to drag the canoes at least one more time—at a spot where the Winter River narrowed before reaching Little Marten Lake. And drag at that spot we did. We also had to drag the canoes two more times, when the water in the Winter River simply disappeared into a rocky stream bed.

When we finally reached Little Marten Lake, we stopped for lunch and waited 45 minutes for the north wind to slacken just a bit. We then paddled toward a point on the east shore, a 1-km crossing of open water. About 3/4 of the way across, the wind and whitecaps returned, slowing our progress to a laboured, worried struggle.

We beached in the shelter of a rocky cove and waited three hours, until 5:00 p.m., before agreeing to end our paddling day. Kathleen and I disagreed slightly with Carey about our wind strategy for tomorrow, but eventually he accepted our preference to be ready to leave at 7:00 a.m. The last few days had been calm in the morning and windy in the afternoon. Kathleen and I thought it would be best to be ready to leave early. This was a significant compromise for Carey, as his methodical, organized approach is to be ready to paddle at 9:00 a.m. Carey seemed somewhat worried about our first day of severe wind problems. In fairness to Carey, though, we were nearly one day behind our tentative itinerary, even though we had paddled on our scheduled rest day. We all knew, however, that this was going to be a challenging adventure.

August 2. Up at 4:00 a.m., with a departure at 6:30 a.m. Cool, with a slight breeze that persisted all last night. No bugs, though. We completed two—almost too windy—open crossings of Little Marten Lake by 11:30 a.m., and paddled up a side current that would take us out of Little Marten Lake.

Moments later, we reached a short (100 m), rock-strewn stream leading to a pond, followed by a second, equally short, rock-strewn stream leading to an unnamed lake that would take us away from the Winter River watershed. Much of the first stream was too shallow to track or drag, so Carey and I portaged the two heaviest packs from each boat to the unnamed lake. We then tied the bow painters of our boats together, and in double harness, Carey and I dragged the more lightly loaded canoes along the soft moss, lichen and Bog Birch shoreline.

Kathleen and Janice offered encouragement by waving from the opposite shore, then walked toward the second pond, where they met us two hours later at the end of the second rock-strewn stream. We were happy with our morning's progress and were now just north of Little Marten Lake, parallel to a striking esker.

We stopped earlier than usual, at 3:00 p.m., at the mouth of the river flowing toward us from Big Lake. A difficult day, but 18 km closer to the height of land, beyond which lay Point Lake. The river leading to Big Lake was wide, with a gentle current. I would be misrepresenting the group's mood to say that we were *expecting* an easy passage upstream to Big Lake. Fairer to say that we were *hoping* for an easy passage upstream to Big Lake, which was only 21 km away.

According to the topographic map, we should be able to paddle all the way to Big Lake on wide streams and lakes. So there was no reason we shouldn't be able to reach Big Lake tomorrow. In fact, I had indicated on the tentative itinerary that only one day's travel lay between the mouth of the river from Big Lake and Big Lake itself. But, as you know, I made up that tentative itinerary at home, on the floor of my bedroom. I had never seen the river leading to Big Lake before. We would see tomorrow what the river to Big Lake actually looked like in real life.

The map indicated that there should be water here somewhere.

August 3. We slept well last night and set off in the morning even more hopeful that this large stream would allow us to reach Big Lake without having to drag or portage any more. After three hours, however, the canoes started scraping and bumping across the rocky stream bed, until we eventually ran out of water not even half way to Big Lake. We were all becoming a bit frustrated, but none of us blamed Carey for having suggested that we begin this trip on the opposite side of the divide between Winter Lake and the Coppermine River. We had all signed up very willingly for this adventure.

We collectively agreed that it would be easier to not bother with a dry river bed, and we simply started portaging straight across the tundra in the general direction of Big Lake. We came across more water, sufficient to float the canoes, after only about 1.5 km.

We gained only 14 km today, including 3 to 4 km by tracking and dragging and the 1.5 km of portaging. We were only two days, I hoped, from Starvation Lake. Kathleen and I used to be backpackers but switched to canoeing for two reasons. One, canoeing allowed us to take more gear for longer periods of time in the wilderness. And, two, canoeing allowed us to generally float through the wilderness without having to carry everything on our backs. An over-the-height-of-land canoe trip, however, is a lot like backpacking, only now we had to carry a canoe as well. I don't remember ever seeing any other backpackers with canoes on their backs. I might have missed it, but I don't think so.

By now the group had become very efficient at portaging. For example, when we reached the end of water on a lake or pond, we didn't just nudge the canoe gently up to shore. Oh sure, we slowed down, but only just a little. When the bow touched shore, we pretty much leaped out of our canoe and dragged it up onto the beach. We then quickly unsnapped the spray deck and chucked all the gear out onto the tundra. Kathleen and I then immediately changed from our wetsuit socks and canvas shoes into our hiking boots, which we packed conveniently at the top of our green Duluth-style canvas pack. *[Note: Each of our three canvas packs is a different colour so that we always know its contents, and who is responsible for portaging it.]*

Now you should know that there were never any actual portage trails. We certainly knew what general direction we wanted to go, but the most direct and easiest route was not always obvious. So the first trip was usually a scouting trip. None of us wanted to carry our heaviest packs, or our canoe, to scout out a potential portage trail if that trail didn't work out. On the other hand, we didn't want to scout completely empty-handed, either.

Kathleen and I always take two white, plastic buckets on canoe trips. One of them is our "kitchen bucket" with stove, pots, pans, plates and cutlery. The other contains food—such as gorp, cheese and crackers—that we would be eating in the next day or two. These white buckets also served as chairs at camp. The primary downside of these buckets is that they are very cumbersome to lug by hand over the portage trail, particularly if one is also burdened with a heavy pack. So as soon as we were ready, Kathleen and I each grabbed a white bucket, donned a light day pack, picked up another hand-held item, such as a fishing pole or paddle, and headed out across the tundra to scout the ideal portage trail.

Once the best route had been determined, particularly on longer portage trails, Carey often assumed the role of Hansel and Gretel. Instead of dropping bread crumbs to mark our route, however, he left little bits of colourful gear along the way to guide us between our beginning and ending points. After Kathleen and I had each carried three loads to the end of the portage trail, we immediately changed from our hiking boots into our wetsuit socks and canvas shoes, repacked the canoe, snapped the spray deck into place, and shoved the canoe back into the next stretch of water. No discussion was necessary. We all knew what needed to be done.

At camp that night, Carey was pleased, chatting merrily away about being on an "elite" wilderness canoe trip. He might have been right. I can't imagine very many people wanting to do this. If the truth be known—and I'm about to make it known right now—I was generally enjoying the trip too. A lot of work, but quite an adventure. *[Note: I don't want to appear too pretentious by claiming elite status, so I must admit that I have read many accounts of wilderness canoeing exploits that were longer and more challenging than this Coppermine story. Even so, Janice, Carey, Kathleen and I were on quite an adventure. You gotta give us that.]*

Kathleen was much happier today, as she joined me in the river tracking and dragging our canoe upstream. She also carried packs over the portage trail. She now felt like a contributing member of the expedition. We were on the water from 8:30 a.m. to 7:45 p.m. As I said, a long and difficult day.

August 4. More of the same today. More hard work. Four more portages and one more drag upstream. Twelve more hours to gain only 12 km. We finally reached Big Lake, though, where we paddled approximately 5 km along its eastern shore to camp at the beginning of the portage to Starvation Lake. Once again, though, there was no "official" or marked beginning of the portage to Starvation Lake. We had merely selected a spot on the east shore of Big Lake that we believed and hoped offered the best route to Starvation Lake.

Our chosen route was not the shortest distance to Starvation Lake yet offered two "large-ish" lakes on which we could paddle part of the portage to Starvation Lake. We would begin our trek to Starvation Lake by portaging about 1 km to the first large-ish lake, across which we intended to paddle east approximately 5 km. Then, almost a 1-km portage to the second large-ish lake, up which we hoped to paddle north a little over 2 km. At that point, we would be only slightly more than 2 km from Starvation Lake, some of which would require portaging but some of which, maybe 600 m, might be paddle-able on a "small-ish" lake.

We had originally hoped to reach Starvation Lake by August 3, which means that we would be two days behind our tentative schedule if we reached Starvation Lake tomorrow. Not too bad. There's still a long way to go on this trip, with many opportunities to make up time. Anyway, my tentative itineraries were indeed tentative. As I mentioned previously, I don't actually expect to follow the itinerary exactly. I make the itinerary primarily to determine if the trip is likely doable in the time available.

Today was rainy, wet and cold. Combined with our struggles, the day had to rate among the least pleasurable wilderness days of my entire life. But then, as I kept reminding myself, we hadn't come on this trip for sheer pleasure. The 5 km of actual paddling on Big Lake, however, did bring some satisfaction. We endured only a slight drizzle, with no wind. We enjoyed a smooth lake surface, with loons calling through the mist.

In August of 1820, Franklin reached Winter Lake and intended to proceed to, and return from, the Arctic coast that summer. Akaitcho argued against Franklin's plan and told him that 40 days would be required to reach the coast. The first 11 days would be through country with no wood. Most importantly, Akaitcho told Franklin that there would be no caribou to hunt, as winter was soon approaching.

Franklin, however, remained confident, and replied, in what I presume was an imperious and condescending manner: "We informed him that we were provided with instruments by which we could tell the state of air and water and we did not imagine the winter to be so near as he supposed."

Oh those British naval captains can be very smug. As we huddled in our wind-bound, cold camp nearly two centuries later, I reflected on Akaitcho's response, as presented in Farley Mowat's book *Tundra*:

> *Well, I have said everything I can to dissuade you from going*
> *on. It seems you wish to sacrifice your own lives as well as the*
> *Indians who might attend you. However, if after all I have said*
> *you are determined, some of my young men shall join your party,*
> *because it shall not be said that we allowed you to die alone*
> *having brought you hither. But from the moment they embark in*
> *the canoes, I and my relatives will lament them as dead.*

Fortunately for Franklin, he accepted Akaitcho's advice and postponed his trip down the Coppermine River to the following spring. If he had not, it is likely that all 20 men, not just 11, would have died.

August 5. Stormbound at Big Lake; 10° with a driving rain, and a howling wind that persisted incessantly throughout the day. Both couples lay in bed in the morning, reluctant to get up unless the other did so first. Kathleen and I slept and dozed until noon. Our enforced rest day was welcomed by our weary bodies, which were so fatigued and tired from the previous two days. I lay in the tent and thought about how it might be kind of nice to paddle in the warmth of Alabama or Georgia. Such paddling excursions might be more relaxing holidays than portaging gear and canoe across the tundra. But again, as I kept telling myself, we hadn't expected this expedition to be relaxing.

In the late afternoon, I joined Carey and Janice beneath the tarp, where they were preparing supper. Each couple alternated cooking supper for the group. Each couple was responsible for their own breakfast, lunch and snacks.

I should mention that Carey is a master at putting up tarps. I like to say that Carey can put up a tarp in a vacant shopping centre parking lot, in the middle of a strong gale. You don't believe me? Wait a minute. I'll be right back.

....

You [☺] are here, in between these lines of dots, waiting patiently for me.

....

OK. I'm back. I've scanned in the slides from our Big Lake camp, and have entered the images on my computer monitor. I can see the tarp and our very bleak camp. I had actually forgotten how extraordinarily bleak and exposed that Big Lake camp was. Let me describe the image on my screen. We're camped on flat tundra "adorned" with a spattering of small to medium-sized boulders. No trees in sight. In fact, the scrubby vegetation barely exceeds 10 cm (4 inches). Whitecaps whip across the surface of Big Lake, shrouded beneath a nearly black sky filled with angry, scudding clouds. I usually don't like to impart emotions like "angry" to weather, which I consider to be emotion free. But I need you to think very bleak and exposed.

On my screen, I can see Kathleen, Janice and Carey huddled beneath the tarp, decked out in rain gear and toques. Yes, although our camp is very similar to a vacant shopping centre parking lot being battered by a gale, there stands the tarp. The side of the tarp facing the wind is nearly at ground level, tied down to the bow and stern thwarts of Carey and Janice's canoe. The middle of the tarp is raised up with Carey's telescoping tripod. The tarp then angles outward toward the front to meet a paddle handle attached to a short line with a clove hitch. Another line, also attached to the paddle handle with a clove hitch, leads downward, where it is tied to the thwart of our canoe using a taut-line hitch. By adjusting the angle of the paddle before tightening the taut-line hitch, the paddle stands firmly and proudly in the wind, without even needing to be driven into the ground. A similarly arranged paddle, tied to a boulder with a taut-line hitch, secures one of the sides of the tarp. This all took only a few minutes. Carey taught me everything I know about putting up tarps.

OK. Now back to the story about me being under the tarp with Carey and Janice that afternoon. I couldn't see out the back of the tarp, as it was nearly at ground level. For some reason, I suddenly decided that I needed to get up, just to look around. Perhaps I had some kind of premonition because as I stood up and looked south, I saw a sow grizzly and her cub heading directly toward the tarp, only 100 m away. Of course, I had left my can of bear spray in the tent. So I just stood there.

The sow halted abruptly as soon as she saw me, then turned and bounded toward the low ridge, stopping periodically to look back in my direction. I turned, stepped back beneath the tarp, and sat down on a white bucket. Trying to remain calm, I said, "You know, Janice and Carey, there's a grizzly bear coming."

"No there's not."

Perhaps I was being too calm. I spoke a little more urgently. "Yes there is. In fact, there's two grizzly bears coming."

This time they believed me. We got out from underneath the tarp just in time to see the mother and cub disappear over the ridge. We all went to our tents to get our respective cans of bear spray. The sow had probably smelled our supper cooking and was coming to investigate. She hadn't been aggressive, but I'm glad I had stepped out from beneath the tarp when I did. If she had come all the way into camp, the incident could have turned out quite differently. It could only have turned out worse. The sow hadn't threatened us, but we were certainly a little more on edge for the next few hours.

August 6. The wind continued to blow all night. Our tent rattled, and the sheltering tarp flapped loudly. A constant din that kept me awake from 2:00 a.m. until my alarm sounded at 3:30 a.m. Yes, I know it sounds goofy to have set an alarm, but I wanted to wake up early to see if the weather conditions had improved. If the weather had improved—if the wind had slackened—we could make an early start on our portage to Starvation Lake.

I heard Carey and Janice talking in their tent, and unzipped our tent fly to look outside. A very blustery, rainy, cold, still very bleak scene. Carey and Janice probably felt the same way, as they didn't seem to be coming out of their tent. I snuggled back down into my mummy bag, next to a sleeping Kathleen.

At 8:00 a.m., Kathleen and I rose, scurried to the shelter of the flapping tarp, hunched over our small Coleman backpacking stove, cooked a breakfast bannock and boiled up a thermos of tea. Still no Carey and Janice. After breakfast, Kathleen and I returned to the warmth of our sleeping bags.

Just before noon I heard Carey calling, from his tent, for a group discussion. Peering out of the barely open cracks of our respective tent doors, the discussion went something like this.

"What do you want to do, Mike?"

"I don't know, Carey, I'm thinking we want to wait until the rain stops."

"Why? It's not raining that hard now."

"Kathleen's worried that I might slip on a wet rock while portaging the canoe and perhaps twist or break an ankle."

I don't think Carey responded directly to this very flimsy excuse for not starting out toward Starvation Lake. It certainly sounded like a weak argument to me. Besides, there's lots of ways I could hurt myself on this trip. Slipping on a wet rock is only one of them. Anyway, we all eventually agreed to break camp and head toward Starvation Lake. We all felt a restlessness to do something positive—even a desperation, you might say—to leave this exposed, windward tundra shore of Big Lake.

Seven hours, two lakes, two portages, and approximately 10 km later, we were camped within sight of Starvation Lake, now less than 2 km away. Another very difficult, miserable day; 12°, boggy terrain, driving rain and a direct headwind. A direct headwind, though, was better for portaging a canoe than a wind coming from either side. It's extremely difficult, almost impossible, to go forward while portaging a canoe when strong winds batter you from the side. So, as you can see, there were some good aspects of the weather conditions today. Also, I didn't slip on any wet rocks. Both of my ankles were fine. Thanks for asking.

Today was actually quite momentous, as we had crossed over the height of land. We were camped at approximately 440 m above sea level, while Starvation Lake is at 433 m. It was all downhill now, only 565 km to the town of Coppermine on the Arctic coast. You might be wondering why we didn't just portage our gear the last 2 km to Starvation Lake if it was all downhill. Good question. Well, the shoreline of Starvation Lake would certainly be quite exposed to the wind. We were now hunkered down in a little gully-like depression behind a ridge that offered some relief from this never-ending onslaught of wind.

About 20 km east of our camp, the returning, weary, starving Franklin party was blocked at Obstruction Rapids for nine days in late September of 1821 as they attempted to cross the Coppermine River. That delay proved extremely costly, as the men began to die in early October, only 68 km from Fort Enterprise. At one time, Carey and I had discussed making a side trip to view Obstruction Rapids. As we crouched beneath the tarp in that tundra gully, however, the topic of side trips didn't seem to come up.

Our group did well today. We persisted, and now rested comfortably, although soggily. We were dining on Kathleen's shepherd's pie while sitting beneath our tarp erected around both canoes and our packs, which all provide additional windbreaks. We would almost certainly reach Starvation Lake tomorrow. We hoped for calm weather that would allow us to paddle its south shore, which is so exposed to the fetch of the prevailing north wind. We needed this calm weather if we were to reach the outlet of the Starvation River, where we would have moving water, and possibly better protection from the wind. We had already endured three days of continuous rain and wind. Surely, we wouldn't be inflicted with a fourth successive day. We were now three days behind our tentative itinerary and would require some good weather to make the town of Coppermine by August 28th.

August 7. The day began as usual: cold (8°), rainy and windy. We lay in the tent, somewhat depressed about our situation. When we arrived here yesterday, Carey announced that we would stay in this leeward camp—in our gully behind the ridge—until the storm broke. Kathleen and I believed that travelling conditions were now slightly better than yesterday, but were content to lie in our sleeping bags, waiting for better weather.

At 8:00 a.m. we headed to the tarp to prepare tea and bannock. Carey and Janice remained silent in their tent. After breakfast we took our tea thermos back to our tent, where Kathleen read a book and I studied our maps. I love looking at maps.

At 11:00 a.m. we joined Carey beneath the breezily flapping tarp, where he was cooking his bannock breakfast. Carey reported that "Janice is stuffing our sleeping bags, just in case the storm should break by 2:00 p.m. We shouldn't leave today, though, unless we're sure of reaching the Starvation River. There probably won't be any suitable camping sites until then."

Carey was probably right about the camping. The shoreline along Starvation Lake was likely very bleak, even without wind. Not much more bleak, though, than our last two camps. Kathleen and I both believed that we could start out now, which would give us more time to reach the Starvation River. It was only 11:00 a.m. We agreed to wait, though.

At 2:00 p.m. exactly, Carey strode to the ridge and returned to announce that everyone should cook a bannock and be prepared to leave for the Starvation River by 3:30. "With some easy paddling on the lake, we should be able to reach the river by 9:00 p.m., even if it means going without supper."

"You know, Carey," I suggested, "I think if we are going to leave today, we should do so now, to maximize our daylight hours."

Kathleen argued against beginning a nearly full day's work at 3:30, and explained that "We're getting a late start today because we got a late start yesterday." She stated, firmly for her, "It's best to begin a full day's work at the beginning of the day."

When asked for her opinion, Janice said, "I'll do whatever Carey and you guys think is best, but I prefer to remain here and dry out."

I repeated that my preference was either to leave now or early in the morning. Kathleen pointed out that even leaving now didn't provide any guarantee that we could paddle down Starvation Lake, which, through our binoculars, still showed whitecaps. The group agreed to stay.

At 6:00 p.m., the sun returned for the first time in four days, the wind died slightly, and a few bugs rose from their ground-hugging retreats. No one likes bugs, but bugs mean calm conditions. Bugs meant that the storm was over. Portaging would now be easier, and paddling would be more pleasant.

Kathleen and I strolled casually across the sun-dappled tundra, seeing scores of caribou. A hunting Short-eared Owl flew a few metres above the ground, and two Arctic Terns angrily chased a pair of predatory Long-tailed Jaegers. It seemed that the calmer weather had energized everyone. I certainly hoped that this weather would hold. We were four days and 55 km behind schedule.

August 8. The day broke with beautiful sunshine and perfect calm. We rose at 4:45 a.m. Ice on the tarp; 0°. Despite the cold, innumerable bugs swarmed upward as soon as they were touched by the sun's rays. Innumerable bugs signified that calm weather had definitely arrived, bringing with it good paddling conditions. Sometimes you have to appreciate, even outright love, innumerable bugs.

We quickly made our way over two short portages, broken conveniently about halfway by a 600-m paddle on the east end of a narrow lake. It felt good to see the lines of people and gear making progress to the end of what we hoped would be the last portage before Point Lake.

On Starvation Lake, we enjoyed a beautiful, joyous, two-hour paddle to the outlet, and the beginning of the Starvation River. I love these tundra lakes when they are quiet and placid. Lake bottom rocks slid by below in crystal clear waters that reflected billowy clouds above. Have we ever had bad weather on this expedition? I don't remember any.

At the outlet to the Starvation River, we immediately faced our third portage of the day. On the Barren Grounds, as in most regions, rapids always occur at the outlets below lakes. It is to be expected. I don't know why I thought, even for a minute, that the portage downhill to Starvation Lake could have been our last portage before Point Lake.

We then paddled a serene, slow-moving channel through willow-lined banks until reaching our fourth portage of the day, to bypass a steep drop in the Starvation River. Six more kilometres put us at a third drop, around a tight corner—another portage. Very soon after that we reached a 250-m chute flowing through a rock-choked channel.

Carey and Janice ran down the chute. Kathleen and I pulled out to portage, dejected at our comparative lack of skill. Our personal defeat dampened what had otherwise been a glorious day of warmth, sun and splendid paddling. We were now only 10 km from Point Lake, leaving us 3.5 days and 60 km behind schedule. Five more sets of rapids lay between us and Point Lake. I hoped Kathleen and I would be able to run at least one of them. As you can probably tell, I was feeling a little discouraged at not having been able to run down that chute.

August 9. We rose at 6:00 a.m. in bright sun to a 4° morning, which quickly warmed to 15° by 8:00 a.m. We had camped halfway through the portage, and Kathleen and I carried our gear across the second half in about 30 minutes. As we waited for Carey and Janice to paddle down to us, we saw scores of caribou cross the river to work their way up the wide, boggy valley. These were soon followed by hundreds more, until 1,000 to 2,000 animals were trailing, snorting and grazing up the valley. All four of us climbed a small knoll to view, photograph and film this natural spectacle, which reminded Kathleen and me of the wildebeest herds we saw on the Serengeti Plains of Kenya.

After returning to the boats, we set our minds to the day's obstacles. The topographic map showed five more marked rapids between us and Point Lake. Based on our experience with the Starvation River yesterday, each of these could require portaging. I'm sure that we were all somewhat resigned to a slow, tedious descent down the Starvation River.

We paddled down to the top of the first of these marked rapids and beached our canoes. Kathleen and I wanted to scout the rapid before paddling it. We headed off downstream while Carey and Janice enjoyed tea and snacks as they sat on a beautiful slab of pink granite. Carey and Janice didn't need to join us as we scouted. They knew that if Kathleen and I decided to run the rapid, that they could run the rapid too. Also, Carey and Janice likely wouldn't run the rapid if Kathleen and I preferred to portage. We were a group, and groups need to stay together. Carey and Janice pulled out yesterday afternoon, only halfway through that 250-m chute, as soon as they noticed that Kathleen and I weren't following them down. So Carey and Janice waited while Kathleen and I decided what we wanted to do. We appreciated their patience.

After scouting the rapid, Kathleen and I returned to the beautiful slab of pink granite to file our report: "We're gonna run this, Carey."

With Carey and Janice in the lead, we set off caroming through the shallow rock gardens until we entered a narrow side channel, only 1 m wide. Our canoe gained momentum as it shot through an overhanging canopy of stream bank brush. Around a tight turn, we suddenly came upon Carey, standing in the water, pulling his grounded canoe off a rock. We were barely able to stop before crashing into Carey's legs. That could have been a lot worse than slipping on a wet rock. All four of us then portaged the remaining 100 m of the rapid. As we loaded the canoes, Carey said, with some surprise in his voice, "That wasn't an easy rapid, Mike."

"I didn't say it was easy, Carey. I said we were gonna run it."

Everyone is entitled to a little bravado once in a while. Even me. Only four portages to go. Maximum.

After two hours we reached the next rapid and pulled out on river left for lunch, and to scout. Kathleen and I agreed to run it, and enjoyed the higher volume of water, which offered easier manoeuvring through the rocks. Only a maximum of three portages to go.

The next rapid was a simple, fairly wide drop. Only a maximum of two portages to go. The following rapid had too little water to paddle, so Carey and I jumped in and guided our boats through 300 m of boulders. Tiring work, but now only a maximum of one portage to go.

The last rapid, where the Starvation River entered Point Lake, dropped steeply but had plenty of water. One narrow chute, however, shot directly into a large boulder, with deep holes on both sides. The left bank was clear of rocks, and had good footing, so Carey and I lined the boats down to Point Lake. Lining downstream is the reverse of tracking upstream. Carey held the bow painter to guide the boat down, while I held the stern painter, making sure that the stern stayed close to shore and did not swing out into the current.

Of five potential portages today, we had to carry our loads a total of only 100 m. A very successful day.

We camped that night on a rock bluff overlooking a completely still Point Lake. We were happy to have completed this leg of our expedition, undaunted that we remained 79 km behind schedule, with approximately 120 km of Point Lake ahead of us. I hoped this fine, calm weather would hold, and that we would be able to paddle Point Lake every day. These large lakes are prone to strong winds that could confine us to camp.

Kathleen and I finally felt like we were on holiday now that the most difficult overland part of our journey was over. Tonight, for the first time since flying into Winter Lake 13 days ago, Kathleen and I bathed, washed our hair (I still had some hair then) and changed clothes. In the tent, we sipped tea, relaxed and applied first aid treatments to the various cuts, gashes and abrasions on our hands and legs. We're having some kind of fun now.

August 10. My alarm sounded at 5:30 a.m., and I easily rose from my warm sleeping bag to try my luck at fishing. Six casts later I landed a 58-cm (23-inch) lake trout. After a leisurely bannock breakfast, we started down Point Lake, towing the lake trout behind my canoe on a short stringer.

At lunch, Kathleen and I saw a Yellow-billed Loon, and a lemming (probably a collared lemming) which scurried away into a rock crevice.

Back on the water, the wind began to blow as soon as we rounded a point. We struggled against waves in a series of large open crossings, which totalled 3 to 5 km. We beached to set up camp at 7:00 p.m., on a peninsula about 8 km west of Keskarrah Bay. *[Note: Keskarrah was one of Sir John Franklin's guides, and was also the father of Greenstockings, whose brief liaison with Robert Hood produced a daughter.]* For supper, we all feasted on the lake trout, smothered in margarine, and complemented with a cornbread bannock.

The day remained warm, at 18°, even at 10:30 p.m. The evening was calm. We paddled 40 km today, but remained 75 km and 2.5 days behind schedule. Two more paddling days like today, though, and we would reach

Kathleen enjoyed her lunch break on Point Lake.

the brink of moving water—and trees—where we could enjoy cooking over a campfire.

August 11. During breakfast, we saw two caribou swimming the 4-km crossing of Point Lake toward our camp. Soon after putting on the water in a calm, 14° morning, we startled a family of flightless Blue-winged Teal. A warm sun shone upon our backs.

We met our first people of the trip today, two tandem canoes, including a guide, from Wanapitei, a company specializing in wilderness canoeing adventures. The paddlers were huddled up against the bank and seemed tired. We paddled over but exchanged no more than cursory pleasantries. I don't remember where they began their trip, although they hadn't gone overland. I also don't remember how far down the Coppermine River they planned to travel. Maybe we didn't even ask them. Maybe they told us, and I wasn't really paying attention. After the brief conversation, we paddled away and never saw them again.

The wind resumed its usual afternoon attack, and we stopped at 4:00 p.m., at the beginning of a 5-km crossing to the large island near the western end of Point Lake. We travelled approximately 30 km today. As this was tentatively scheduled to be a rest day, we were now only 1.5 days and 45 km behind schedule.

August 12. We rose at 3:30 a.m. and put on the water at 6:15, attempting to begin our day before the wind began its day. Our clever ruse, however, failed miserably. The wind apparently never truly sleeps, and must have been watching us all night. By 8:30 we struggled into a strong headwind, taking rollers over the spray deck on several occasions. This is another reason why we always travel with spray decks. You might think that spray decks are useful primarily for running rapids with large waves, and you're probably right. But large waves on exposed, wind-battered lakes can also swamp open canoes.

I have a friend, Tom Stuart, with whom I shared a house in graduate school. Tom had recently read our Thelon River book when he asked me the following question: "You say that you like wilderness canoeing, but where in that book were you actually having fun?"

In retrospect, Tom had made a good point. There's a lot of talk in our Thelon River book about wind, bugs, rapids, portages and other sorts of physical challenges. The sorts of challenges wilderness canoeists always face. I have to say, though, that our Thelon River adventure was much more idyllic, relaxing and out-and-out enjoyable than this Coppermine River trip. So far, pretty much every day had been hard work. We never just lounge around.

Moreover, having to organize this hard work around other people's needs and expectations adds an additional layer of challenge. This morning, Kathleen complained that she doesn't even feel connected to me. I assume that Carey and Janice were experiencing some of the same feelings. Again, though, it's the price to pay for having companions, and I was very satisfied to be travelling with Carey and Janice.

We took off the water at 4:30 this afternoon, in an area indicated on the map as being forested. The map exaggerated reality, as only a small grove of spruce stood on a boggy shore opposite our camp. After supper, Carey and Janice canoed over to the stand and collected approximately one day's supply of firewood. This was a very welcome addition to our fuel supply, as we had only three days of white gas left. This actually represented fairly good planning on our part, as we brought only a little bit more white gas than we thought would be necessary. We certainly didn't want to bring an extra seven to ten days of gas, which would have added unnecessarily to the weight and volume of items required to carry over the portage trails.

And, in fact, we expected to find wood soon. My 1:250,000 topographic map indicated that we would enter forested country at Redrock Lake, which we planned to reach tomorrow. The Northwest Territories brief *Explorer's Guide to the Coppermine River* refers to the "meandering and spruce wooded shores" from Redrock Lake to Rocknest Lake. Mary McCreadie's book, *Canoeing Canada's Northwest Territories: A Paddler's Guide*, says that the shores of Redrock Lake "are wooded with black spruce." *[Note: For the rest of this chapter, I will refer to this guide as simply the* Paddler's Guide.*]* Based on all this information, we would be more than just a little disappointed if trees didn't show up at Redrock Lake.

We progressed 35 km today, leaving us still 1.5 days, but now only 37 km, behind our tentative itinerary.

August 13. A beautiful, sunny morning, with calm conditions. On the water at 6:45 a.m. Point Lake offered a satisfying exit to its strenuous paddling, often across deep, windy bays. We were exhilarated with the current emptying into Redrock Lake, and we slowly meandered along its spruce-lined shore, in the lee of a slight breeze, with the sun on our backs.

For lunch, we lay on a cobblestone beach, warming and dozing in its 30° surface heat. Only reluctantly did we climb back into the canoes to begin our final two open crossings on Redrock Lake. The wind had obviously been waiting for us to make these open crossings, as it immediately sprang up.

As we turned north, a cluster of buildings on the opposite shore came into view. This surprised us very much, as no buildings were indicated on the 1:250,000 map, and we had never read or heard about any buildings on Redrock Lake. Through binoculars, we saw that the little community was pretty darn elaborate and fancy—perhaps a little too fancy to be a remote Northwest Territories fishing lodge. As we continued to study the opposite shore, a powerboat came across the lake to greet us, and its three occupants invited us to come on over for coffee.

"I don't think we can," I said. "It's getting late, and we need to find a good campsite."

"You can stay with us. You could have a shower if you like."

The three visitors seemed to be upping the ante. Our group of wilderness adventurers seemed to be wavering. Even so, I didn't want to unpack and then repack just to have a shower.

"It's a long way over there," I continued. "And it's windy. It would take us several kilometres out of our way. It would cost us valuable time."

Time was important to us. We were behind schedule, you know.

"We'll tow your canoes."

This was a nice offer, but sometimes being towed by powerboats can be disastrous. Capsizes often result.

We looked at each other. Carey and Janice seemed eager. Kathleen also appeared to welcome the opportunity. I was wavering a bit myself.

"OK, then. That sounds great. Just don't go too fast."

A few minutes later, we stepped into a completely unexpected world filled with luxury and convenience. A very elegant lady introduced herself as Marjorie.

"Welcome. Come on in. We've been waiting lunch for you."

Carey, Janice, Kathleen and I sat down at a large, linen-covered table to enjoy the promised cup of coffee, plus a hot, homemade pizza topped with fresh vegetables and shrimp. What the heck was this place? It was like a dream. Was this actually happening to us way out here on the Coppermine River?

After finishing our meal, we wandered around the dining room looking at photographs on the walls. Most of them featured airplanes, including some that bore the insignia of Wardair. It then slowly dawned on us that we were being hosted at the private lodge (well, it wasn't likely a public camp, was it?) owned by Marjorie and Max Ward, founder of Wardair, which was later purchased by Canadian Airlines.

We then met Max himself, who led us to our sleeping quarters—a very large, red and white striped circus tent. "You guys should put your gear in here and get what you need for your shower. I'll show you where the facilities are."

A person probably shouldn't use terms like "jaw dropping" to describe shower facilities. But see what you think. Remember, we were way out there on the Coppermine River. Carey, Janice, Kathleen and I each had our own separate stainless steel shower stall. The common areas of the bathroom were also stainless steel. "There's plenty of water," Max said. "You could all shower at once if you wanted to. Be sure to get your laundry going."

[Note: I didn't write these details in my diary, so I might be embellishing just a little. And, in fact, I am relying quite a bit on Kathleen's memory of that day. If we are wrong about some of these physical details, try to remember that we were probably still in somewhat of a daze at this point.]

"After you've cleaned up," Max continued, "come on over to the dining room for happy hour at 6:00 p.m. Supper begins at 7:00."

This was truly unbelievable. I didn't use an exclamation point in the last sentence, and I don't think I needed to. Even without the exclamation point, I'm sure that you understand the excitement that we four wilderness adventurers felt.

After showering, I strolled around the compound and met Max hauling some cots down the boardwalk to our sleeping quarters. "Have you seen in any of the cottages?" he asked.

"No I haven't."

"Well, why don't you go over to the one over there and let yourself in. Doors aren't locked around here."

So that's what I did. I went over, opened the door, and stepped inside.

A woman, approximately 30 years old, stood in the centre of the room, only partially dressed. She didn't actually scream, but she was quite adamant that I should leave. She seemed upset. I didn't get a very good look at the cottage. Heck, I didn't even have time to get a very good look at the young woman. And that's not like me.

After a brief nap and rest in our very large, red and white striped circus tent, Carey, Janice, Kathleen and I wandered over to the dining room, which featured teak furniture with china place settings on the tables. Vases of fresh gladiolus, flown in from Yellowknife, provided colourful centre pieces. The four of us had arrived exactly at 6:00 p.m. for happy hour. Two weeks in the wilderness had destroyed any desire on our part to arrive fashionably late. Any drink was ours, simply by asking. While I sipped a glass of white wine, Max came over to ensure that everything was fine.

"Couldn't be better. We really appreciate this, Max. I can tell you, we certainly didn't expect it. We had no idea that this place even existed."

"When I was a bush pilot, I fell in love with this spot, which I call Rockhaven. I met a lot of people in the airline business, and I used to bring executives from Boeing up here to go fishing. In fact, the large tent that you're staying in was the tent that we originally used. So, did you get a chance to see inside that cottage?"

"Well, I went in, as you suggested. But there was a woman in there getting dressed. She told me to get out."

"That wasn't very hospitable of her, was it?"

I don't know what Max meant by that. What was the woman whose privacy I had invaded supposed to do, in his opinion? How hospitable was she supposed to be? Ever since then, I have always wondered if Max knew that the woman was in the cottage. At the time, he seemed to have an impish gleam in his eye.

"You know, Max, when I got out of the shower, I stepped on the scales, and was surprised to see that I have lost 12 pounds since we landed at Winter Lake a couple of weeks ago." (The scales read in pounds only. I had lost 5.4 kg.)

*We had no idea that Max Ward had a luxurious retreat,
way out here, on Redrock Lake.*

"What do you expect? You've been working hard."

Even so, I was quite surprised. I had never felt hungry after supper, and always went to bed feeling full. But, as Max said, we were working hard, in damp, cool weather, often wading in cold rivers for hours at a time. And our diet was lean. No alcohol. No snacks other than gorp. Before the trip, Kathleen had dehydrated all of our suppers, which store much longer if they contain no fat. For suppers such as shepherd's pie, which include meat, Kathleen began by cooking very lean meat, and then draining off all the fat before dehydrating. We have actually kept unused, dehydrated meals at home in our closet for two years, and then used them on the next canoe trip.

Carey, who stood over six feet (1.8 m) tall, had told Kathleen and me that he would need 6,000 calories a day to maintain his body weight. Difficult to provide on a lean, relatively fat-free diet. After the trip, Carey told me that he had lost 16 pounds (7 kg) by the time we reached the Ward compound. Wilderness canoeing is a great way to lose weight, particularly if you go over the height of land.

"When your boat came to get us this afternoon, Max," I continued, "I was reluctant to come over here."

"My man said that all of you looked very comfortable out there. Most people coming down the Coppermine look pretty tired by the time they get here."

"How could I not look comfortable? I was in my canoe. I love being in my canoe."

Between 6:30 and 7:00 the other guests began to arrive. Throughout the summer, Marjorie and Max host week-long events, each intended for a particular group of people. For example, last week had been set aside for immediate family members. This week featured business associates of his son, most of whom were from eastern Canada, particularly Toronto.

It turns out that the Wards purposefully scan Redrock Lake looking for paddlers to entertain their guests. If I remember correctly, there were six tables that night, each of which had eight settings. Carey, Janice, Kathleen and I each sat at a different table so as to spread our entertainment value among as many guests as possible. Supper was stuffed chicken breasts with shrimp, chilled pasta with garlic, and Bavarian mousse with fresh strawberries. It was a sumptuous feast, served by waiters dressed in white coats and black bow ties. Toward the end of the meal, a very well-dressed, nicely perfumed woman asked me, "How were you able to take baths out there?"

"We weren't able to take baths. But I think it was on day 13 that I actually washed my face."

I wasn't being facetious. Just trying to answer her question as factually as possible. I had the impression, though, that any appeal wilderness canoeing might have held for her instantly evaporated. Another guest asked me about clothing, as in how much clothing do I take on a 30-day trip. I listed off the number of shirts and socks, the kinds of footwear, and eventually got on to underwear. "I normally take two pairs of underwear."

"Only two pairs? For 30 days? How can that be?"

As I always say when answering this question, "Well, how many pairs of underwear do you wear at one time? Only one, I suspect. When that pair gets dirty, you wash it and put on the other pair. No sense taking clothes and gear you don't need."

Silent incredulity enveloped my table. I hoped I was being sufficiently entertaining. Although I didn't tell my table mates, I actually usually take three pairs of underwear on wilderness canoe trips, just in case one pair is lost or otherwise damaged. I sometimes even wear the third pair, but not all at once.

In case you were wondering, I didn't recognize any of the Toronto women in the dining room that night as being the woman whose privacy I had invaded. But then again, I didn't get a good look at her. Somewhat disappointingly, she didn't introduce herself to me. I could have explained to her that it wasn't my fault. Max told me to go into her room.

After supper, Kathleen and I lay in the red and white striped circus tent, reflecting on our day. "You know, Michael, most days on this trip have been very unpredictable and unexpected, but always in a bad way. Our canoe capsizing on the first day. Running out of water on the river to Big Lake. Waiting out wind storms. But in my wildest dreams, I never could have imagined such an end to today."

We now had a complete set of clean clothes, were freshly bathed, and physically refreshed. It was like starting the trip all over, even though we were about halfway through. Nevertheless, a luxurious location like Rockhaven did intrude upon, and interrupt, a wilderness experience. We were now 25 km and less than a full day behind schedule.

August 14. The next morning we arrived early at the breakfast table. No other guests were there. I guess none of them were behind schedule. The waiter asked us what we wanted to eat, and I requested bacon, eggs, toast, fruit and juice. I could have asked for bannock, I suppose, but a change of pace seemed appropriate. I didn't write in my diary what Carey, Janice and Kathleen had for breakfast, but I can assure you that it was a made-to-order breakfast of exactly what they wanted.

During our meal, Max came by to wish us well on the rest of our journey down the Coppermine River. "There's a lot of rapids on the Coppermine," he said. "Many of them quite difficult."

"We know that. But we expect that we can run all of them, except, of course, Bloody Falls."

I don't know if it was Carey or me who said that. Could have been either one of us. Carey can run just about anything. I can't, but always believe I can, at least until I get there. You probably remember that Kathleen and I had already portaged one rapid that Janice and Carey ran.

Max looked skeptical. "Oh really? There's a set of very difficult rapids about 50 km north of here. And they're not the worst on the Coppermine. There's been several times that canoeists get to these rapids and realize they can't handle the Coppermine. They paddle back here, and I fly them out to Yellowknife."

Well, I thought. I still expect to run them all. This was not bravado on my part. It's just what I expected.

As we waited for our breakfast, Kathleen read aloud from the *Paddler's Guide*. We were interested in what the guide had to say about these rapids. Carey objected, suggesting something like we shouldn't put too much value in guidebook descriptions of rapids. He was right, of course. But Kathleen and I like to read the descriptions anyway. I said something like, "It's interesting to hear what other people have to say. We don't necessarily accept everything they say. But we want to read it."

We paddled away from Rockhaven at 9:00 a.m. and travelled through Redrock and Rocknest Lakes comfortably and easily, beneath a blue sky dotted with pleasant, fluffy clouds. A few kilometres upstream from the Napaktolik River, we pulled out on river left at 3:45, on a long, beautiful beach. A very relaxing day. Although I certainly enjoyed the interlude at the Wards' lodge, I much preferred the beauty and serenity of our riverside camp.

In the tent, Kathleen read to me from Samuel Hearne's diary, as presented in Farley Mowat's book *Tundra*. Samuel Hearne was the first European to travel to the Coppermine River, reaching Bloody Falls in 1771. He had tried and failed on two previous occasions to reach the Coppermine River from Fort Prince of Wales on Hudson Bay. For his third attempt, Hearne arranged to be led by the native hunter Matonabbee, who was shocked to hear that the British did not travel with women. Matonabbee explained his position:

> For when all the men are heavy laden they can neither hunt nor travel any distance. And in case they should meet with some success in hunting, who is to carry the produce of their labour? Women were made for labour. One of them can carry or haul as much as two men. They also pitch our tents, make and mend our clothes, keep us warm at night—and in fact there is no such thing as traveling any considerable distance without their assistance. More than this, women can be maintained at trifling expense, for as they always cook, the very licking of their fingers in scarce times is sufficient for their sustenance.

This kind of attitude wouldn't go over too well today. I like to believe, however, that Matonabbee's perspective reflected the immeasurable value of women to the success of Inuit and Dene societies. European diaries, written by the expedition leaders, such as Franklin, largely ignored the contributions of people who did most of the work and who provided all of the local knowledge and expertise.

After our slide show presentations in the Vancouver area, we always entertain questions from the audience. At one such presentation featuring this Coppermine River trip, at the Dogwood Canoe Club's Burnaby clubhouse, a man raised his hand to ask, "So where do I find those kinds of women that Matonabbee talked about? Wilderness canoeing would be a whole lot easier."

He got a good laugh. But I don't think such women—women who are willing to serve essentially as slaves to their men—exist anymore. At least not in the canoeing circles in which I have paddled.

Tomorrow we will reach moving water on the Coppermine River. Kathleen and I were anxious about the rapids just north of the Napaktolik River. The *Paddler's Guide* indicated that there were four rapids in an 8-km stretch, the "first real whitewater challenge paddlers will encounter" on the Coppermine River. "The rapids are characterized by boulder fans which create hazardous shallows, large standing waves and ledges. This section requires technical paddling, lining and/or portaging."

These are likely the rapids Max Ward said are very difficult, and which occasionally send paddlers back to Rockhaven to be flown out to Yellowknife. Despite our anxiety, Kathleen and I were confident that we would perform well. After 30 km today, we remained a little over one day and 45 km behind schedule.

August 15. We've enjoyed a second successive short day of paddling, 30 km from 8:00 a.m. to 3:00 p.m. I would have liked to have travelled a bit farther, but Carey and Janice had been pressing for earlier starts with shorter days. They first began mentioning looking for a good campsite at 2:00 p.m. Kathleen and I were happy to stop, though. By now, we certainly deserved to savour some leisurely days.

At 8:30 p.m., Kathleen and I were sitting in our tent, pitched on an esker ridge, overlooking an unnamed lake, with the western sun streaming into our front door. Stripped to our underwear, we basked in the 24° heat.

While Kathleen read from Sir John Richardson's diary, I eagerly and quickly devoured my daily ration of gorp. Since leaving Rockhaven, I seemed to be always hungry. Interesting how I was never hungry during the overland trek, when I had worked hard and long in cold weather. Now with shorter, easier, warmer days, I couldn't wait until my next meal or snack.

One reason we all agreed to stop early today, I believe, was the harrowing experience in the rapids after the confluence with the Napaktolik River. The first one featured a quite strong, pushy current and large, diagonal waves that we needed to cross to reach the inside bend. As both canoes rested in the eddy, Carey said, "See, Mike. That wasn't as hard as the guidebook suggested."

"Well, actually, Carey, it was harder than I expected."

The real difficulty for us occurred in the Class III rapid in the west-trending portion of the Coppermine, about 5 km below the Napaktolik River. As we approached the rapid from up against the left bank, Carey suggested that we "back" around a very large rock jutting out from shore. The rock outcrop was large enough that we couldn't see what lay behind. Our experience had virtually always been, however, that an eddy lies behind such large rocks projecting into a river.

"We can get in the eddy," Carey said, "and then get out to scout if we want to, or run, if it looks OK."

"Sounds good to me, Carey."

Now, "backing" is a lot like lining. The two paddlers ensure that the stern stays pointed to shore so that the canoe does not swing around broadside in the strong current. Backing would also allow us to simply back into the eddy, stern first, as soon as we cleared the boulder. This contrasts with the "normal" way of hitting an eddy, which is to drive the bow into the top of the eddy. We didn't want to do that, however, as we were in strong current and wanted to make sure that the stern would not swing out into even more powerful current. Besides, backing around obstacles, particularly in tight turns, is fun. Well, it's fun most of the time.

The Coppermine is a big river, with impressive hydraulics. We backed around, quite nicely, I might say. But there was no "normal," calm eddy behind the boulder. Instead, as the Coppermine raced around the boulder, it filled the void behind the boulder by reversing its current—what is known as a back eddy. We were immediately thrust back out into the main current and were now headed toward the middle of a rapid that didn't look like anything Kathleen and I would ever want to run. Particularly on a wilderness canoe trip. This didn't look good.

I know people often exaggerate their exploits, but I'm telling you the truth. Huge holes and diagonal waves reared up to greet us. There were no downstream Vs or any apparent routes through. We would just have to wing it and hope for the best. Kathleen and I plunged over a ledge and into a hole that seemed like a 1.5-m drop. We powered out of the hole but were slammed by a diagonal wave that spun the canoe around. We were still upright, though.

We then plunged, stern first, into another hole, but somehow came out, still right side up.

I turned my head around to see that we were hurtling toward another hole, perhaps larger than the last. As you can imagine, we didn't like the idea of plunging into holes or over ledges going backwards. Our stern was now passing by a wide boulder with a somewhat calm eddy behind it. Calmer than the current, anyway. That's all we needed. I plunged my paddle into the eddy, held on, and the boat swung around, like swinging around a fulcrum. We were now going bow first. That was very good. The bow glanced hard off the edge of a boulder and plummeted into a huge hole below. Our spray skirts blew off the cockpit coaming, and water poured into the canoe.

We were still upright, though. We could see Carey and Janice, on river left, up against a cliff bank. They were bailing water in a very small eddy, perhaps no wider than a canoe. We headed over, hit the eddy (in the "normal" way), and bailed the water out of our canoe.

We looked downriver. We were only about halfway through the rapid. Janice looked at Carey and said, "I'm not getting back in the boat."

I don't remember if Carey replied. Didn't really need to. Everyone had to get back in the boat. We were up against a steep, high cliff. There was no real shore that we could walk on to line the boats. The only way out was to paddle the rapid.

We forward-ferried 100 m across the river to put ourselves beyond the huge haystacks at the bottom of the drop. We then turned down and finally reached calm water on river right. We beached our canoes and got out to rest our nerves. Janice was shaking, claiming that it was the most horrendous rapid she had ever run. And that's saying something. On many day trips with our Beaver Canoe Club, we had seen Carey and Janice paddle stuff that Kathleen and I only sat on shore to watch.

Before we got back in our canoes, Janice made Carey promise that we weren't going to run any more rapids unless we scouted first. Carey agreed. But I know Carey. He scouts from the boat. As long as he can see his next place to get off the river, he continues paddling. Even so, we did scout the next rapid from shore. After all, Carey had promised—a promise that he quickly cast aside. Except for Muskox Rapids and the very serious Rocky Defile and Escape Rapids, that was the last rapid we scouted on the trip.

In the afternoon, as we sat around the campfire, all four of us chatted happily about our success. Carey said that when he and Janice were in that sliver eddy, he told Janice to "Hurry up and bail. We need to get back out there to rescue Mike and Kathleen. They aren't going to make this."

Carey knew our skills. He expected us to capsize.

We had made it, though. Kathleen and I have excellent balance in the canoe. We get a low centre of gravity. We have strong bracing strokes. We certainly got lucky with that eddy behind the boulder, which allowed us to get turned around bow first. Without that, we would never have been able to make the sliver eddy on river left. We then would not have been able to bail. We then would not have been able to ferry to river right. We then almost certainly would have capsized in the large haystacks at the bottom of the run. No telling how long it would have taken Carey and Janice to catch up with us. No telling if Kathleen and I and our canoe would even have been able to stay together as the current flushed us downriver. I don't like to think about these "what-ifs" too much. We paddled well, and we made it. As we mentioned to Max Ward, we expected to run all the rapids.

We had reached dense stands of spruce at Redrock Lake, and were happy that we no longer needed to rely on our now meagre supply of white gas to heat our food. Meals cooked over a campfire are so much more relaxed, social and aesthetic compared to those cooked on small, one-burner, white-gas stoves. Kathleen and I always bring a grate—with collapsible, adjustable legs—that provides a relatively flat cooking surface, even on uneven ground. This grate is large enough to heat supper and boil tea and cooking water at the same time. On most mornings, before breakfast, Janice and Kathleen organized gear for the paddling day. Carey and I were responsible for cooking breakfast. We enjoyed squatting over the grate. Just two guys, simultaneously cooking and admiring our respective bannocks.

In our evening tent, Kathleen read from Farley Mowat's book *Tundra*. In the chapter summarizing Sir John Franklin's 1821 descent of the Coppermine River, there is obvious reference to the same rapids that we ran today:

> *We embarked at 9:00 am ... and descended a succession of*
> *strong rapids for three miles. We were carried along with*
> *extraordinary rapidity, shooting over large stones, upon which*
> *a single stroke would have been destructive to the canoes. They*
> *plunged very much, and on one occasion, the first canoe was*
> *almost filled with waves. But there was no retreating after we*
> *had once launched into the stream, and our safety depended on*
> *the skill and dexterity of the bowmen and steersmen.*

The voyageurs stayed up late that night repairing the damaged canoes. The next morning, Franklin's journal, as edited by C. Stuart Houston in the book *Journey to the Polar Sea*, indicates that "before embarking I issued an order that no rapid should in future be descended until the bowman had examined it and decided upon it being safe to run."

Interesting how Janice and Franklin reached the same conclusion. We had certainly read this passage several times before the trip. Perhaps we should have read it again yesterday. On the other hand, running rapids in birchbark canoes differs greatly from running rapids in shorter, plastic canoes. No direct comparison exists. And, as we told Max Ward, we expected to run all the rapids. All I know for sure is that the Franklin expedition survived the rapid without scouting first, as did the Robson/Pitt expedition.

We remained 47 km and 1.5 days behind schedule. Only 336 km, however, lay between us and the community of Coppermine. Even if we took three rest days, we would still have ten paddling days left. We would need to average only a very manageable 34 km per paddling day to reach our goal on time.

August 16. Today we paddled from 8:00 a.m. to 5:00 p.m. and completed 50 km, including nine rapids, the last of which extended more than 1 km. It was shallow with strong current pushing through a boulder field. I don't understand how commercial recreational companies can advertise the

Coppermine River as suitable for novice canoeists. On the west shore of the lake opposite the White Sandy River, where Franklin's party had camped, a shiny object lying on the beach attracted our attention. We stopped to visit the carcass of an aluminum Grumman canoe. This was the second canoe fatality we had seen, the first occurring halfway down the Starvation River. Yesterday we so very nearly added our canoe to these shoreside reminders of misjudgments or inadequate skill. Both Janice and Kathleen acknowledged today that they had trouble sleeping last night, as they reflected on our near catastrophe.

As we paddled north of the Fairy Lake River, in calm water, searching for this evening's campsite, we came upon six elegant, white Tundra Swans floating serenely down the river. We were now only about half a day and 25 km behind our schedule. No more rapids for 130 km, until we reach the Rocky Defile. Any rapid with a name has just got to be taken seriously.

August 17. A leisurely 8.5-hour paddling day, covering 42 km, leaving us still half a day and 30 km behind schedule. We faced a brisk, 18° north wind all day but enjoyed the sun in the afternoon as we paddled across the Arctic Circle. One moose, Tundra Swans and scenic riverbanks of lacustrine clay added to the day's enjoyment.

The particular place to camp each day was selected by the couple responsible for making supper. That meant that either Janice or Kathleen usually chose our campsites.

When it was Kathleen's turn to choose the campsite, she and Carey got out of their canoes and tromped up the beach. They wandered around for a while to determine if the potential site had an appropriate cooking area, a good supply of wood, suitable spots for our two tents, and an area where canoes and gear could be stowed for the night.

After a few minutes, Kathleen would hopefully say, "OK, I like this place," as she pointed to where she wanted her cooking area. She and Carey then tossed their PFDs on the spot each had chosen for their tent.

At this signal, Janice and I started to unsnap our spray decks as Kathleen and Carey returned to the canoes to help unload the gear and carry the appropriate packs to either the kitchen, tent site, or overnight storage area. I then gathered rocks for our campfire and placed a pot of water on our cooking grate. I then started the fire with kindling and wood that Carey and Janice had been bringing back to camp.

All four of us then sat down for a bit of a break while we enjoyed tea, after which Carey and I set up the tarp. Each couple then organized their tent and sleeping bags for the evening before returning to the campfire, where we discussed the day's adventures while watching—and occasionally helping—Kathleen heat up our supper. Afterwards, Kathleen and I boiled more water for tea and for washing the cooking and eating utensils.

We altered this routine when it was Janice's turn to select the campsite. On those days, Janice and I got out of the canoes to assess the site. If Janice decided "yes," then Kathleen and I collected firewood while Carey and Janice organized the cooking area and supper. This camp set-up became a comfortable nightly routine that gave a predictably satisfying end to the paddling day—particularly after having reached spruce forests and firewood.

August 18. We paddled 50 km from 8:00 a.m. to 4:30 p.m. beneath grey, somber clouds, joined by a brisk east wind, which made the 16° day seem cold. Because today was tentatively scheduled as a rest day, we were now 20 km ahead of schedule. Ten days remained for us to cover 200 km. We should easily reach Coppermine sooner than our intended August 28 arrival.

For the first time since the Starvation River, we saw many groups of caribou, often swimming across the river right in front of our canoes. We were also treated to a large male grizzly ambling along the beach; unfortunately, we were upwind, and he retreated to cover, far in advance of a photo opportunity.

We passed by the Hook River, leading to Great Bear Lake. It was here that Franklin met with Hook, one of Akaitcho's hunters who were supplying food for the expedition. Franklin arranged for Hook and his men to meet him at Great Bear Lake should the Franklin expedition return by that route.

Because today was our once-a-week brandy day, Kathleen and I retreated to the tent soon after supper. We enjoyed fruitcake with our libation, studied our maps, read from Richardson's diary, and contemplated the approaching four rapids named Rocky Defile, Muskox, Sandstone and Escape.

August 19. We woke to 10°, and an overcast sky, which progressively cleared throughout the day. By the time we put to shore to set up camp at 4:00 p.m., we basked in 24° warmth, beneath a clear, blue sky.

During the paddling day, as we approached the Big Bend, the river narrowed and wound through very scenic gorges, with caribou and one muskox feeding along the bank. As we turned north around Big Bend, the Coppermine River suddenly seemed very eager to reach the Coronation Gulf, as we sped through the last 6 km in only 30 minutes.

Kathleen seemed to be enjoying the adventure more now. She laughed and smiled tonight in the tent as she read from Richardson's journal and compared his comments with our experiences. Nonetheless, we both sometimes felt that this journey was like a task, something we must accomplish. We had become very regimented. My wristwatch alarm beeps 30 times at 5:30 a.m. Up at 5:45. Cook and eat bannock at 6:00. Begin packing canoes at 7:00. Paddle away from the beach at 8:00. Stop for lunch at 11:30. Munch gorp while floating in the canoe at 2:00 p.m. Begin looking for campsite at 3:00.

Despite this regimentation, today was one of our most enjoyable paddling days so far. It might be our last relaxing paddle, however, as we will reach the first ominously named rapid tomorrow around noon—the Rocky Defile. I hope we're able to run it. I know that I told Max Ward that we expected to run all rapids, but the following description from the *Paddler's Guide* does sound intimidating:

> *To avoid getting swept into the canyon at Rocky Defile,*
> *paddlers should pull out on river right well above the entrance*
> *to the defile. This rapid is 500 m long and ... the well-used*
> *portage trail on river right starts from a rocky cove before the*
> *cliffs begin. Scouting this rapid is difficult from the heights*

*of the canyon and impossible from water level. Only expert
paddlers should attempt this canyon because of the large
standing waves, whirlpools and ledges. Several people have
lost their lives in Rocky Defile and anyone who capsizes risks a
long, cold and possibly fatal swim.*

That didn't sound easy. Kathleen and I consider ourselves to be highly competent paddlers, but perhaps not expert paddlers. We covered 37 km today, leaving us 6 km ahead of schedule. Only 170 km to go to reach the town of Coppermine.

August 20. We made it. We paddled through the Rocky Defile today and are lying in our tent at the confluence with the Kendall River, with a marvellous view eastward to the September Mountains.

We experienced a highly varied day. We began paddling in a wide, calm stretch of the river, in a cool (8°) morning. Mist evaporating from last evening's gentle rain. As we entered swift-flowing water, the morning sun shone brightly and warmly as we quickly covered 26 km through some scenic narrows toward the Rocky Defile rapids. As we neared the canyon, an ominous north wind blew strongly. Two river bends later, the river dropped quickly to the narrow, red chasm, so aptly and picturesquely named the Rocky Defile.

We stopped to scout. My heartbeat quickened in anticipation. We lunched in noon-hour heat, at a cairn erected in memory of David and Carol Jones, who died here. The plaque read, "David and Carol Jones drowned in these rapids August 14, 1972. They loved the north and its people. They respected honesty and truth."

I can't remember where, but I have read that at least six other people had drowned in the Rocky Defile between 1972 and when we arrived in 1995. I wonder if these people inadvertently missed the takeout on river right and were accidentally swept into the rapid. Or perhaps they miscalculated their paddling abilities.

Their fate heightened my anxiety as we trudged back down to river level and stood peering around the corner of the canyon.

"The river's moving like a freight train," Carey said.

I looked at Kathleen. She appeared confident.

"You know, Kathleen, we don't have to run this if you don't want to."

"I think we can run it, Michael."

"We don't have to, though."

If the truth be known, I was trying to get her to say she didn't want to run the Rocky Defile. I wasn't completely positive we could do it.

"No, we can run it. We just have to make one move. All we need to do is paddle out a little bit to get our angle, and then power over to the point there, and cross the eddy line to the inside bend."

She was right, but I remained worried. Back in the canoe, we stroked strongly toward the 1.5-m waves piling off the entry to the canyon on the inside bend. We powered through the trough leading to the eddy behind the point, and just like that, we were in the eddy. That wasn't so bad. We then sneaked down on river right, right up against the canyon wall in relatively calm water, easily avoiding the ledges, holes and whirlpools spread

Kathleen assessed the entry to the Rocky Defile rapid:
"We can do this, Michael."

throughout the rapid between river centre and the left bank. As is often the case, the reality of the rapid fell short of the self-inflicted terror created by fantasy and worry.

We then drifted easily on a strong current, without rapids, 10 km in one hour to the Kendall River, where we set up camp at an apparently abandoned, or intermittently used, fishing camp. We enjoyed the amenities that had been left behind: tables, chairs, a real fire pit with a large grate, and plenty of large spruce rounds already bucked up for firewood. All four of us felt nearly as pampered as we had at the Ward compound.

For hors d'oeuvres, we enjoyed an Arctic grayling that I caught at the confluence with the Kendall River. Minestrone soup, bannock and vanilla pudding, courtesy of Janice, comprised supper and dessert. After supper, in the tent, Kathleen and I sipped tea and nibbled on fruitcake. I was feeling quite content.

We travelled 36 km today, and are now one full day ahead of schedule. We plan to take our scheduled rest day tomorrow, the first time our group has actually enjoyed the luxury of choosing our own rest day. All other layover days had been imposed by bad weather. Only 130 km from Coppermine, which we will probably reach on August 26, two days ahead of schedule.

August 21. A beautifully restful day. Just like a rest day is supposed to be. We woke late—8:30 a.m.—and enjoyed Janice's breakfast of pancakes, strawberries and whipped cream. Well, actually, it was Dream Whip, but mighty, mighty satisfying. We then put into our canoes to paddle 20 minutes up the slow-moving Kendall River, past crumbling sedimentary cliff walls, to the first rapid. We quickly caught five Arctic grayling, ate lunch in the 24° afternoon sun, and drifted casually downstream back to camp.

While Kathleen and I dozed in the warmth of our tent, Carey caught a 66-cm (26-inch) lake trout, which we eagerly consumed at supper. Way to go, Carey! After stuffing ourselves, Carey and I cooked up the Arctic grayling for tomorrow's supper.

We'll be back on the water tomorrow, one day ahead of schedule. Only two marked rapids appear in the 48 km between us and tomorrow's destination of Melville Creek.

August 22. We paddled away at 8:15 a.m. in a cool (4°), autumnal breeze. Around the first bend, we sighted a grizzly bear foraging on a mid-channel island. We beached on the opposite shore to take pictures as the bear stood up on its hind legs, looking in our direction. Moments later, he lumbered away, stopping periodically to peer back to make sure we weren't following. Or so it seemed. He forded the river, shook himself dry, looked back again, and then ran up the bank, eventually disappearing into a thin stand of spruce on the ridge.

The northwest wind increased, sending chills into our bodies as we paddled by beautiful limestone and basalt cliffs framed by a crystal blue sky. After lunch, we turned north past Melville Creek, directly into an even stronger wind, and entered an extended, quick, shallow, rocky rapid. We stopped at 4:15 p.m. to scramble up a boulder-strewn cliff to camp in the lee of a hanging meadow drained by a small, burbling stream, probably Burnt Creek. If that's where we were, then we had completed 58 km today, leaving us only 75 km from Coppermine. We were now approximately 58 km, and more than one day ahead of schedule.

We easily negotiated the three marked rapids today, all of which were little more than fast-flowing ripples over a few rocks. Based on the lateness of the season, and the height above the river where the more-or-less permanent vegetation occurred, we were quite certain that we were paddling at low water levels. This was good. I was glad not to be paddling the Coppermine River at high water, which would certainly have produced pushier water with larger standing waves at the bottom of rapids. Only 22 marked rapids to go, including the named rapids of Muskox, Sandstone and Escape.

[Note: I just checked the monthly mean discharge for the Coppermine River at the outlet of Point Lake, between 1965 and 2011, as reported by the Water Survey of Canada. The second highest average monthly discharge occurs in August, at 202 m³/s (7,130 ft³/s). The average discharge in August

1995, when we were on the Coppermine River, was 170 m³/s. We were indeed paddling on water levels less than normal for August.]

Each night, Kathleen read from the Franklin party's diaries for descriptions of the upcoming section of river. She said she wished she hadn't tonight, as a notation on one of their maps pretty much indicated that the rest of the trip down to Bloody Falls contained "rapids frequent and dangerous." As always, this worried us. Even so, as I told Max Ward, we expected to run them.

August 23. And run them we did. Today we paddled numerous unmarked rapids and 19 marked rapids, including Muskox, Sandstone and Escape. We scouted Muskox Rapids before easily running on the left bank and then punching across the wave train deflecting off the point, to reach the eddy. As always, Carey and Janice went first, and were on shore watching our progress. When we reached the eddy, Carey yelled out, "Good job, Mike." High praise from Carey. I naturally felt pleased with myself.

A man and a woman from Colorado were camped at Muskox Rapids, and we exchanged a few bits of conversation before putting back on the river. About 10 km later, we paddled through Sandstone Rapids. No scouting. No worry. No problem.

We stopped for lunch in a calm section of the river, and our conversation focused on Escape Rapids, which was reported to be a Class IV drop. Let me remind you about Class IV, which, according to the International River Rating Scale:

> *... has long, difficult rapids with constricted passages that often require precise maneuvering in very turbulent waters. Scouting from shore is often necessary and conditions make rescue difficult. Generally not possible for open canoes. Paddlers in covered canoes and kayaks should be able to do the Eskimo roll.*

I have never seen two people in a tandem canoe do an Eskimo roll. I doubt if it's even realistically possible in a tandem canoe fully loaded with gear.

After lunch, we ran three difficult rapids. So difficult that we wondered if we had already paddled through Escape Rapids without realizing it. That was not likely, though. We would recognize a Class IV drop, even at low water levels. It was not possible that we had already paddled through Escape Rapids without knowing it.

The rapids came in quick succession now, until Escape Rapids obviously came into view. My spirits plummeted. The opening to the canyon looked intimidating. This would certainly require a portage. Franklin's party ran this rapid in 1821 and reported that "we barely escaped foundering."

The following description of Escape Rapids is from the *Paddler's Guide*:

> *This is the most difficult rapid of the trip and should be carefully scouted. The river flows through an S-curve gorge creating turbulence near the canyon walls on the outside curves. Two metre waves roll across the left limit at the first bend and a large ledge blocks passage on river right. Canoeists who decide to run this rapid should do so in empty boats.*

There's no way we would take the advice offered in the last sentence. Running in an empty boat would mean that we would have portaged all the rest of the gear anyway. If we portage all of the gear, we might as well also portage the canoe. No, we would not run in an empty boat. We would run or portage, not a combination of the two. Besides, a fully loaded boat is more stable than an empty boat. Maybe not as manoeuvrable, but more stable.

We beached our canoes on river left and trudged along the cliff edge. I began to change my mind. This might be runnable. In fact, I thought it was runnable. We needed only to ferry over toward river right to avoid the large waves at the entry on river left and then ferry very aggressively back toward river left, using an eddy behind those large boulders. This would allow us to avoid the ledge extending out from river right.

Carey and I agreed on the route. Carey seemed confident. Of course, he always does. I was not completely confident, though. "Do you think I'm underestimating the rapid, Carey? We're a long way up, and the waves are certainly larger than they appear from here. Do you really think Kathleen and I can do this?"

If I remember correctly, Carey seemed noncommittal. Certainly the decision to run or not to run belonged to Kathleen and me. No one should ever run simply because someone else says they can. Carey left the decision to us.

Back in the boats, we forward-ferried over toward river right, slowly dropping down below the large waves on river left. We then began forward-ferrying back toward river left, hoping to drop just below those large waves. I was stroking very hard. I felt a genuine urgency to get back to river left to avoid going over the ledge on river right. You would have felt the same urgency, I'm sure. I grunted involuntarily with each stroke, like a tennis player on television, putting everything I had into every stroke. We were now close to the boulder eddy, and gaining on Carey and Janice. How could we be gaining on Carey and Janice? We don't gain on Carey and Janice. Perhaps we were too close to the eddy and should back off. No, that can't be it. Everyone knows it's almost always best to hit an eddy as high as possible. I stroked and grunted, stroked and grunted some more, and ran into the stern of Carey and Janice. We didn't bump them hard, or on purpose. We just wanted to get into that eddy.

Seconds later we were in that eddy. We turned downstream and paddled out of Escape Rapids.

Kathleen and I celebrated in the tent that night with fruitcake and brandy. Only three marked rapids and 34 km to go. We should be in Coppermine in two days, a full three days ahead of schedule.

August 24. Kathleen and I camped at Bloody Falls, named by Samuel Hearne after his guide Matonabbee led his Dene hunters into a massacre of Inuit as they lay sleeping in their tents on the left bank. We reached the portage trail at 11:00 a.m. after 2.5 hours on the water. Following a leisurely lunch, all four of us completed the portage by 2:30 p.m. Along the way, we

On the portage above Bloody Falls.

made a brief hike to the ridge top, which afforded spectacular views south up the Coppermine River and north to the Arctic Ocean. I suggested to Carey that it was a beautiful day for a portage.

"It's never a good day," he grumbled, "for a portage."

Perhaps he was right. The late Bill Mason, Canada's iconic wilderness canoeist, has been quoted as saying that "Anyone who says they like portaging is either a liar or crazy."

I am neither crazy nor a liar, but under the right conditions, I sometimes like portaging. As Bill Mason wrote in his classic book *Path of the Paddle: An Illustrated Guide to the Art of Canoeing*:

> *Portaging can be a welcome change from paddling and a chance to stretch your legs. The trip back for a second load gives you a perspective and a closeness with the land that you don't get from a canoe.*

That's exactly how I felt about our portage of Bloody Falls. I actually enjoyed it. And I repeat. I am neither a liar nor crazy.

At the bottom of Bloody Falls, we said goodbye to Carey and Janice, who continued on to Coppermine, hoping to catch tomorrow's early flight on NWT Air to Yellowknife. Kathleen and I stayed behind to absorb the place and spirit of Kugluktuk, "place where the river drops." I fished in the same spot where Inuit have fished for thousands of years before me. While Kathleen organized camp, I attempted to catch a whitefish for supper. Although I hooked one every 15 minutes or so, their mouths are very soft, and the strong current kept tearing the hook away. At least that's how I explain my lack of success. After persevering for two hours, however, I finally kept my promise that we would have fish for supper.

Kathleen and I were enjoying being all alone on the river. Soon after our meal, however, four groups from town arrived by powerboat. Five people stood on the left bank. Nine people clambered up the right bank. They had come to fish at the falls. Our few hours of being alone on the river were over. We shared short conversations, during which Rachel told us that she worked for NWT Air, the company that we planned to fly with back to Yellowknife. After quickly saying goodnight to our visitors, Kathleen and I crawled into the tent and zipped up the door. Sixteen kilometres to go to Coppermine, but it felt like we were already there.

August 25. No journal entry today. Way too busy. Please proceed directly to August 26.

August 26. I'm sitting in Yellowknife, enjoying pizza and red wine, out of the wind, with a showered body and clean clothes. Yesterday, we left Bloody Falls at 8:45 a.m. beneath blue skies. Moments later, the sky darkened, bringing a gentle rain and a beneficial southerly tailwind.

We drifted between the left bank and an island, and dropped through a series of unmarked, easy rapids. Nonetheless, a diagonal wave slapped over the gunwale, struck me disdainfully in the face, and funnelled into my lap. I guess I should have still been wearing my spray skirt. After all, we were still on the river. We were not actually in Coppermine yet.

Kathleen and I paddled contentedly on a wide, smoothly flowing river that unceremoniously ended its journey at the Arctic coast. No last rapids. No last drops or ledges. The Coppermine River just simply disappeared into the Coronation Gulf. We turned left around a point and headed west toward the town of Coppermine. Between sandy shoals and the shore, the water depth provided only a few centimetres (inches) of draft, and minutes later we were dragging our canoe across the tidal flats, in the rain. Our last physical struggle on the Coppermine River. But the worst was yet to come.

We had read in a brochure that the town of Coppermine had recently built a campsite to accommodate paddlers coming off the river. How convenient and considerate. We beached at the designated location, only to discover, with disappointment, that the toilet facilities were still just a shell, not yet serviceable, and that no running water was available. To compound our disappointment, a strong wind now blew from the northeast, sending waves and chill across the completely exposed, potential campsite of the distant future.

Oh well, Coppermine, with a population of slightly more than 1,000 people, seemed like a bustling, interesting place. We'd just get a room at either the Coppermine Inn or one of the two Bed & Breakfasts. We planned to spend two days there, and were quite prepared to pay the advertised $250.00 nightly accommodation rate.

We sauntered up the slope and came first to the Coppermine Inn. We walked inside and inquired about a room.

"We don't have any rooms available until September."

Not to worry. We just continued up the hill to the nearest Bed & Breakfast, where we were told, "We don't have any rooms available until next Wednesday."

Now if you're reading this book without a 1995 calendar at your side, I should tell you that August 25 was a Friday. A room next Wednesday would not meet our needs. We now had only one option left.

"That's too bad," I said. "What about the other Bed & Breakfast in town?"

"They're closed."

Uh-oh. This wasn't working out too well. We had arrived in town thinking that there were four potential places to stay. Less than an hour later, we had nowhere to stay.

We knew that the next NWT Air flight out of Coppermine wasn't until next Monday. Until then, 2.5 days from now, we were homeless in a windswept Arctic community. We walked slowly back to our canoe on the beach and discovered that someone had already gone through our gear, likely looking for alcohol. Kathleen and I had finished the trip with some brandy left. We always carry our brandy in an unbreakable, red Sigg fuel bottle, which the potential thieves didn't realize contained booze. Nothing was missing. Even so, we wouldn't feel comfortable camping there.

We then walked over to the NWT Air office just after noon, hoping to ask Rachel for assistance and advice. The office was closed for the rest of the day. Kathleen sat on the steps and cried slightly at our misfortune. I tried to encourage her with the unsatisfactory suggestion that camping on the beach perhaps wouldn't be all that bad. "We could use the NWT Air restroom during the day, and could probably get fresh water at the hotel."

We then wandered over to the office of First Air, where a sign in the window said closed until 2:00 p.m. We waited, and were pleased when the agent returned exactly at 2:00 p.m. We followed him into his office to ask about shipping our canoe out and whether we could get space on their next scheduled flight, which we believed to be Sunday.

"Sure," he said.

We told our story of having no place to stay. A young native man working in the back room overheard us and came to the front desk to say, "You can stay in my house. I will be away hunting caribou for the weekend. Just come on in and make yourself comfortable."

"That's very generous. We just might do that."

I preferred to get out of town, though, hopefully tomorrow. From previous research, we knew that no one had scheduled flights to Yellowknife on Saturday. It didn't hurt to ask, though. Our previous information about a campground in town turned out to not be true. Maybe our information about Saturday flights was also wrong.

"Do you or anyone else, such as Ptarmigan Air, fly on Saturday?"

"No. No one flies on Saturday, but we have a flight to Yellowknife tonight."

"You do? We didn't know that. We'll take it!"

So here we are, our second night as tourists in Yellowknife, eating pizza and drinking wine, when only two days ago we were struggling in rapids and portaging Bloody Falls. Twenty-eight days by canoe from Winter Lake to Coppermine. Ninety minutes by jet from Coppermine to Yellowknife.

Already, the marvellous memories of the expedition, particularly pride of accomplishment, were beginning to dominate our thoughts and conversation about the Coppermine River. We were already talking about our next canoeing adventure, perhaps the Horton River, another one of mainland Canada's most northerly rivers. No matter what river, however, next time Kathleen and

I will paddle alone so that we can savour the landscape according to our own whims and desires.

Before then, though, I must thank our paddling companions—and fellow adventurers—Carey and Janice, for inviting us on this "epic wilderness canoe trip." Kathleen and I likely wouldn't have—perhaps couldn't have—done it without them.

PROPOSED COPPERMINE RIVER ITINERARY (1995)

Date	Activity	Kilometres Daily	Kilometres Total	Miles Daily	Miles Total
July 28	Fly to bay at NW end of Winter Lake	0	0	0	0
July 29	Visiting Fort Enterprise	0	0	0	0
July 30	Fishing & hiking at Winter Lake	0	0	0	0
July 31	Head of lake north of Lastfire Lake	17	17	11	11
Aug. 1	Mouth of river from Big Lake	27	44	17	28
Aug. 2	Big Lake	21	65	13	41
Aug. 3	Starvation Lake	15	80	9	50
Aug. 4	Starvation River	12	92	7	57
Aug. 5	Point Lake	18	110	11	68
Aug. 6	Fishing & hiking at Point Lake	0	110	0	68
Aug. 7	Cove on east shore of Point Lake's first bay	25	135	16	84
Aug. 8	Small, narrow bay on north shore of Point Lake	25	160	16	100
Aug. 9	SE shore of "large island" in Point Lake	35	195	22	122
Aug. 10	Narrows to Redrock Lake	33	228	20	142
Aug. 11	Fishing & hiking at narrows to Redrock Lake	0	228	0	142
Aug. 12	Narrows to Rocknest Lake	27	255	17	159
Aug. 13	Napaktolik River	24	279	15	174
Aug. 14	Lake below "3-rapids Island"	38	317	24	198
Aug. 15	Fairy Lake River	29	346	18	216
Aug. 16	Left-bank tributary	28	374	17	233
Aug. 17	Entry to wide, sandy channel	47	421	29	262
Aug. 18	Resting at entry to wide, sandy channel	0	421	0	262
Aug. 19	Big Bend	50	471	31	293
Aug. 20	Rocky Defile Rapids	32	503	20	313

Aug. 21	Scouting/portaging/paddling to Kendall River	10	513	6	319
Aug. 22	Fishing & hiking at Kendall River	0	513	0	319
Aug. 23	Melville Creek	48	561	30	349
Aug. 24	Sandstone Rapids	25	586	16	365
Aug. 25	Escape Rapids	26	612	16	381
Aug. 26	Scouting/portaging/paddling to Bloody Falls	17	629	11	392
Aug. 27	Portaging Bloody Falls	1	630	1	393
Aug. 28	Coppermine (now Kugluktuk)	16	645	10	403

MAPS FROM THE
CANADIAN NATIONAL TOPOGRAPHIC SYSTEM

These 1:50,000 maps were essential for the overland section between
Winter Lake and Point Lake:

86 A/6 Fort Enterprise   86 A/15 Starvation Lake

86 A/11 Angelique Lake   86 H/1 Lake Providence

86 A/10 Shaw Lake

1:250,000

86 A Winter Lake   86 K Sloan River

86 G Redrock Lake   86 N Dismal Lakes

86 H Point Lake   86 O Coppermine

86 J Hepburn Lake

1:1,000,000

NQ-9,10,11,12 Great Bear River

CHAPTER 3

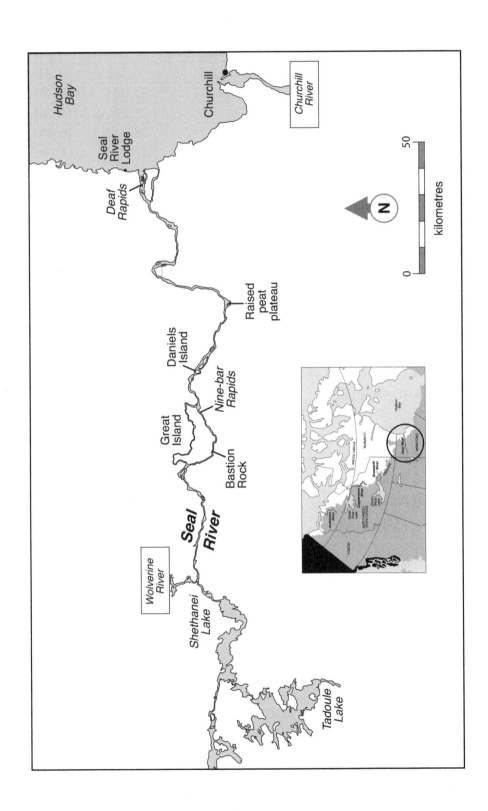

THE SEAL RIVER

Plans A & B

The canoe took me away from the crowds and introduced me to places that had remained unchanged for centuries. And in the going I discovered a sense of freedom that has never been equaled in any other way.

These words by Bill Mason in his book *Song of the Paddle* describe so well why Kathleen and I canoe wilderness rivers. Wilderness canoe trips have given us the opportunity to live free from the intrusions, noises and demands of modern civilization. And, as you will find in this story of the Seal River, some, if not most, wilderness canoe trips serve up completely unexpected adventures.

You might remember at the end of our 1995 Coppermine River trip, while enjoying pizza and red wine in Yellowknife, that I mentioned the Horton River in the Northwest Territories as our most likely next adventure. Sometimes, though, events conspire to change my plans.

Kathleen and I have been very fortunate in our professional careers. As part of the management team in Information Technology Services at the University of British Columbia (UBC), Kathleen received six weeks of yearly vacation. That was plenty of time for us to drive up to northern Canada, paddle for a month, and get back to Vancouver before her holiday time ran out.

As Associate Professor and Associate Dean for Student Affairs in Agricultural Sciences at UBC, I enjoyed only four weeks of paid vacation. As you can immediately see, this was not enough time to be able to drive up to northern Canada, paddle for a month, and get back to Vancouver before my holiday time ran out.

I suppose I need to explain myself. Now, I don't wish to sound like a martyr, nor do I expect you to feel sorry for me, but like most faculty members responsible for research, teaching, administration and community service, I worked pretty much seven days a week, including most evenings. The public impression that university professors just hang out pontificating and generally having a good time during summer is absolutely false. In fact, research is the primary responsibility for all faculty members at major universities like UBC. The axiom "publish or perish" is entirely and unequivocally true. Successful research requires nearly constant applications for grants, supervision of graduate students, writing papers, and making presentations at conferences. If one is not totally committed to the process, then one will simply not succeed in the academic world.

As part of my commitment, I estimate that I worked, on average, 60 to 70 hours per week. There was no overtime pay. In the years that I didn't paddle in Canada's north, I usually took no more than two weeks of vacation time. There was no banking of unused holiday time. The holiday time simply vanished. The reward for my commitment, hopefully, would be academic success. UBC's motto, *Tuum Est,* translates to "It is yours," or "It is up to you." So, if I wanted to reward myself with an extra week or two of vacation to go on a canoe trip, it was "up to me." If my absence lowered my research productivity or success, it was "up to me."

And in fact, my passion for wilderness canoeing did affect my career negatively, even though I allowed myself an extended trip only once every two years. It was just too much time away from my academic and research demands. Do you feel sorry for me yet? Probably not. And you shouldn't. I loved wilderness canoeing. And, as a colleague of mine once said, "On their death bed, no one ever wishes they had more publications." I don't know how he knew that. But it could be true.

Anyway, I didn't go on a wilderness canoe trip in 1996. Had to concentrate on my research, you know. Canoeing would have to wait until 1997. It turns out that in mid-June of 1997, I would be in Winnipeg, as co-chair of the Grassland Biodiversity Session of the International Grasslands Congress. This was a problem. Mid-June would be close to when I would be getting ready to head north to paddle the Horton River. Certainly, I would want to be getting ready no later than late June. The timing of paddling the Horton River and being in Winnipeg just didn't seem ideal.

Well, I thought, since I needed to be in Winnipeg anyway, maybe Kathleen and I should paddle a river in Manitoba. We could have all our gear and food ready, load up the van, drive to Winnipeg, attend the conference, and then head to the river. Heck of an idea, wouldn't you say? We could paddle the Horton River another year.

I sent away for the appropriate topographic maps and planned our tentative itinerary. The Seal River would be a relatively short trip. It should take us only about two weeks to reach Hudson Bay from our starting point at Shethanei Lake.

You might remember from the Introduction that the Seal River enters Hudson Bay about 70 km north of the town of Churchill, which lies across the river from Fort Prince of Wales. Kathleen and I thought it would be fantastic to visit Churchill, which was constructed by the Hudson Bay Company between 1733 and 1771. At the time, Fort Prince of Wales was the largest fort in North America, and together with Fort York, served as Canada's economic centre for more than a century. Lots of history there. We gotta go to Churchill and Fort Prince of Wales.

We also felt a latent association with Fort Prince of Wales because of Samuel Hearne, whose path we had crossed at Bloody Falls on the Coppermine River in 1995. Hearne began his 1770–1771 overland trip to the Arctic coast from Fort Prince of Wales, as did many other European explorers of northern Canada. Visiting Fort Prince of Wales would connect us more closely to these iconic stories and historic adventurers.

First of all, though, we needed to find out when the ice went out of Hudson Bay. We needed to know when it would be possible to paddle from the mouth of the Seal River to Churchill. After a little investigation, I learned of a man named Mike Reimer, who owned the Seal River Heritage Lodge, located just 6 km north of the mouth of the Seal River. He would know when the ice went out of Hudson Bay. He would also be a great contact for additional local advice.

I called him up and got straight to the point. "I'm going to be in Winnipeg in mid-June and would like to paddle the Seal River a few days after that. When does the ice go out of Hudson Bay?"

"Where do you plan to start on the Seal, and when would you arrive at the bay?"

"We plan to start at Shethanei Lake and should reach the mouth of the Seal River near the end of June."

"That's too soon. The ice usually doesn't go out until the first week of July, sometimes even later. I recommend that you don't get to Hudson Bay any sooner than July 15."

This was useful, if not welcome information. This meant that we couldn't leave for the Seal River immediately after the conference. If I wanted to paddle the Seal River, I would have to go to Winnipeg, return home to North Vancouver, and wait more than a week before driving back out to Manitoba. The main reason we selected the Seal River was because of the potential convenient timing with the conference. Now the timing wasn't convenient at all. Too late to change rivers, though. Too late to go back to our original plan to paddle the Horton River in 1997. I already had the maps for the Seal River. Once I have maps—once I have studied those maps—once I have dreamed about those maps—I become committed. I would be paddling the Seal River in 1997.

"Well," I said. "Thanks for the advice, Mike. We will adjust our plans."

"What do you plan to do," Mike asked, "when you get to Hudson Bay?"

"We're going to paddle down to Churchill."

Mike's response came immediately. "Don't do it. We're tired of fishing dead bodies out of the bay."

Not much equivocation there. Mike didn't even want to talk about it anymore. Just in case you're wondering, I am not making any of this up. Mike really said, "Don't do it. We're tired of fishing dead bodies out of the bay."

Mike Reimer's warning supported the information contained in a Canadian Heritage Rivers System brochure for the Seal River, which said that Hudson Bay features "treacherous shoals ... [which] ... canoeists and kayakers cannot do safely. All river travellers are advised to arrange for water taxi or aircraft pickup from the Seal River estuary."

Still, I remained undaunted. It could be that the authors of the brochure were just trying to protect themselves from potential legal liability. If Kathleen and I capsized, or perhaps even drowned, we had at least been warned. They told us so.

In my experience, people who aren't canoeists really don't know much about canoeing. They don't really know what water conditions a canoe is capable of handling. On the other hand, Mike Reimer did refer to dead bodies in the bay. It is possible these dead bodies belonged to canoeists, maybe even experienced canoeists. Mike didn't provide any more details.

He continued to discourage us from paddling to Churchill. "I open my lodge on July 15. You should paddle up to the lodge and stay a few days. We can then fly you to Churchill. Don't try to paddle. If we don't happen to be there, just come in to use the radio phone, and we will come get you."

"OK. Thanks."

I didn't really like this advice. I wanted to paddle to Churchill. Paddling to Churchill would make the adventure complete. Although I said "OK" about coming up to the Seal River Lodge, I hadn't really meant it. I still intended to paddle to Churchill. And, not surprisingly, it has been done. I had recently read an article by Hap Wilson, published in the Winter 1995 edition of *Kanawa*. Hap and his group paddled the Seal River in 1994, a trip made memorable by a huge wildfire that literally chased them down the river. The dramatic cover on that *Kanawa* issue shows two paddlers on the river, with an exploding, smoke-spewing, fire-ravaged forest on the opposite shore. Truly exciting, but not what Kathleen and I would want as part of a wilderness canoe trip. We're not adrenaline junkies, after all. We just want to paddle to Churchill.

Hap's article offered insight about paddling from the Seal River to Churchill: "Some locals asserted grimly that no one had ever done it yet and lived to tell the tale! An over-exaggeration, perhaps."

As you know, I tended to agree with Hap's perspective about over-exaggeration. People who don't canoe don't really know what a canoe, experience and skill can accomplish. In fact, Hap and his companions did paddle to Churchill. I called Hap in early June to ask him about the experience. He said they had "been favoured with calm conditions, but that the tidal flats were very muddy and very extensive."

He didn't encourage or discourage me from paddling to Churchill. During the conversation, I learned that Hap, along with his wife Stephanie Aykroyd, was writing a guidebook to the wilderness rivers of Manitoba. He offered to send me photocopied pages of his "navigation charts" for the Seal River.

"That would be great, Hap. I look forward to receiving them."

I had also recently read a fantastic book, *Kabloona in the Yellow Kayak*, by the late Victoria Jason. In 1991, Victoria and her two companions had kayaked north from Churchill, at the beginning of her four-summer expedition through the Northwest Passage. Victoria had courage, skill and experience. She knew what she was doing. She knew what a kayak, and by implication a canoe, could do. Surely Victoria would tell me "Just go ahead. Don't pay any attention to those naysayers. They don't know what they're talking about anyway."

Victoria lived in Winnipeg. I called her the day after I arrived in Winnipeg for my conference. "So, Victoria. What do you think? Should I paddle from the mouth of the Seal River to Churchill?"

"Don't do it. You'll die."

Like Mike Reimer, Victoria showed no hesitation or equivocation in offering this advice.

"But you did it."

"But we were lucky."

"So why is it so dangerous?"

"The tides go out 10 km, and very strong winds often come up very quickly."

This still didn't sound so bad to me.

"I've been on lots of large lakes subject to strong winds. If the winds come up, why can't I just get out of the canoe, set up camp, and wait for the wind to stop?"

"To keep water deep enough for paddling, you have to go beyond some ledges, and beyond the shallow flats. If the winds come up then, you are committed. You can't just get out and set up camp."

"I'd still like to try, though."

"Well, if you insist, I suggest that you put on the water two hours before high tide, and take out two hours after high tide. That way you will always been in sight of land and would not put yourself at risk from sudden storms far out on the bay. You could probably do that."

"I like that approach, Victoria. Thanks!"

Kathleen and I have allowed four days to paddle the 70 km from the mouth of the Seal River to Churchill. We could travel approximately 17.5 km in each four-hour sprint. At two tides per day, we would need only four of eight tides to bring favourable paddling weather. This was our Plan A. If Hudson Bay looked too dangerous or uninviting when we got there, we would follow Mike Reimer's advice to paddle 6 km north to the Seal River Lodge. This was Plan B. I felt very good about this.

After the conference, back in North Vancouver, I called Jack Batstone, who lived in Churchill and offered a pickup service by barge at the mouth of the Seal River. I read that Jack built a plywood shack just north of the Seal River to provide his clients with some protection from polar bears. It might be nice to stay in his shack when we reached Hudson Bay.

"So, Jack. Kathleen and I will be paddling the Seal River this summer and were wondering how much it costs to stay in your cabin."

"Am I picking you up?"

"No. We plan to paddle either to Churchill or up to the Seal River Lodge."

"Well, then you can't stay."

Doesn't anyone equivocate anymore?

"Not even if we pay you to stay?"

"No. Only the people I pick up can stay there."

This was disappointing news, but at least Jack didn't tell us not to try paddling to Churchill.

"I'm sorry to hear that, Jack. Thanks, though."

Maybe we wouldn't be stopping at the mouth of the Seal River anyway. It would depend a little on the timing of the tides when we reached Hudson Bay. Kathleen and I took along a laminated sheet of tide tables for Churchill for the period from July 11 to July 29. This easily covered the dates when we expected to be paddling to Churchill.

As we planned the trip, I told Kathleen that the paddling would be very easy. I probably said something like, "There's only a few rapids on the Seal River, Kathleen, and they're not very difficult." I don't know why I say these things. I always do, though. I don't try to purposefully mislead Kathleen. I actually believe what I'm saying when I'm saying it. I believed paddling on the Seal River would be easy, despite obvious evidence to the contrary.

Hap Wilson's navigation charts for the Seal River arrived about a week before we left for Manitoba. His beautifully illustrated diagrams listed 39 sets of rapids between our intended starting point on Shethanei Lake and

Hudson Bay. Fifteen of these rapids were rated as Class III or IV, including 14 km of continuous whitewater leading up to Deadly Rapids. You might remember that Class III is suitable only for expert paddlers, while Class IV has long difficult rapids that are not suitable for open canoes. From this information I concluded that, "There's only a few rapids, Kathleen, and they're not very difficult." I don't know why I tend to downplay the challenges. I really don't.

I then reread Hap's article in *Kanawa*. The second paragraph of his article stated "We had just finished running Nine-bar Rapids, a notorious 3.5-km long, hair-raising roller coaster ride, classed as a Class V rapid by Parks Canada."

Hap, Hap, Hap. (You don't mind if I call you Hap, do you?) Are you serious? You're telling me that you just ran a Class V rapid? On a very isolated, wilderness canoe trip?

At this point, I just gotta repeat, for you, the reader, the description of a Class V rapid:

> *"Extremely difficult, long and violent rapids with complicated routes that should be scouted from shore. There is a significant hazard to life in the event of mishap. It is essential to be able to Eskimo roll."*

You must be one hell of a paddler, Hap, or Parks Canada has overstated the rapid's difficulty. In fact, later in the article, Hap wrote that "we were using ... background study information which was compiled in 1986 when the Seal became a candidate for Canadian Heritage River designation. The study indicated 42 rapids up to Class VI. The resource study, although informative, was not very accurate."

That's what I thought. In my experience, people tend to overrate the difficulty of rapids. I don't know why, but it seems to happen a lot.

Even later in the article, Hap wrote that "one of the inherent problems with the international grading system for rapids, is inexperienced people setting rather vague standards to identify them. Much of the volume on [our

Seal River] runs kept centre profile but we always seemed to manage to find easier slots on either side, usually with a few minor ferries and a *&$#-load of bracing."

Now that's more like it, Hap. Big rivers often have so-called "sneak routes" down the bank, particularly on the inside bend. Even so, Hap's discussion of Nine-bar Rapids indicated that, "Everyone we had talked to said that we would have to portage Nine-bar Rapids, but we ran it in its gruesome entirety."

Gruesome sounds challenging, no matter what classification. Even the CHRS brochure says that Nine-bar Rapids is a "possible 3-km portage."

All of this information provided even more contradiction of my original assertion to Kathleen that "There's only a few rapids on the Seal River, and they're not very difficult." I don't know if I mentioned this contradiction to Kathleen. At this point in the adventure, though, while sitting in North Vancouver, the rapids were a long way off. As always, I felt confident that we could run them.

So, Kathleen and I had Plans A & B, a tentative itinerary, tide tables, Hap Wilson's navigation charts and the appropriate topographic maps from the Canadian National Topographic Series. We were ready.

We arrived in Lynn Lake, Manitoba on July 1 after driving 2,830 km from our home in North Vancouver. We knew very little about the history of Manitoba, or of Lynn Lake, and were surprised to see that about one-third of the buildings were boarded up and vacant. We learned later that Lynn Lake was founded in 1950 after a deposit of nickel ore was discovered. The mine opened in 1953, and the population of Lynn Lake peaked at approximately 3,000 people in 1975. After the mine closed in 1976, the population quickly declined, and by 2001 stood at only 700 people.

We had arranged to stay at Betty's Bed & Breakfast, where we enjoyed the pleasant accommodation all to ourselves. Not even Betty spent the night at Betty's Bed & Breakfast. We had also made arrangements to fly to Shethanei Lake the next day with La Ronge Air, and called around 4:00 p.m. to inquire what time we should be ready. There was no answer, so we left a message.

We hadn't heard anything by 7:00, so I called Betty to see if she knew of any potential problems.

"It's Canada Day. They're all probably at the big town celebration."

Oh yeah. We had forgotten. July 1. Canada Day.

We still had not heard anything by 9:00 p.m., and so assumed that we would not be getting an early start tomorrow. That was OK with us, though. We could sleep in, enjoy a leisurely breakfast, and likely fly to Shethanei Lake tomorrow afternoon. We organized our gear a bit and went to bed. The ringing phone woke us at 10:00 p.m. It was La Ronge Air.

"Be down at the float plane dock for a 6:00 a.m. flight."

Good news. We didn't come to sleep in. We had come to paddle the Seal River, down to Hudson Bay, and then on to Churchill.

"I have a question for you. After our canoe trip, we plan to take the overnight train from Churchill to Thompson. Is there any way that you could drive our van to Thompson and leave it there for us?"

"Sure. That would work out fine for us. We often travel to Thompson for shopping and grocery supplies. We'll leave your van at the airport parking lot. There's good security there."

This was very good news for us. It's about 320 km from Thompson to Lynn Lake. To get back to Lynn Lake would mean that one of us would have to take the bus while the other stayed behind at a motel with the gear and canoe. This would have added a day or two of inconvenience. This trip was working out very well.

"Also," I said, "about 100 km south of Lynn Lake, a truck passed us and showered us with gravel, which broke our side-view mirror. Is it possible that you could get this repaired in Thompson?"

"No problem."

"We're certainly happy to pay for gas and your time."

"OK. How 'bout fifty bucks."

"That sounds much more than fair."

This trip was working out very well, indeed.

July 2. We stood on the dock in the early morning warmth, watching the crew load our gear into the de Havilland Beaver float plane, after which they tied our canoe to the pilot-side pontoon.

"So, are you ready to go?" the pilot asked.

"Yep, we're ready. We've checked three times in our van. I think we have everything. I don't think we've left anything behind."

"I'm glad to see that you've brought a rifle. We fly in so many city people who mistakenly think that bears won't bother you if you don't bother them. It just ain't so. You're almost certain to see polar bears when you get to Hudson Bay. Keep your guard up. Keep your rifle handy."

"We will."

Let me tell you a little story before we actually take off for Shethanei Lake. It pertains to my rifle and my hunting prowess. Once, when I was about 14 years old, in the coast mountains of California, I had spent a whole day fishing without catching a single rainbow trout. It was along a stream that I had fished many times before and had always caught my daily limit of ten. Well, if you don't report me to the conservation officer, I will confess that I usually caught more than my daily limit of ten. Most of these week-end backpacking/fishing trips were with my father, younger sister Susan, and occasionally a friend. I was an aggressive angler. I threw my line into only the holes I knew were most likely to yield results. I raced along the stream, casting and catching, casting and catching. The fishing party generally called it a day when the group's total daily limit was reached. I couldn't help it if I caught trout faster than anyone else on the river.

So, on this particular day, I didn't catch anything. I still don't understand how that could have happened. After all, I was the group's premier angler. I was very depressed. The next day, I refused to go fishing. Not very mature of me, but as I said, I was only about 14 years old. I stayed in camp to pout. In mid-morning, two Steller's Jays slipped into camp and hopped about among the pots and pans looking for crumbs and tidbits. My father's .22 rifle sat leaning up against a tree. Without thinking, and perhaps for no other reason than retribution for the rainbow trout that had refused to enter my creel, I picked up the rifle and fired, mortally wounding one of the jays. I went over to investigate as it lay flapping and dying on the ground. Its partner jay glided over to sit at its side. The wounded jay looked at its companion, turned to stare at me, and died. I buried the Steller's Jay in a shallow grave, leaned the .22 rifle back up against the tree, and crawled into my sleeping bag, feeling quite guilty.

I can tell you that I still feel very bad about my actions that day, which was probably in 1962. I didn't fire at another animal again until half a century later, in 2012. And I fired then, only because I believed I had no choice. Kathleen and I had moved to rural Saskatchewan and had assumed responsibility for four older sled dogs from Inuvik. Three of them had been "quilled" quite badly in 2008, following their discussion with a porcupine about territorial rights and restrictions. The discussions did not go well at all for the dogs. In the fall of 2012, I noticed a porcupine moseying near our house. I couldn't have that. I had no choice.

I apologized to the porcupine and explained my position. "I know you're just minding your own business. It wouldn't be your fault at all if my dogs attacked you. But I just can't have you here. The pain you could inflict on my dogs, and on me, is just too terrible. I am truly sorry." I still feel bad about shooting that porcupine.

So you see, I am not a hunter. I have packed a lever-action, .308 rifle and am certainly willing to use it if charged by a polar bear. Can I bring down a charging polar bear? I have no idea. I hope I don't have to find out. As additional protection, Kathleen and I are each armed with a can of pepper spray. Kathleen also carries a "bear banger," a pen-sized launcher with screw-in explosives that make one heck of a loud noise.

Anyway, back to the Seal River story. Kathleen climbed into the back seat of the float plane, and I joined the pilot in the cockpit. The plane taxied down the lake, lifted off at 7:00 a.m., and headed northeast, flying low over the infinite boreal forest. Although Kathleen and I felt relaxed throughout the flight, we both silently wondered what adventures this new country would bring to us.

Two hours later we landed within a few kilometres of where Samuel Hearne camped in March and April of 1770 on his second attempt to reach the Coppermine River. At least that is where we think we landed, according to our topographic map and the four-page Canadian Heritage River System description of the Seal River. As far as I know, there is no actual formal designation of where Hearne camped.

We set up our camp and spent most of the day just relaxing, sauntering and enjoying the quiet stillness. After supper that evening, we climbed a low knoll for a better view of Shethanei Lake and to survey the surroundings of our new home. I felt very satisfied to be back in Canada's northern wilderness and was only a little worried about polar bears, the Hudson Bay tidal flats and Hap Wilson's 39 sets of rapids. All wilderness canoe trips include separation from civilization, which signifies a new beginning. Kathleen and I had separated. Our adventure was now beginning. Its story and ending remained unknown.

We set up our camp on Shethanei Lake and spent most of the day just relaxing, sauntering and enjoying the quiet stillness.

July 3. This morning I thoroughly enjoyed one of my favourite activities on wilderness canoe trips—cooking a breakfast bannock and then smothering it in jam and margarine to share with Kathleen.

After breakfast, we loaded the canoe and paddled 2 km east to wander freely and aimlessly along an esker, certainly standing in the same spots where Hearne had stood and gazed upon the same scenes 227 years before us. As you might know, eskers began as rivers running below the surface of the melting glacier. The tube in the glacier eventually filled with gravel and sand, and when the glacier finally melted, the esker became a ridge raised above the landscape. Eskers, because they drain quickly, are drier than the surrounding habitats, and generally do not support dense tree or shrub growth; consequently, they provide ideal travel corridors for both people and wildlife.

Moreover, such elevated ridges, exposed to the wind, often keep the mosquitoes and black flies at bay. A windy esker becomes a refuge from mosquitoes and black flies. Given a choice, Kathleen and I would prefer not to camp

We wandered freely and aimlessly along an esker, likely standing in the same spots where Samuel Hearne had stood and gazed upon the same scenes 227 years before us.

with mosquitoes and black flies. Eskers give us that choice, and we love to camp on them.

We anticipated a leisurely journey to Hudson Bay. The day was warm. We had no inclination or need to rush, so we spent about an hour photographing plants and just wandering along the esker.

Back on the beach, at the foot of the esker, we discussed whether we should camp early to enjoy the sun or paddle east to the next esker indicated on the topographic map. The day was calm. No wind. We concluded that it was best to head east to take advantage of the excellent paddling conditions.

We paddled easily along the north shore, encountering Yellow Warblers, Lesser Yellowlegs, Common Redpolls, Common Loons and Red-breasted Mergansers. At one point, a white wolf followed us along the shore for nearly 1 km. Samuel Hearne, in his diary, reported that the Chipewyan Indians "believed that the wolf did not eat its prey raw, but by a wonderful wiseness, peculiar to itself, has devised a method of cooking its food without the aid of fire."

Hearne didn't provide any details about the actual cooking method.

Kathleen and I didn't reach our intended esker camping spot, however, as early in the afternoon, a strong wind forced us to shore, where we set up camp in an area burned by the 1994 wildfire. The Heritage River brochure about the Seal River reported "excellent fishing" on Shethanei Lake. Good news, and, as I tell Kathleen, "I can catch fish, anywhere, any time."

Except, of course, on that day 35 years ago when I was only 14. Kathleen waited patiently with her camera to photograph supper. I don't know what happened. But now there are two days in my life when I couldn't catch fish.

I'm a little more mature now than I was on that day back in 1962. I pouted only a little bit while Kathleen prepared one of our dehydrated meals for supper.

We had begun our day at 5° but now baked on the open, charred beach at 28°. Too uncomfortable to linger by the fire. Also, the wind had died, and the bugs were becoming annoying. We retired early, stripped off our hot clothes, and lay in the sauna of our tent. Later in the evening we emerged briefly to enjoy the long shadows of a northern sunset. A cool breeze drifted across our camp. Only a few bugs remained. Maybe it wouldn't be too windy to paddle tomorrow. Kathleen said it didn't matter to her. "The river will bring us a variety of conditions and experiences. We should try to enjoy each of them as they come."

July 4. Our 16th wedding anniversary, and I forgot to pack a card. Very poor planning. I improvised the following, which Kathleen seemed to like:

> *Dear Kathleen:*
> *Adventuring together;*
> *Meeting physical, emotional and mental challenges*
> *together;*
> *These nomadic, wilderness paddles characterize our*
> *marriage;*
> *I can't imagine completing my life's journey with anyone*
> *other than you;*
> *Meeting physical, emotional and mental challenges*
> *together;*
> *Adventuring together;*
> *For all of these reasons I am always happy that you are my*
> *partner and my wife.*
> *Happy Anniversary!*

I have to admit that I am a little embarrassed reading this "anniversary card" 17 years later. It sounds a bit lame and trite to me. All I can say in my defence is that the card was hastily prepared. Too late to write a better one now. I am forever stuck with what I actually presented to Kathleen on the river. I have learned my lesson. Next time I won't forget to bring a card and a present.

The weather deteriorated overnight, and we woke to a blustery, grey morning. We spent much of the morning in the tent listening to rain being driven before howling winds. The rain stopped by late morning, and we wandered around, waiting for the wind to die. Blackened stems of spruce, killed by the 1994 wildfire, lay haphazardly across our aimless path. The fire also renewed life, however. Bunchberry grew vigorously from beneath and among the dead spruce. And everywhere above the rocky beach, Pink Corydalis sprouted through the ash-covered soil. According to MacKinnon et al. (1992), Pink Corydalis "is most abundant for a few years after disturbances such as wildfire." It can apparently bank "its seeds in the forest floor for decades or even centuries, until germination is triggered by disturbance, exposure, and warming of the soil."

After lunch we loaded the canoe, and set out around 1:00 p.m. By 4:00 p.m we had gained about 15 km, to a point 1 km past the esker at the tip of the peninsula dividing Shethanei Lake. We paddled around the point but were driven back by strong north-by-northwest winds.

We had plenty of time in our schedule, though, and were content to stop for the day to enjoy the clouds racing across the horizon. We were glad that we decided yesterday to paddle when the weather was favourable. Large lakes, with unpredictable winds, must be paddled when they grant permission.

July 5. The wind remained strong throughout the night. I rose late, made a fire, boiled water, and took a thermos of tea to Kathleen in the tent. The storm intensified during our breakfast bannock, and we spent most of the morning lying in the tent, lingering around the campfire, and lounging on the beach.

After lunch I decided to practice with my .308 rifle. As you know by now, I have no hunting experience, so I always practice at least once on every canoe trip. I found a rusted piece of tin measuring about 20 cm x 25 cm (8 x 10 inches). I hung it on a branch, and walked back about 50 m. This is the distance that I visualize shooting at a charging bear. With my back to the tin, I wheeled and fired four quick shots. I am pleased to report that every shot hit the mark, in a pretty darn tight cluster.

[Note: I actually practice firing my rifle a couple of times per year. I always hit the targets. Practice is good, and I have become completely confident that if I am ever to be charged by anything made of tin, that I will be able to bring the rusty brute to its knees. I am not nearly so certain, however,

The storm intensified during our breakfast bannock, and we spent most of the morning lying in the tent, lingering around the campfire, and lounging on the beach.

that I could actually take down a growling, teeth-gnashing, angry, menacing bear. Such an encounter would make a great story, though.]

In the late afternoon, the storm seemed to be dissipating, and we began to think of packing up and leaving our beach. We were camped on the lee side of the point and couldn't actually tell if the wind was calm enough on the open part of Shethanei Lake to travel. We climbed into our empty canoe and paddled out to the point where the wind had driven us back yesterday. Only a slight breeze. We were free! We quickly returned to camp, loaded our gear, and paddled away into a very beautiful evening at 8:00 p.m.

We headed across Shethanei Lake, angling toward the east shore. We hoped to reach the lake's outlet, about 12 km away, before nightfall. It would be good to be on moving water. It would be good to be off the lake. It would be good to escape the wind.

As darkness approached, however, we were still nearly 3 km from the outlet, paddling along a boggy, rocky, dense shoreline. We paddled slowly and close to shore, peering into the deepening darkness, hoping to find a suitable campsite. It didn't look promising. We preferred not to camp in a bog or on top of rocks or wedged in between shrubs, but maybe we wouldn't have any choice. Suddenly, though, just before 11:00, out of the gloom, a sandy beach beckoned. We beached the canoe just as night settled beneath a crimson sunset.

July **6.** We broke camp in the sunshine on our fourth morning of the trip. We were excited that we would soon escape the winds that had plagued us on Shethanei Lake.

We paddled away at 11:00 a.m. and reached moving water on the Seal River in 45 minutes. A new phase of our adventure had now begun. We stopped for lunch at the confluence with the Wolverine River, which Samuel Hearne followed north to the Barren Grounds after wintering at Shethanei Lake. Hearne failed in this, his second attempt to reach the Coppermine River, and arrived back at Fort Prince of Wales on November 25. Undaunted, Hearne set out on December 7, 1770, with Matonabbee as his guide. On this third attempt, Hearne finally reached the Coppermine River.

For lunch, Kathleen and I enjoyed a mug of Top Raman soup prepared with water that had been kept hot in a thermos since breakfast. Cheese on crackers completed our mid-day meal. Before heading back to the canoe, we referred to our topographic maps and Hap Wilson's navigation charts.

Our maps indicated an esker on the east side of Zayets Lake that should provide good camping. In fact, Hap's navigation chart included a symbol on this esker in the shape of a tent, which indicated a "large" campsite. Obviously, this would be the place to camp. We love camping on eskers, you know.

Just before the esker, though, Hap's chart indicated a Class II–Class III rapid. The topographic map also showed a series of rapids extending nearly 1 km. Our first whitewater challenge of the trip.

We approached the rapid about an hour after leaving the Wolverine River. We drifted slowly closer, wondering if we should beach to scout. Class III rapids are generally at the limit of our comfort zone, particularly when we are all alone on a wilderness river.

"This doesn't look so bad to me, Kathleen. What do you think?"

"Doesn't look so bad to me, either. Let's keep going closer."

I stood up in the canoe to get a better look at the rapid. OK. I hear some of you saying, "What? You're not supposed to stand up in canoes. They're tippy, you know."

I've heard that too. But canoes are not tippy if your weight is evenly balanced on both feet. A loaded canoe, like ours, is even more stable. I have never tipped standing up in a canoe. Moreover, many canoeists enjoy the art of "poling" up and down rivers. Polers always stand up. They wouldn't enjoy their sport nearly as much if they were always tipping over and thrashing about in the water.

Anyway, I scouted the rapid while standing up in the canoe.

"Doesn't look bad at all, Kathleen. Let's go."

I kneeled back down. Kathleen and I both exchanged our light wooden paddles for our whitewater paddles with plastic blades and light, aluminum shafts. These paddles are heavier than wooden paddles but their more rigid blades move the canoe more forcefully. We easily ran through the rapids and pulled out on river left at the base of our intended camp up on the esker.

"What did you think, Kathleen? Certainly not a Class III. Maybe not even on the high end of Class II."

"That wasn't hard at all."

We felt quite pleased. Maybe all the rapids on Hap's navigation charts are overrated. I'm not saying that Hap overrated the rapids. When he paddled the Seal River in 1994, this rapid might indeed have included sections of Class III. Rivers change by the year and by the season. We both felt confident, though, that we would be able to run most, if not all, of the rapids between us and Hudson Bay.

We tied the canoe to some riverside shrubs and put on our hiking boots. I should say that I always tie my canoe to shrubs or rocks, even if I intend to be away for only a minute or two. We have all heard the old saying about being "up the creek without a paddle." This particular predicament, however, is not really so terrible. You can always fashion a serviceable paddle from driftwood (assuming you are not on the Barren Grounds). Being "up the river without a canoe, or your gear, or your tent, or your food," on the other hand, would be truly horrible. I have actually seen sudden gusts of wind blow canoes off the beach and into the river, where they easily floated away. I would feel pretty sheepish, bordering on stupidly careless, if this ever happened to me.

Anyway, after tying our canoe to some riverside shrubs, Kathleen and I clambered up the esker to investigate camping potentials. Our expectations, and Hap Wilson's recommendation, were confirmed. The esker afforded a large and spectacular camping area, with fantastic views over the Seal River. Our best campsite of the trip so far. Way to go, Hap!

As we began to set up camp, we noticed a plaque, erected to Bill Mason, which read, "The River, The Canoe, The Paddle, The Man. Bill Mason. Seal River Trip 1988. His Spirit Will Come Through."

We read later that the plaque was placed there by some of Bill's friends in 1989 to commemorate a planned trip with him down the Seal River in 1988. Bill had to cancel, however, as he had contracted duodenal cancer, which claimed his life that October, at only 59 years of age. For those of you who might not know, Bill Mason arguably remains Canada's most famous canoeist because of his prolific career as an acclaimed artist, author and film-maker about wilderness canoeing.

After lugging all of our gear, including the canoe, up on the esker, I began to think about my self-proclaimed fishing excellence.

"You know, Kathleen, that place where I fished a few days ago really wasn't a good place. I know I said that I can catch fish anywhere, any time, but that place had absolutely no potential for fish. The water along the shore was covered in rocks and was barely deep enough to float a fish. I fished there only because we were camped there. I didn't really expect to catch a fish."

"It would be great to have fish for supper, Michael."

"Then, my dear wife, you shall have fish for supper. I'll even cook the fish myself."

I put my rod together and scrambled down the esker to the river. Cast. Cast. Cast. Cast some more. Cast a bunch more times. After 30 minutes, not a single fish had struck my lure. What the heck had happened to me? There were now three days in my life when I couldn't catch a fish.

So once again, Kathleen prepared a meal from our selection of suppers that she had dehydrated at home. She said she didn't mind, though.

"You cooking a fish would have been nice, Michael."

But, as she pointed out, dehydrated meals are actually easier than preparing a fish. She'd already cooked the dehydrated meal at home. "All I gotta do, Michael, is warm it up."

After supper, we hiked on the esker that snaked away from our camp, seemingly endlessly, above the boreal forest. Pierre-Esprit Radisson and his partner Groseilliers, in the mid-17th century, were among the first Europeans to travel extensively through the pristine forests of northern Canada. As Kathleen and I viewed our isolated surroundings, I recalled the feelings of Radisson, whose words, expressed more than 300 years ago, still apply to two paddlers standing all alone in the boreal vastness: "We are as caesars of the wilderness, there being nobody to contradict us."

Kathleen and I strolled back to camp through open stands of spruce. The boreal forest extends around the northern hemisphere and comprises the world's largest vegetation type. I enjoyed the fact that most of the boreal forest still remained unbroken by major cities and highways.

July 7. A great day on the river, as we put in a lot of distance, paddling about 44 km to reach the west end of the Great Island at 6:00 p.m. Along the way, we also successfully ran all 11 of Hap Wilson's marked rapids. Two of them were listed as Class III, and we did eddy out on river left to scout the first one. The Seal River was wide, and the most challenging part of the rapid, with large, standing waves, extended from river centre to river right. We easily sneaked down on river left, up against the bank, in nearly smooth water.

The day was not perfect, however. At the end of that first Class III rapid, there was a jumble of small ledges and back eddies. Lots of pools that would be filled gill-to-gill with hungry fish feasting on insects trapped forever in the recirculating pools. I knew this from my vast angling experience.

"You know, Kathleen, we should paddle over to some of those ledges. I could stand on one of those ledges, right above those pools. I know I can catch a fish there. In fact, if I can't catch fish there, then I can't catch fish anywhere."

I put my rod together. We paddled over. Kathleen and I stepped out of the canoe onto the ledge. Cast. Cast. Cast. Cast some more. Cast a bunch more times. Grit my teeth. Wipe my brow. Cast a whole bunch more times. After watching me cast without success for about 30 minutes, Kathleen got up, walked over to the canoe, and said, "Let's go, Michael. It seems that you can't catch fish anywhere."

Oh, that hurt. I was truly embarrassed for myself. There were now four days in my life when I couldn't catch a fish. I was beginning to hate the Seal River.

July 8. We rose late (8:30 a.m.), enjoyed a leisurely bannock break-fast, and spent the day bathing, washing clothes and relaxing. We also enjoyed the ever-popular game of "toss-Kathleen's-diamond-earring-into-a-carpet-of-lichen-and-moss-and-see-if-you-can-find-it."

You might be asking, "Why was Kathleen wearing diamond earrings on a wilderness canoe trip?" Let me explain. Kathleen has pierced ears. She likes to wear something in her pierced ears. That's why she has pierced ears. She obviously wouldn't be wearing large, expensive, diamond earrings on a wilderness canoe trip. Rather, she chose to wear small diamond studs—studs small enough that they wouldn't get caught on shrubs and branches—studs small enough to be comfortable while sleeping. Her diamond studs were the smallest studs she owned.

Anyway, while relaxing at the west end of the Great Island, Kathleen swatted at a mosquito buzzing so very irritatingly around her face. I think she missed the mosquito but scored a direct hit on the diamond stud, sending it flying who-knows-where. We searched for over an hour, with no success. But if you are ever camped at the west end of the Great Island, you might stumble upon Kathleen's diamond earring. If so, Kathleen says you are welcome to keep it. Or, if you like, you can mail it back to us. That would make a great story, wouldn't it?

After lunch, we strolled downriver a short distance to view a rapid listed by Hap as Class II. We agreed that we could run it. Agreement is essential for Kathleen and me. Our policy is that we portage a rapid if either one of us is leery of running. And, if we choose to run, then we must also agree on the best route.

At this point, Kathleen says that I begged her to give me one more chance to catch fish. I need to set the record straight, though. I don't have to beg to catch a fish. In fact, she already knew that I intended to fish at the bottom of the rapid. After all, I had brought my fishing rod with me. What did she think I was going to do with it?

I stood at the bottom of the rapid, scanning the water for the most likely places that fish would congregate. Based on my vast experience and fishing prowess, I knew, almost intuitively, where the fish would be.

Cast. One Arctic grayling. Cast. A second Arctic grayling. I guess I had proven my point. I can, indeed, catch fish—anywhere—any time.

After our supper of FISH, complemented with cornbread bannock, we retreated from the bugs to the tent to plot tomorrow's 40-km paddle to the east end of the Great Island. We naturally reviewed Hap Wilson's navigation charts, which listed seven rapids along our route. The second, at Bastion Rock, was rated as Class II to Class IV, while the last, Nine-bar Rapids, was supposed to be 3 km of "gruesome" Class III & IV.

This unsettled us a little, as we are not really whitewater junkies and do not look forward to long, difficult rapids. You might say, "But you've read this before. You weren't worried then. Why are you worried now?"

Well, this was the first time we had read about these rapids when they were pretty much just around the corner. Easy to be cavalier when the danger was weeks or days away. Less easy to be cavalier when the danger is tomorrow.

During the evening coolness, which drove most of the black flies into retreat, we strolled across the Great Island to enjoy the vistas and landscapes of the boreal forest. While we sat on a large boulder, Kathleen read again about Thanadelthur, a Chipewyan woman who had been captured by the Cree Indians as a young girl. The Cree were southern Indians who enjoyed virtually all of the trade with the Hudson Bay Company. The company, however, hoped to also trade with the northern Chipewyan but were prevented from doing so because of the traditional hostilities between the two nations. In 1715 the Hudson Bay Company in Fort York sent out a party led by Thanadelthur to broker a peace between the Cree and the Chipewyan people.

The mission was plagued by misfortune, sickness and starvation, and many of the Cree deserted. Only Thanadelthur's influence caused the others to remain. She persuaded the Cree to wait exactly 10 days as she trekked out alone to contact her people. On the 10th day, she returned with more than 100 Chipewyan to negotiate a peace treaty, which, according to the Manitoba Parks Branch's *Land of Little Sticks Routes*, might have occurred right there, at the west end of the Great Island.

July 9. We loaded up the canoe and set off in a calm, sunny morning toward Bastion Rock, a little less than 15 km away. After trending southeast from our camp for a couple of hours, the Seal River turned due east. We were now just a little more than 1 km from Bastion Rock. A few minutes later, the river turned abruptly due south and the "Rock" soon came into view. Hap's navigation chart indicated that the Class IV portion of the water was in river centre, with Class II on river right. The navigation chart also suggested a 250-m portage on river right.

Bastion Rock, now only 100 m away, sat at the bottom of the channel. Most of the water deflected back toward river centre, with high standing waves. Kathleen and I hugged the right bank and beached our canoe at the top of the side channel that swept around and below Bastion Rock on river right.

As a river-running policy, Kathleen and I (almost) never enter side channels without scouting. Side channels have less water and are often clogged with debris and log jams. We got out, tied the canoe to some riverside rocks, and sauntered downstream to scout. Just as Hap suggested, the side channel offered Class II water, with a low ledge at the bottom of the drop.

"What do you think? Run or portage?"

"Run."

Back in the canoe, we paddled down the side channel and re-entered the main current only minutes later, safely below the Class IV water. Way to go, Hap. Your navigation chart was bang on. Of course, that's the way we would have run Bastion Rock anyway. Navigation chart or no navigation chart.

Two kilometres later we reached the next rapid, a river-wide ledge with a drop of maybe 1 to 1.5 m. Hap listed the rapid as "Class IV, scout!" The rapid consisted only of the ledge. No rock gardens. I believe that we could have powered over the ledge right up against the left bank and paddled hard to escape the recirculating water at the bottom of the ledge. We have paddled ledges like this before. But not on wilderness canoe trips. Not when we are so isolated. As I've said before, Kathleen and I don't capsize on wilderness canoe trips. Besides, the portage was only a few metres. No big deal.

After reloading the canoe, Kathleen and I enjoyed lunch, sunning ourselves on the rocky shore. Our greatest challenge of the day waited for us only about 10 km down the Seal River. Nine-bar Rapids, which the CHRS brochure indicated was a "possible 3 km portage." Nine-bar Rapids, which Hap Wilson reported to be 3 km of "gruesome" Class III & IV. Rapids with names always command my attention.

Less than two hours later, the land up ahead dropped away as we approached Nine-bar Rapids. We paddled cautiously along the inside bend of the left bank as we approached foreboding, turbulent ribbons of white. We eddied out, wrapped the bow line around a large, stream-side boulder, and hiked down the bank to scout Nine-bar Rapids.

We walked single file, without speaking, both of us independently assessing the cascading challenge before us. The Seal River glowed beneath the lengthening, sunlit shadows of early evening. Golden-green tongues of water surged through an armada of impassive, dark, angular, rocky outcrops. Curling sheets of foam sparkled throughout.

We continued down the north bank until we reached a calm cove about halfway through Nine-bar Rapids. "What do you think so far, Kathleen? Are you wanting to run or portage?"

"I think we can run what we've seen so far, Michael. Let's go back to the canoe. We can paddle down to this cove and then scout the rest of the rapid."

"OK."

We trudged back slowly along the north bank, planning our intended route. "I think this rapid requires only two major moves, Kathleen. First, we need to make a strong ferry out to the eddy behind the large rock at the top of the rapid. From there we can drift by the first jumble of rocks next to shore. Then we need to drive back hard to the left to avoid the ledge in the centre of the channel."

Kathleen nodded. "I was thinking the same thing. After that we should be able to sneak along the left shore. The rest of that entire stretch down to the cove seems to have downstream Vs between all the rocks."

We headed back to our canoe, turning around frequently to memorize the changing perspective of our checkpoints throughout the run. "See that greyish-looking, pyramid-shaped rock? We've got to stay just right of that before beginning to head back left. If we head back any sooner, we'll never get through that first wall of rocks."

"I see it. Are you confident with our choice to paddle this?"

"Yes."

"Let's go, then."

Back in our canoe we stretched our spray skirts snugly over the coaming of the spray deck cockpits. We glanced back one last time down the rapid, picked up our whitewater paddles, and then sat quietly, facing upstream. Kathleen on the left, me on the right. As usual, at the beginning of every difficult rapid, my mouth dried like a discarded chunk of Styrofoam baking in the summer sun. "It's your lean, Kathleen."

"I know. You just make sure you're powering hard when we cross the eddy line."

We took a deep breath and thrust our blades fully into the water. With short, purposeful strokes, we ratcheted our canoe up to the top of the eddy. We crossed the eddy line at full speed, angled slightly outward, both of us leaning lightly downstream. The racing current grabbed the hull of our canoe, from bow to stern, and propelled us outward, across the rapid, toward the mid-channel eddy below the entry rock. With a few forward strokes, we rested safely in the haven of our first checkpoint. On either side of us the Seal River churned in a nerve jangling, clamorous din.

We cocked our heads downstream, searching for the greyish-looking, pyramid-shaped rock. "There it is," said Kathleen, "but it certainly seems a lot more in river centre and closer to the ledge than when we were standing on shore."

"Things always look different from the river. Do you want to leave the eddy on river right or river left?"

Seconds later we re-entered the rock-studded maelstrom, slowly working our way down to the greyish-looking, pyramid-shaped rock. We rode a narrow tongue of green water between two rounded boulders, slipped past the greyish-looking, pyramid-shaped rock, and angled our canoe toward the left bank. The ledge loomed ominously, its jaws wide open, only four canoe lengths below.

"Forward. Forward. More power!"

Knifing through the eddy below the greyish-looking, pyramid-shaped rock, our canoe sped toward the left shore. "OK. Enough power. We're by the ledge. Let's straighten out."

We then ran with the current along the shore, slowing our descent by sideslipping into eddies below scattered rocks that offered clear, obvious passages. Moments later, we easily glided into the shallow, still water of the welcome cove. Halfway through. Only 1.5 km to go.

I stood up to scan downriver. It seemed that several routes existed, as far as we could see, anyway. "This doesn't look so bad, Kathleen. Not many rocks at all. Mostly shallow gravel bars, and some standing waves no more than a metre high. What do you want to do? Do you want to walk down the shore to scout the rest of the rapid?"

"The first half wasn't so bad, Michael. And this looks better. Why don't we just work our way down. The water's not too pushy. We'll just go from one eddy to the next. We can always get off if we can't see the next eddy."

We settled back into the canoe, and the rest of the rapid proved fairly easy, except for a lift-over at the ledge at the end of the run. We then paddled into the calm water at the east end of the Great Island at 8:30 p.m. After our successful run of Nine-bar Rapids, we were feeling quite relaxed, floating comfortably in the early evening. As we slipped past a fairly large rock, its top suddenly rose up and leaped into the water. Quite startling. We normally don't expect rocks to rise up and leap. Although we were nearly 140 km from Hudson Bay, the leaping rock was a seal, which are common on the river, and for which the river was named.

This leaping seal reminded Kathleen and me of the time in 1991 when we were sitting on a veranda overlooking the Mara River in Kenya. The brown river flowed sluggishly between five or six large, round rocks. We chatted about what it would be like to paddle the Mara. Then the "rocks" began to move. Then they stood up to become hippopotamuses. Now that would be truly startling. Imagine eddying out behind a large rock, only to put yourself face-to-face with a 2,500-kg (5,500 lb.) hippo. I'd much rather be startled by a seal jumping off the top of a rock.

Just before 10:00 p.m., after 11 hours on the water, we arrived at the Environment Canada water monitoring cabin, which was rebuilt after the 1994 wildfire that burned for three months and consumed 250,000 ha (620,000 acres). As no one was home, we moved in to enjoy the luxury and comfort of sitting on chairs while eating our supper at a table. Just before crawling into our sleeping bags, we toasted our day's success with a glass of brandy, savoured beneath the bright light of a Coleman lantern. Almost like sitting in one of the fashionable pubs along Vancouver's upscale Robson Street. Well, not quite. We didn't cradle elegant brandy snifters in our hands.

There is a limit to how elegant I can feel while drinking brandy from a plastic cup.

[Note: I just looked up the 1997 water levels for the Seal River. A direct comparison of water levels for our trip in 1997 and Hap Wilson's trip in 1994 would have been interesting in terms of Hap's rating of the rapids. For some reason, though, there were no data for 1997 from June 13 to September 19. For the rest of September 1997, daily discharge ranged between 575 and 611 m^3/second (20,300 and 21,575 ft^3/second). When Hap Wilson paddled the Seal River, average daily discharge in September was only 186 m^3/s. Does this mean that Kathleen and I paddled the Seal River at higher water levels than Hap Wilson? Maybe, but not necessarily. Perhaps there had just been more rain than usual during late July to mid-August in 1997.]

Kathleen and I slept fitfully in the cabin, as mosquitoes harassed us all night. Very few bush cabins, if any, are bug free. We talked briefly about going outside to put up our bug-proof tent. That seemed like a lot of trouble, though. We applied more bug dope, burrowed deep into our sleeping bags, and toughed it out until morning. Bush cabins are often not as comfortable as you might think or hope.

July 10. We left the Environment Canada water monitoring cabin at noon and drifted lazily, about 12 km, down to Daniels Island, where we stopped for a snack at 2:00 p.m. We dozed in the shade, out of the 38° heat. For those of you who prefer imperial units, that's 100° F. That's hot. That's triple digit hot. Kathleen hates hot weather. And by hot, I mean pretty much anything over 25°. Obviously, 38° was too hot to paddle, and we decided to make camp. We lugged our gear up on the ridge to pitch our tent in the shade of a few trees. A cow moose, with two calves, foraged along the water's edge.

During supper, we decided to forgo our one remaining scheduled rest day on the river and push on to Hudson Bay. That would give us one full day at the bay to assess its potential for paddling to Churchill.

The sun shone unbearably hot all afternoon, most of which we spent seeking shelter in the shade. At 10:30 p.m., a moose, likely to escape the heat and the bugs, swam into the river and crossed beneath the blazing sun, which was sinking slowly toward the northwest. We hoped tomorrow would cool off.

July 11. We woke to a cool 8° morning. The wind had shifted to blow in from the east, bringing fog and mist from Hudson Bay, which now, for the first time, seemed to lie, ominously, in wait for us.

We left camp at 10:30 and drifted past Lavarie Island, where we surprised a family of moose and eight seals. *[Note: The moose and seals weren't a family. There was a family of moose, and there were also eight seals.]* Late in the afternoon, we approached the "raised peat plateau" indicated on Hap Wilson's navigation chart. Based on information in E. C. Pielou's book *A Naturalists' Guide to the Arctic*, the peat plateau likely formed 5,000 to 10,000 years ago. I paraphrase:

> *When the accumulating peat from dying, but not decaying sphagnum moss becomes thick enough, it fails to thaw in summer, becoming a flat slab of permafrost. The ground above the frozen slab starts to rise, (1) because the water in the peat expands on freezing, and (2) more water migrates toward the expanding slab. These expansions cause a raised dome to appear.*

We beached our canoe at the base of the peat dome and climbed up, maybe 15 to 30 m to the top. Cloudberry and Labrador Tea, plants that prefer acidic, peaty soils, spread out before our feet, interspersed with large patches of bare, eroding ground. Again, according to Pielou, this particular peat dome seemed to be entering the final stages of its existence. I quote:

> *As it rises, the dome becomes better drained and starts to dry out in summer. Its surface cracks; rain and warm air reach its frozen core, and before long the centre thaws and the whole structure then erodes and collapses.*

As Kathleen and I stood on the peat plateau, looking down the Seal

River, the sun appeared for the first time that day. We hoped that the hot, sunny weather that we'd been cursing only yesterday would soon return. You might remember that on July 3, Kathleen said, "The river will bring us a variety of conditions and experiences. We should try to enjoy each of them as they come."

Despite what she said then, we wished for warm, sunny weather now.

After paddling about 35 km today, we stopped to camp at 6:00 p.m., just north of the raised peat plateau. This is the same location listed as "End of rapids after southern dip in river" in the tentative itinerary for July 11. So Kathleen and I are exactly on schedule. We also successfully ran six more of Hap's rapids, including a Class III and a Class III–IV. At our water levels, we would not have rated either of these rapids as that difficult.

We both felt tired and ate a simple supper of cheese, plus soup cooked quickly on our stove rather than over a campfire. We retired to the tent immediately afterward to sip brandy, to munch on fruitcake, and to study our plant books and maps. Although tired, I was satisfied and content. I was even comforted by the thunder rolling toward us from across unbroken tracts of boreal forest.

For the second evening in a row, a mist formed over the river, perhaps an influence of Hudson Bay, which now lay only 60 km due east. Approximately 90 km away by river.

July 12. We woke to find ourselves completely enveloped in dense fog. We could no longer see the opposite shore. We dozed, then lazed through breakfast, hoping for the fog to lift. We finally paddled away at 12:30, despite the poor visibility and a slight but steady headwind. After 90 minutes the fog lifted to a grey sky as the headwind intensified. After struggling until a little after 4:00 p.m., we camped at the "alluvial deltaic island" indicated on Hap Wilson's navigation chart, approximately 17 km downriver from last night's camp. I was curious to know why Hap referred to this island as deltaic. We were still a pretty long way from the Seal River delta. If I ever meet Hap I will ask him. *[Note: I just emailed Hap Wilson, and he responded that "the terminology ... was taken from the Parks Canada description in their Heritage Rivers inventory." So I still don't know why this island is called deltaic. I probably never will know, as I don't have any idea who in Parks Canada I could ask. Sorry about that.]*

I felt very content in our home stretched along the banks of the Seal River. For me, it only takes a few days of living—in the open—on the river— before I become enveloped by quiet exhilaration. It is as though the very power of the earth and the wind penetrate to my soul, and I never feel so free, so strong, and so alive as when I am paddling down a wilderness river.

We enjoyed a stroll down the 1.5-km sandy beach before our supper of chili and tea. We stopped to appreciate and photograph plants such as Mouse-ear Chickweed and Rock Cranberry. Rock Cranberry is also commonly called Lingonberry. Kathleen says she prefers Rock Cranberry as more descriptive. And, as she asks, somewhat rhetorically, "Who knows what a Lingonberry is anyway?" Apparently, Kathleen doesn't.

We woke to find ourselves completely enveloped in dense fog.

For the first time on the trip, the entire day was cool, reaching a high of only 12°. With the wind and fog, we felt cold and longed for some heat. We would even have welcomed the 38° heat that afflicted us two days ago. By 9:30 p.m. fog completely surrounded our camp once again.

July 13. We lay in the tent at 9:00 p.m. The rain had continued, nearly without interruption, since 4:00 a.m. this morning. We spent the day in the tent, reading, napping, snuggling, snacking and waiting for the rain to leave us alone. We also contemplated the difficulty of the 13 rapids that remained between us and Hudson Bay. We hoped to run them but believed that the last, Deaf Rapids (Class IV), likely presented the greatest possibility of a portage, maybe as long as 500 m.

We also reviewed our Plans A & B for reaching Churchill. As you well know by now, we had allowed four days to paddle the 70 km to Churchill, and could travel approximately 17.5 km in each four-hour sprint. At two tides per day, we needed only four of eight tides to bring favourable paddling weather. This was Plan A, as suggested by the late Victoria Jason.

During the past three mornings, however, the fog had been too dense to risk paddling on the bay, such that we would have lost the morning tide. Also, the afternoons had been windy, perhaps preventing us from paddling the bay on the afternoon tide. The closer we got to Hudson Bay, the worse the weather had become. We had now spent our last tentative "rest day" in camp, and would no longer have a full day at Hudson Bay to assess the potential for paddling to Churchill.

So it seemed that our plan for sprinting to Churchill was in some jeopardy. For the first time, Kathleen and I talked seriously about pursuing back-up Plan B to paddle 6 km north, up the Hudson Bay coast to the Seal River Lodge. We were happy that we confirmed with Mike Reimer that the lodge would be open on July 15, and that we might arrive between July 16 and July 19.

Before heading downriver, though, ever closer to the malevolent bay, we took one last walk along the beach to enjoy the evening mist and stillness.

July 14. We successfully paddled the 14 km of continuous rapids known as the Felsenmeer—German, for "sea of rock"—which included the Class IV Deadly Rapids. Difficult rapids never seem to have friendly names. There are no Class IV rapids known as Winnie-the-Pooh Rapids, or Yummy-Chocolate-Pudding Rapids. No. Difficult rapids always have ominous names, such as "Deadly."

Anyway, when we arrived at Deadly Rapids, we beached on river right to scout. The rapids were, after all, called "Deadly." Kathleen and I consider ourselves to be prudent canoeists. Prudent canoeists scout Class IV rapids called "Deadly." Besides, the rapid truly did look serious as we approached by canoe.

We scrambled down the rocky shore in a light rain and a dense mist. "Deadly" had high volume in the middle and two serious ledges on river right halfway down. We agreed on a plan to ferry out very near to the large waves in river centre. This would put us beyond the immediate threat of going over the ledges. Then, to avoid being swept into the large waves in mid-channel, we would turn down and head hard right to eddy out just below the second ledge halfway down the rapid. Only two necessary moves. Three, if you count the eddy turn below the ledge. We should be able to do it.

We both felt confident as we climbed back into the canoe, snugged our spray skirts over the cockpit coaming, and began our ferry out to river centre. I stroked hard all the way, worried about those ledges. From the bow, Kathleen yelled out, "Michael. What are you doing? Head down. Go right. We're too far out!"

"But where are the ledges? I can't see 'em."

"Just go right!"

I went right, as Kathleen instructed. She knows what she's doing. Still, though, I asked one more time, "Where are the ledges?"

"We're OK. Just keep going right."

Moments later we eddied out behind the ledge and rested in the calm water.

"Michael. What was the matter? Why couldn't you see those ledges?"

"My glasses were all fogged up because of the rain. I couldn't see, so I took them off."

I should tell you that I wear glasses for a reason. With my foggy glasses off, I still couldn't see all that well.

Apparently telling the truth doesn't always impress my paddling partner. In retelling the story, Kathleen likes to say, "Next time you're going to run a Class IV rapid blind, you could at least tell me so I can get out of the boat."

She didn't actually say that at the time, but it makes a good story. And, she actually might have been thinking it at the time.

We camped that evening on a beautiful tundra ridge, on the left bank, approximately 8 km downstream from Deadly Rapids.

The day had been generally overcast, with some fog, but mostly dry and mostly calm. We ran all the rapids successfully, and were certainly pleased with ourselves. Only six more rapids before Hudson Bay, which was now only 20 km down the Seal River. Deaf Rapids, right near the bay, is alleged to be the most difficult of the entire journey. We intend to camp tomorrow on Hudson Bay itself, and then likely head north to the Seal River Lodge the following morning.

During the day, we saw a few more seals and several flocks of elegant Tundra Swans. By 9:30 p.m., our tent was once again enveloped in mist drifting over from Hudson Bay.

July 15. I woke just before 5:00 a.m. and was encouraged to see a small patch of blue piercing the dense fog that surrounded our camp all night. We enjoyed another bannock breakfast, photographed an elegant Northern Bog Violet, and put on the water at 9:30. In a little over an hour, we reached the entry rapid to the Seal River delta. The sun hinted that it might break through to dissipate the mist. The fog reasserted its dominance, however, and we peered into the grey gloom as we ran downriver.

The fog and mist grew even more dense, with visibility sometimes down to only 50 m. But we hoped to reach Hudson Bay today, and we paddled on, until it became obvious that we were running rapids based primarily on sound, intuition and reaction. Not very wise, as we definitely heard—but could not see—what sounded like a very large rapid just downstream. We pulled off the river to have a better look at the rapid from shore. This was a good idea—in principle. We still couldn't see the rapid, however, because of the dense fog. We portaged across a wet, slippery boulder field, about 500 m around the rapid.

We studied our topographic map before getting back into the canoe. The Seal River delta has many islands and bays, which made it difficult to know exactly where we were. Very dense fog added to our uncertainty about how close we might actually be to Deaf Rapids. We paddled on. Straining to see. Straining to hear. At one point, because we couldn't see any river banks, we thought that perhaps we had entered the mouth of the Seal River and were approaching Hudson Bay.

Just wishful thinking on our part, though. We couldn't see river banks only because fog obscured them. And besides, it was very unlikely, even ludicrous, that we had paddled through Class IV Deaf Rapids without knowing it.

We paddled on until we heard a threatening roar downriver. "This could be Deaf Rapids, Michael."

"Yeah. Could be."

Visibility had again dropped to only 50 m. We headed to shore. Best to run Deaf Rapids when we could actually see Deaf Rapids. You might remember the incident at Deadly Rapids, when Kathleen said, "Next time you're going to run a Class IV rapid blind, you could at least tell me so I can get out of the boat."

I preferred to have Kathleen in the canoe when we ran Deaf Rapids. She's a very good bow paddler.

So, we ended our paddling day at 6:30 p.m. to set up camp on a very wet and boggy flat that undulated like a waterbed. Kathleen heated soup for supper, after which we crawled into the tent for tea.

Our very soggy, boggy home for the night was among the all-time worst campsites I have ever "enjoyed." Even so, I was glad to have stopped, and to

We set up camp on a very wet and boggy flat that undulated like a waterbed.

rest from struggling against fog, wind and rapids. We didn't reach Hudson Bay today, and we thought we were still about 2 km above Deaf Rapids. Despite these adversities and anxieties, however, we were thoroughly enjoying our trip. Life on the river might not always be easy, but life on the river is always simple. Like all obstacles, we would deal with Deaf Rapids when we got there. We would run them if we could. We would portage them if we must. We would just have to wait to see what it looked like when we arrived tomorrow morning. Maybe we would even paddle all the way to the Seal River Lodge tomorrow. If Deaf Rapids were just downstream, then we were only 10 km from the Seal River Lodge.

July 16. We left our soggy, boggy, undulating, waterbed camp at 10:00 a.m., beneath a low sky, but no mist on the water. We ran two rapids down to Deaf Rapids, and got out to scout on river right. Very high, threatening waves throughout. From our vantage point, it looked like there was a potential "sneak route" right up against the bank on river left.

"Do you want to ferry over there, Kathleen, and see what it's like?"

"No. I want to portage."

We lugged all of our gear past Deaf Rapids on a fairly well-defined trail through low shrubs. We stood next to our canoe, and stared to the east, across the mouth of the Seal River, which was filled with ledges everywhere. The Hudson Bay shoreline has been rebounding at a rate of about 0.5 to 3.0 metres per century since it was released from the weight of the ice that covered this landscape during the last glacial advance. This rebounding has created numerous, jumbled, haphazard ledges in virtually all directions. No obvious route existed through this last obstacle between us and Hudson Bay.

Kathleen and I picked our way east for another 45 minutes through the maze of ledges, rocks and rapids. And then, two weeks and nearly 280 km after leaving Shethanei Lake, we finally paddled into Hudson Bay, where we startled half a dozen seals sunning themselves on the rocks.

We filled our water bottles and plastic water jug with the last fresh water from the Seal River, paddled north around the point, and reached Jack

Deaf Rapids: What should we do? Portage or run?

Batstone's plywood shack at 5:00 p.m., only 25 minutes before high tide. Excellent timing on our part, even if not entirely planned.

We pulled the canoe high up on the beach, tied it to some willows, and walked up to the shack. No lock on the door. No one home. We moved in. Yes, I remember that Jack said we couldn't stay here unless he was picking us up. I also remember that he built this plywood shack so that his clients didn't get eaten by polar bears. Even though we weren't Jack's clients, we still didn't want to get eaten by polar bears. We moved in. And besides, when we get to Churchill, we'll find Jack and offer again to pay him for our night's accommodation. I promise.

We thoroughly enjoyed a spaghetti supper, and congratulated ourselves with brandy. We lay snug and warm in our sleeping bags, and discussed Plans A & B. Today had been relatively calm, with a few minutes of sunshine. Perhaps we should opt for the more exciting Plan A, to paddle to Churchill. The wind, however, seemed to be intensifying. Perhaps we should pursue the more prudent Plan B, to paddle to the Seal River Lodge. Either way, we wouldn't start paddling until about two hours before the evening high tide at 6:30 p.m. So we had all day tomorrow to decide.

July 17. We slept late and savoured another great bannock breakfast in the morning sun—our nicest day in a week. High cloud—no hint of rain or fog. Just before low tide, at noon, we strolled down to where the water rose at yesterday's high tide. Even through the binoculars, we couldn't see any water out on Hudson Bay. Just rocks and mud. Truly impressive, as people had suggested to us. It was one thing to hear that the tides go out 10 km. It was quite another thing to actually see for yourself.

Hudson Bay is much more than just another ordinary bay. In fact, it is the world's second largest bay, exceeded in size only by the Bay of Bengal. Hudson Bay's maximum length and width equal 1,500 km and 830 km, respectively (930 miles and 515 miles). Its total area equals 1,230,000 km^2 (470,000 square miles). For a Canadian perspective, Hudson Bay is nearly twice the size of my home province, Saskatchewan. For an American

Just like Victoria had told us. The tides on Hudson Bay go out 10 km.

perspective, Hudson Bay is nearly three times the size of California (where I was born). Hudson Bay is shallow, with an average depth of only 100 m. The long fetch, with strong winds and shallow water would make very formidable and challenging canoeing.

We turned back toward Jack's shack and saw a polar bear, much closer to the shack—and its safety—than we were. We didn't want to run, and we certainly didn't want to get any closer to the bear. So we just stood there and watched, with rifle in hand, as the bear slowly ambled north into the wind. It stopped briefly to look at us, rolled in some willows, and disappeared over a small ridge. We had seen many black bears and grizzly bears on previous backpacking and canoe trips. We had become accustomed to bears being black or brown. So startling to see a white bear for the first time.

We scurried over to the shack and stood outside to see if the bear were circling back. It seemed, though, that we were all alone. At least for the time being, anyway. We sat on the steps of the shack, sunning ourselves, sipping tea, and learning the names of some of the vibrant flowers dominating these

Marsh Ragwort on the Hudson Bay coast.

scenic Hudson Bay Lowlands: Marsh Ragwort, Purple Paintbrush and Sea-shore Chamomile.

The weather continued to improve throughout the afternoon as we photographed plants and the landscape and watched the tide rising over the glacial rocks strewn all along the shore of Hudson Bay. Kathleen and I had both looked forward to reaching Hudson Bay. Now we needed to decide whether we would paddle south to Churchill or north to the Seal River Lodge.

Through the binoculars, the lodge looked very inviting. Even though the lodge was 6 km away, it seemed to tower above the rock-strewn mud-flats. I'm not exaggerating. The lodge looked really tall. Really tall like a sky scraper. Let me explain with the following information provided by E. C. Pielou. I quote:

> *Light travels slightly faster through warm air than through*
> *cold, causing a light ray, as it passes from cooler to warmer*
> *air, to curve back toward the cooler air. To somebody*
> *observing a distant object through air that is warmer above*

than below…it will be elongated vertically, making it seem
taller than it really is. This is a superior image, seen across a
cold surface, and the kind likely to be seen in the Arctic.

Now do you believe me?

So, it was time for a decision. What would you do if you were part of our expedition? Here are the attributes of Plan A: paddle 70 km over four days, in four-hour sprints south to Churchill, risking fog, wind, mudflats, rocky shores, polar bears and extensive tides.

Here are the attributes of Plan B: paddle 6 km for one afternoon, north to the Seal River Lodge, where we could shower, sleep in a bed, eat prepared meals while sitting at tables, perhaps enjoy a glass of wine, share our stories with fellow guests, and then fly to Churchill.

You probably noticed that I asked what would you do in our situation. When Kathleen and I give our Seal River slide show, we always ask the audience to vote on what they would do. It's generally nearly unanimous that the audience prefers Plan B, to paddle to the Seal River Lodge. This is what we expect.

Well, when we presented our first Seal River slide show to our Beaver Canoe Club, we phrased the question differently, in that we asked, "What should we (as in Kathleen and I) do?" Most of the audience preferred Plan A, to paddle to Churchill. After the presentation, while chatting with club members, I talked to Dan Burnett, who had raised his hand in favour of paddling to Churchill. "Would you really have paddled to Churchill if you had been on the trip, Dan?"

"No, but I wanted to see you paddle to Churchill."

That's why, ever since that first presentation, I always ask, "What would you do?"

So, if you were standing there with Kathleen and me at Jack Batstone's shack, what would you recommend that we do? I'll wait for your decision. You've already decided? That's what I thought. So we've all decided on Plan B. We will paddle to the Seal River Lodge. It seemed prudent, and so much easier. We have experienced a very enjoyable trip down the Seal River. Let's

Waiting for the afternoon high tide.

call this trip done, and go to the lodge. And we still get to paddle a little bit on Hudson Bay, even without canoeing all the way to Churchill.

Our decision made, we waited for the tide to return. Two hours and 45 minutes before high tide, we began carrying gear and canoe across the mud-flats to meet the rising tide. We started to load the boat at 3:45 p.m., and set out in a slightly windy, choppy, swelling ocean toward the Seal River Lodge, clearly visible to the north.

After 1 hour and 45 minutes, the lodge was distinctly visible, but we couldn't see any people. That struck us as odd. You would think that the lodge guests would be excited about a lone canoe paddling north. You would think that the lodge guests would be standing on the beach, waiting to welcome us, ready to offer us elegant glasses filled with wine.

We paddled on, a little perplexed. A few minutes later, we could see that the windows and doors of the Seal River Lodge were still boarded up with plywood. At 6:32, exactly two minutes after high tide, we paddled into the cove in front of the still vacant Seal River Lodge. We had executed Plan B perfectly, but now found ourselves in a bit of a predicament. Are you still happy with your choice of Plan B?

Oh well, Mike Reimer told us that there was a radio phone in the kitchen. Too soon for us to start worrying. I removed two Robertson screws from a side door plywood shutter, and we entered the main lodge. (Yes, I had a Robertson screwdriver with me. I always carry a variety of tools in my repair kit. You never know.) We strolled over to the kitchen and saw the radio phone, exactly where it was supposed to be. This was good. Plan B was still working. We depressed the call button, and spoke into the transmitter.

"Two canoeists at Seal River Lodge. Over."

No response. We tried again.

"Two canoeists at Seal River Lodge. Over."

Again. No response. We studied the radio phone.

"There must be an on-off switch, Michael. Maybe this is it."

Good. No reason to have left the radio on when there's no one here. Plan B was still working.

We again depressed the call button and spoke into the transmitter.

"Two canoeists at Seal River Lodge. Over."

No response. We tried again.

"Two canoeists at Seal River Lodge. Over."

Again. No response. We turned off the radio phone.

Maybe we don't know how to use the radio phone. I started to look for an instruction manual when Kathleen noticed that the radio wasn't plugged in. That makes sense. No reason to plug it in when no one was there. We attached the radio phone to an adjacent battery, turned it on, and were rewarded with sounds and lights. This was very good. I was beginning to love Plan B.

We spent the next several minutes repeating ourselves.

"Two canoeists at Seal River Lodge. Over."

We must have transmitted and then listened two dozen times. The last six times or so, we added greater urgency.

"Two canoeists STRANDED at the Seal River Lodge. Over."

The radio remained silent. Perhaps no one was listening to the frequency.

But then, Reimer had told us to use the radio phone if he wasn't there. He knew approximately when we were coming. He owned an ecotourism business. He must have been listening. Plan B was not looking as wonderful as it had only a few minutes ago.

Just then, Kathleen noticed (she notices everything, doesn't she?) that the cable leading away from the radio phone led to a hole in the floor. The end of the cable, however, didn't actually go through the floor but just lay there, not attached to anything. What could this mean?

I crawled under the lodge, found the other end, and poked it back up through the kitchen floor. The two ends seem to have been severed. The cable included an outer set of wires around an inner set of wires encased in a tube. This was not like electrical cord at all. Not like the cord I could just easily twist back together and then secure with electrician's tape, which I always carry in my repair kit. I learned later that this set of wires was coaxial cable. Although I try to be prepared for anything, I don't yet carry any equipment in my repair kit to splice coaxial cable back together. Call me ill-prepared if you want.

Nevertheless, we tried our best. I held the two ends together while Kathleen transmitted and listened a dozen or so times.

"Two canoeists STRANDED at the Seal River Lodge. Over."

No response. Just silence. Obviously, the radio phone was not going to work. We don't know why the cable had been severed. Perhaps one of the very numerous Arctic ground squirrels had chewed the cable, just to see what it tasted like. Don't know why the squirrels would do that. I can't think of any other reason why the cable would have been severed, though. The damage must have happened over the winter, as certainly Reimer would have fixed the cable had he known last summer or fall that it had been severed.

We now had no communication, no pre-arranged pickup, and were 76 km from Churchill with only six tides remaining before we were scheduled to be in Churchill. Besides that, we now had canoed 6 km on Hudson Bay and knew firsthand that it could be dangerous, even with relatively calm conditions. We had paddled broadside to the incoming tide, and struggled to avoid rocks and shoals, while still making progress along the shore. If there were high winds driving a surging tide, we could be forced broadside up against the rocks, where our canoe might pin, or even capsize.

Kathleen and I spread our sleeping bags on mattresses in one of the bedrooms and fell asleep, more than just a little uneasy about our situation. I had taken a decided dislike to Plan B. Maybe we should have tried to paddle to Churchill.

As I lay in bed, though, I also thought about the many highlights of our day. We had successfully paddled the open shore of Hudson Bay. For the first time in our lives, we had witnessed the effects of a superior mirage, which made the Seal River Lodge appear to be several stories high. And, best of all, during our morning walk, we had seen our first polar bear. Yes, despite being the only residents at the Seal River Lodge, Kathleen and I had enjoyed a good day. Maybe Mike Riemer would come to open his lodge tomorrow. He had likely just been a little delayed for some reason.

July 18. I slept well during the night and was dozing when Kathleen rose just before 9:00 a.m. to go outside. Moments later she yelled out, "Michael. A plane is coming!"

I quickly dressed, rushed up the observation tower, and saw two float planes, flying low, from the south, heading directly toward the lodge. Maybe someone had heard our distress call. These planes must be coming to see us!

As the planes passed overhead we waved excitedly, and the lead plane tipped its wings in response. They continued to fly low, and I kept expecting them to circle back and land. Instead, they simply continued flying north, and were soon out of sight and sound. I guess they thought we were just saying hello. We were at a lodge. There would be no reason for them to assume that we were "stranded." Moments later, a third plane, with wheels, flew low, just to the west of the Seal River Lodge. It also soon disappeared. We remained alone, with only the wind and the falling tide as company.

We spent our day resting and reading. We also tried more carefully to splice the cable back together with duct tape, but were apparently still unable to transmit, as we received no response. In the afternoon, we went for a tundra hike. When we reached a small lake about 1 km west of the lodge, to collect fresh water, Kathleen spotted a polar bear approaching from Hudson Bay. We walked quickly back to the lodge, climbed the observation tower, and watched the bear enter the tide and swim away toward the south.

We ate our chili supper at 5:00 p.m. and repacked all of our gear just in case a boat should arrive at high tide at 7:25. No luck, however. High tide came, covered the rocks, and then ebbed away, with no boat coming to our aid. Looked like we would spend a second night at the Seal River Lodge. We retired to our beds at 8:00 p.m., for reading, brandy and fruitcake. We had looked forward to each high tide, hoping that the Seal River Lodge owners would come to open their lodge. But, on our first full day at the lodge, July 18, the morning and evening tides came and left, without any sign of any boats anywhere on Hudson Bay.

July 19. We woke early to another morning of sunshine and a day of hope that someone would come by boat to the lodge. We were again disappointed when the 7:40 morning high tide left without bringing any boats up from Churchill.

Before lunch, we walked 1 km to the lake to collect drinking water. We spent the afternoon reading, looking at plants, playing cribbage, checking the condition of the polar bear fence that completely encircled our prison/haven, and regularly looking south toward Churchill.

We weren't fully able to enjoy the area's beauty, as we thought only of how long it would be before any boat passed by the lodge. Our canoe trip was over. We were at a resort. Yet, we were now dealing with the greatest adversity of the trip. Just like being windbound, we had virtually no control over our destiny. Surely, someone would come by someday to take a message to Churchill for us.

During supper of shepherd's pie, we discussed our concerns and discomfort. We were warm, dry, had plenty of fuel, food and water, and were in absolutely no danger. Yet we felt uncomfortable. Here we were, living safe and secure in a lodge, doing nothing more than just waiting to be rescued. Somehow, just waiting and hoping seemed wrong. We thought maybe we should try to make a break for Churchill. We quickly agreed, however, that if it was inappropriate to paddle to Churchill two days ago, then it was even more inappropriate to paddle to Churchill now, just because we felt trapped. And, we had actually been seen by someone in those float planes. Perhaps they will have returned to Churchill and might mention to Reimer, or someone who knows Reimer, that "guests" were at his lodge. That might trigger Reimer's memory that he had encouraged us to come to his lodge. Also, we had filed a trip report with the RCMP that indicated we might be at the lodge on these dates. The RCMP might notify Reimer. Could we have planned this trip any better? Was our predicament our fault? Had we failed somehow? I didn't think so.

Our intent (Plan A) had been to assess Hudson Bay before deciding whether or not to paddle to Churchill. We could not, therefore, have pre-arranged for a pickup at the mouth of the Seal River. If we had pre-arranged for a pickup, we could not have paddled to Churchill. Our backup (Plan B) was to paddle to the Seal River Lodge, whose owners told us they open on July 15. They also indicated that we could use the radio phone if no one was at the lodge. I also talked to the owners just before leaving North Vancouver to report that we might arrive between July 16 and 19. They said, "Fine. Canoeists often drop by."

Based on all this planning and preparation, we believed it was reasonable to wait for help, which would surely come someday. Even so, I felt sheepish and to blame for our situation. For the first time on any canoe trip, we were hoping to see boats and people. Also for the first time on any canoe trip, we had seen no one since the pilot left us at Shethanei Lake, nearly three weeks ago.

Twenty minutes before high tide, 8:00 p.m. No one came.

Reading books in the lodge, we learned of a traditional Inuit saying: "Good luck nearly always follows after misfortune. If this were not so, all the people would die."

Kathleen and I now waited patiently for our good luck.

Maybe tonight, like last night, we would see the northern lights. Assuming of course that we actually got up during the night. Some of the joy had gone out of this canoe trip. We tried to remind ourselves of what Kathleen said way back on July 3: "The river will bring us a variety of conditions and experiences. We should try to enjoy each of them as they come."

July 20. We woke to another sunny, calm morning, and discussed whether we should try to paddle 40 km south to the Dymond Lake Lodge, also run by Mike Reimer. Maybe Mike was at the Dymond Lake Lodge. Goofy idea, though. It would likely take us two days to paddle to the Dymond Lake Lodge, and it might also be vacant. Then nobody would know for sure where we were. We could leave a note here, but it was probably safer and wiser to just stay where we were.

Kathleen suggested that we pack up all of our gear to be ready.

"When we first arrived here, I assumed that the owners of the lodge would come in a day or two. Now I think that they're probably not coming at all, and that it will only be happenstance that someone might come at a high tide. We need to be ready to leave in a hurry."

Sounded like a good plan. Besides, it would give us something to do. Something that would make us feel more in control.

About 8:30 a.m. we left the lodge to walk 1 km to that small lake to collect more drinking water. After reaching only halfway, we heard, then saw a helicopter circling and hovering near the mouth of the Seal River. As it began to fly north, we quickly ran back toward the lodge to intercept its flight path. As we neared the helicopter landing pad, the chopper circled low overhead. We waved wildly, and made downward-sweeping motions, illustrating to the pilot that we would like him to land. The helicopter banked toward us, revealing its markings as a Canadian Coast Guard helicopter. Our hopes soared. Surely they were coming to find us!

The chopper dipped to acknowledge our presence and then sped away rapidly toward the north. Kathleen started to cry. In frustration, I scolded her.

"Be a man, Kathleen. No need to cry."

I felt embarrassed for myself, for three reasons. First, she can cry if she wants to. The situation seemed to warrant a few tears. Second, "being a man" doesn't preclude crying. Men cry too. Third, and perhaps most important, I wouldn't want Kathleen to actually be a man. I liked her very much just the way she was.

Immensely deflated, Kathleen and I returned to the lodge to play cribbage and solitaire. After lunch, we again set out to the lake for drinking water. On our return trip, approximately halfway back, and still 500 m from the lodge, Kathleen spotted a polar bear in the willows, only 200 to 300 m to our left. We had read that polar bears never run during the heat of summer. So much the better for us. As best as we could carrying a heavy jug of water, we ran to the lodge and scurried through the gate just before the bear reached the fence. For the next 20 minutes, the bear circled the compound, repeatedly trying to gain entry under, over and through the fence.

I had heard before that the Inuit have many names for the polar bear, depending on its age, sex and reproductive status. And in fact, reading a book in the lodge, we learned that *atiqtalaaq* refers to a newborn cub. *Atiqtaq* indicates a cub able to join its mother away from the den. *Angujjuaq* means a fully grown male. It seems that the broader term for polar bear, *Nanuk*, has a variety of meanings, including "the ever-wandering one," "the one who walks on ice," "the great white one," and "an animal worthy of great respect."

We certainly held a great deal of respect for this animal circling our compound, and wondered what the words would be for "polar bear trying to get stranded canoeists inside the fence." After taking a few pictures of the bear, Kathleen and I climbed the stairs to the observation tower and stood ready, with rifle in hand. If the bear did gain entry and came after us up the stairs, he would be somewhat confined, and I could get more focused shots. I much preferred this strategy compared to the potential chaos of all three of us racing around the compound, with perhaps two of us in panic mode.

The polar bear eventually lost interest, wandered toward Hudson Bay, and lay down in a small tidal pool where it splashed and cooled itself. The

*Polar bears added excitement during our
one-kilometre hikes to collect fresh drinking water.*

bear then continued its journey to the ocean, where it was joined by another polar bear at the water's edge.

Back in the main part of the lodge, playing cribbage, we again heard the motor of an aircraft. We rushed outside to see a float plane disappearing to the south, likely returning to Churchill.

Back in the lodge to resume our cribbage game, we were quite dejected and wondered how much longer we would remain stranded at the Seal River Lodge. "I think we're going to have to unpack some of our gear, Kathleen. I'm getting hungry. Maybe we should cook supper. I think we should also get our sleeping bags out. It doesn't seem like we'll be going anywhere today."

Moments later, about 6:00 p.m., we once again heard the unmistakable sound of a helicopter approaching from the north. Again, we rushed outside to see two helicopters flying directly toward the lodge. We ran toward the landing pad, rifle in hand.

*We wondered what the Inuit words would be for
"polar bear trying to get stranded canoeists inside the fence."*

Just in case you were wondering, I had rifle in hand for polar bears, not to shoot down the helicopters. We weren't that desperate yet.

Kathleen and I made very exaggerated motions for the pilots to land. Certainly we must not have looked like normal ecotourists. Certainly we looked somewhat crazed and in need of some assistance. The two helicopters passed overhead, circled around, and then, so very beautifully, landed 100 m away!

I have been told by a professional writer that the use of exclamation points in modern literature is frowned upon. (Are you frowning right now?) Rather, the content of the words, the strength of the prose itself, should express exclamation. Well, two points about that. First, I am not a professional writer. And second, it was damned exciting when those helicopters landed.

Such excitement called for an exclamation point. Modern, professional writers should just be thankful that I didn't use two or more exclamation points.

We walked up to the pilot and shook hands.

"You got a problem here?"

We blurted out our story. "Open July 15—boarded up—Robertson screws—radio phone—coaxial cable—Arctic ground squirrel—four days."

"Well," he said, "If you want to go to Churchill, get in. I don't have room for any gear, though. I can only take you and your wife."

"Well maybe you should just take Kathleen, then. I should probably stay here and guard the gear. Once she's in Churchill, Kathleen can arrange for someone to come get me by boat."

"First of all," the pilot responded, "I'm going to take both of you or neither of you. Second of all, you tell me you've been here for four days and haven't seen anyone come to the lodge. Who exactly are you guarding your gear from?"

He made a reasonable point. We ran back into the lodge and grabbed our overnight cases. We screwed the plywood shutters back on the side door, jumped into the helicopter, and lifted up over Hudson Bay. Immediately, nearly 1,000 beluga whales came into view in the shallow water below. (Notice that I didn't use an exclamation point. I wanted to, though.) Well, maybe we saw only hundreds of beluga whales. But, it could have been a thousand. According to the Canadian Heritage Rivers System brochure, the Seal River Estuary "is the calving and breeding grounds for 3,000 beluga whales."

Moments later, we approached the Batstone shack at the mouth of the Seal River and noticed how bleak the trip would have been had we tried to paddle to Churchill in four-hour sprints. Even near high tide, with the current good weather and wind conditions, the mudflats were extensive and appeared inhospitable for canoeing and camping.

We flew wonderfully and elegantly down the coast, past the still vacant and boarded up Dymond Lake Lodge. And then, only 30 minutes after feeling completely abandoned at the Seal River Lodge, we neared Fort Prince of Wales on the opposite side of the river from the town of Churchill. We landed at the Churchill airport and took a taxi to the La Perouse House Bed & Breakfast, where we had pre-arranged accommodation for the night of July 20. We had arrived exactly on the day originally planned. (Pencil in an exclamation point at the end of that last sentence if you wish. In fact, I encourage it. Modern, professional writers be damned, I exclaim!)

We knocked on the door and were welcomed in by our host, a very gracious woman. "I'm glad to see you," she said. "I mentioned to my son, who works for the Department of Natural Resources, that I was expecting guests this afternoon."

Apparently this news perplexed her son, as it's not easy to get to Churchill. There are no roads to Churchill. And, if I remember correctly, the train arrived only three days per week. Similarly, only a limited number of commercial flights served Churchill on any given day. Her son was probably thinking that on a late Sunday afternoon, everyone who was going to be in Churchill was already in Churchill.

"How are they getting here?" the son asked his mother. (I apologize for not remembering their names.)

"They're canoeing down from the Seal River."

And her son's response? You guessed it. "They can't do that. They'll die."

"I was getting worried about you," she told us. "I'm glad that you made it."

"We are very glad to be here."

We told her about our four days at the Seal River Lodge, and the helicopters, and how we had to leave all our gear behind, including clean clothes.

"That's OK," she said. "Take those dirty clothes off. I'll put some bathrobes in your room. While you're showering, I'll put your clothes in the washer and dryer."

Yep. Kathleen and I were very glad to be at the La Perouse House Bed & Breakfast.

Two hours later, Kathleen and I sauntered to the restaurant. We marvelled at how quickly our situation had changed. At 6:00 p.m. we were stuck in the lodge, seemingly forever. By 9:30 we were strolling casually to the pub for hamburgers and fries.

We sat down and asked the waitress to bring us a beer. Didn't make any difference what kind of beer. Just bring us a beer. "And we would also like some French fries and a cheeseburger. Lots of gravy on those fries, please."

A few minutes later, our rescue helicopter pilots sat down at the next table. "I'm glad you saw us," I said. "No telling how much longer we would have been at the lodge if you hadn't seen us."

"Well, we didn't see you at all. Unless you're looking for people on the ground, you almost never seem them. We turned back only because we wanted a closer look at the lodge."

Dang. That was lucky for us. "You know," I continued, "We had an EPIRB with us, but we never considered using it, even for a second. Just out of curiosity, if we had set the EPIRB off, would we have been charged? How much would it have been?"

"Well, for almost all rescues, there is no charge. Your situation was different though. You were at a lodge. You weren't hurt. You weren't sick. You probably had a month's supply of food in the pantry. If you had set the EPIRB off, it would have been only because you were tired of being there and wanted to go home. They might not have charged you, but it could have been as much as $20,000."

Well, as I said, we never considered using the EPIRB. It would have been too embarrassing. I would have to be pretty much already dead before I would set it off. We ordered another beer. Life was again beautiful. Plan C, hitching a ride on a helicopter to Churchill, worked to perfection.

July 21. Last night, while Kathleen was in the shower, I called Mike Reimer. I didn't write down the conversation in my diary, so the following is what I remember 17 years later. The gist of the conversation, I believe, is accurate.

"Hello, Mike. This is Mike from Vancouver. I talked to you about a month ago, about my wife and I canoeing down the Seal River, and our plan to paddle all the way to Churchill. Do you remember?"

"Yeah."

"You told us that it was too dangerous to paddle to Churchill, and that we should come up to the Seal River Lodge, which would be open on July 15. Remember that?"

"Yeah."

"Well, we arrived on July 17, but no one was there."

"We decided not to open on July 15."

"Anyway, Mike, some helicopter guys brought us back to Churchill this afternoon, but our canoe and all our gear are still back up at your lodge. Can we hire you tomorrow to take us back up there to retrieve all our stuff?"

"I don't have time."

It was a friendly conversation, even though unproductive from my point of view. Some people have suggested that I should have been angry with Mike Reimer, but I wasn't at all. We were not Mike's responsibility. As far as he knew, we might have changed our minds about paddling the Seal River. As far as he knew, we might have paddled to Churchill. After all, that's what we told him we were going to do. Mike had a business to run. It wasn't his job to interrupt his work to go up to the Seal River Lodge on the off chance that Kathleen and I might be there.

Anyway, after talking to Mike, I called Jack Batstone. "Hello, Jack. My name is Mike. My wife and I paddled down the Seal River and arrived at the Seal River Lodge on July 17, expecting that Mike Reimer and his guests would be there. It was still boarded up from the winter, though. Some helicopter guys saw us there and have brought us to Churchill. But our canoe and all our gear are still back up at the lodge. We were hoping that we could hire you tomorrow to take us back up there on your barge to get all our stuff."

"I don't know if I want to go up there tomorrow. I'd have to find out when high tide is."

"Jack, I've been staring at the tide tables for four days. Tomorrow morning's high tide is at 9:20 a.m."

"OK. I'll pick you up at eight o'clock tomorrow morning. My cost is $250.00."

I already knew about Jack's cost. Two-hundred-and fifty dollars was his advertised price per canoe for picking people up at the mouth of the Seal River.

Jack showed up exactly at eight. We climbed into the truck. Jack looked at us and said, somewhat sternly, "You better bring a coat. It's going to be cold and wet out there."

"I told you, Jack. All our gear is at the lodge. These are the only clothes we have."

Jack grumbled. When we boarded his high-bowed barge, he handed us some rain gear. Jack was right. The trip across Hudson Bay to the lodge was cold and wet.

We arrived at the lodge at 9:35, 15 minutes after high tide. "I'm going to set you on shore," Jack said. "I can't tie up. The tide's going out. You'll have to canoe back out to me. I hope you don't take very long to get back here."

"It won't take long at all, Jack. Our stuff is already all packed up."

I removed the Robertson screws from the plywood shutter on the side door. Fifteen minutes later, all of our gear was at the water's edge. I screwed the shutter back on the side door. We loaded the canoe and paddled out to Jack, who helped us transfer canoe and packs onto his barge. Only 10:00 a.m., and we were heading back to Churchill.

About halfway across the bay, Jack said, "You know, $250.00 is what I normally charge for each canoe when I pick people up. Usually I pick up at least three canoes on each trip. But you're only one canoe."

"You should charge what you think is fair, Jack."

Jack thought for a moment, and then continued. "You know, I had to miss a half day of work this morning."

"Be fair to yourself, Jack. Charge what you think is fair."

Back in town, Jack swung by the train station. "We'll leave your canoe here," he said. "No reason to take it to the B & B just to bring it back again."

"But what if someone steals it, Jack?"

"Who's gonna steal it? There's no way to get a canoe out of town except by train. Everyone would see them. No one's gonna steal your canoe."

At 11:45, Jack dropped us off at the La Perouse House Bed & Breakfast.

"You know," he said, "To put you on shore at the lodge, I damaged my propeller on the rocks. Normally I don't get anywhere close to shore when I'm picking up canoeists. They always paddle out to me. I think $250.00 is too low a price."

"Jack. I understand. Just tell us what you think is a fair price."

"I think another $50.00 would be fair."

"We were thinking more like an extra $100.00, Jack."

Jack seemed pleased. I would have paid even more if Jack had asked. He had helped us out of a very difficult situation, and we very much appreciated his efforts.

So, by noon we were back in Churchill to become tourists as we headed out on the road to Fort Prince of Wales. The men who had lived at the fort worked as clerks, tradesmen and administrators for the Hudson Bay Company. Company journals and reports indicate that alcoholism was a major problem. I'm sure that there wasn't much else to do during those long, lonely, boring, bleak winters on the frozen shores of Hudson Bay.

Forty cannons were placed to protect the fort from attack. According to the tour guide, 10 men were needed to operate each cannon. But only 39 men lived at Fort Prince of Wales in 1782 when a French naval force under the leadership of Jean-François de Galaup, comte de La Pérouse besieged the fort. Samuel Hearne surrendered without firing a single shot in defence. I don't know why I'm telling you this. It just seemed such an ignominious defeat for what had been the largest fort in North America.

July 22/23. After breakfast, Kathleen and I wandered over to the train station. My canoe was still there. I know Jack told me that no one would steal it. I just wanted to be sure.

We hired a guide, who boated us over to Sloop Clove, where we viewed Samuel Hearne's signature, which was carved into the rock in 1767. I still admired Samuel Hearne despite his quick surrender to de La Pérouse. There was little else that Hearne could have done, however. According to Farley Mowat, in his book *Tundra*, "The French had four hundred men, and Hearne had thirty-nine. The uncompleted fort was, as La Pérouse noted, indefensible, and Hearne had no choice but to surrender."

The Hudson Bay Company used Sloop Cove to secure their boats safely from the ice during winter. Because of the rebounding land, however, Sloop Cove is now high and dry, less than 250 years later. On our return back across the river, we boated among hundreds of beluga whales, who swam right up to the edge of the boat to let us pat them on the head. You should have been there. It was so overwhelmingly cute.

Kathleen and I boarded the train for Thompson, Manitoba at 11:00 p.m. At the station, we met Brian and Penny, who had just finished paddling the Thlewiaza River, which enters Hudson Bay 150 km north of the Seal River. We settled into our seats and chatted away about our respective adventures. Brian and Penny were kindred canoeing spirits—our Plans A, B, and ultimately C seemed to resonate very well with them.

Just before noon, our overnight train pulled into Thompson, Manitoba. I taxied out to the airport parking lot to get our van. The side-view mirror had been fixed, just as La Ronge Air had promised. Back at the train depot, Kathleen and I loaded the van, drove into town for lunch, and then headed west, back toward North Vancouver.

You might be thinking that our Seal River adventure was now over. But for me, it will always remain unfinished. Those four days at the Seal River Lodge were calm and sunny. We could have made it to Churchill in four-hour sprints. Even as I write these words 17 years later, I regret that we hadn't at least tried.

PROPOSED SEAL RIVER ITINERARY (1997)

Date	Activity	Kilometres Daily	Total	Miles Daily	Total
Plan A					
July 2	Fly to Shethanei Lake	0	0	0	0
July 3	Hiking at Shethanei Lake	0	0	0	0
July 4	South end of peninsula dividing Shethanei Lake	28	17	17	28
July 5	Cove north of Wozniak Lake	24	52	15	32
July 6	End of rapids east of Steel River	23	75	14	46
July 7	Cove south of St. Croix Island	27	102	17	63
July 8	Hiking, resting & fishing	0	102	0	63
July 9	Beginning of rapids near end of Great Island	32	134	20	83
July 10	North end of Daniels Island	21	155	13	96
July 11	End of rapids after southern dip of river	33	188	21	117
July 12	Northern bend of river	35	223	22	139
July 13	Hiking, fishing & resting	0	223	0	139
July 14	End of Tambany Rapids	21	244	13	152
July 15	Fork of Seal River nearing delta	18	262	11	163
July 16	Hudson Bay	15	277	9	172
July 17	Resting & viewing Hudson Bay	0	277	0	172
July 18	Dymond Lake	35	312	22	194
July 19	Resting & viewing Hudson Bay	0	312	0	194
July 20	Churchill	35	347	22	216
Or, Plan B					
July 16	Hudson Bay	15	277	9	172
July 17	Resting & viewing Hudson Bay	0	277	0	172
July 18	Seal River Lodge	6	283	4	176
July 19	Resting & viewing Hudson Bay	0	283	0	176
July 20	Barge or fly to Churchill				

MAPS FROM THE
CANADIAN NATIONAL TOPOGRAPHIC SYSTEM

1:50,000

64 J/16 Frame Lake

64 I/13 Dawes Lake

64 I/12 Stanley River

64 I/14 Steel River

64 I/15 Wither Lake

64 I/16 Meades Lake

54 L/13 Eppler Lake

54 M/4 Warner Lake

54 M/3 Sothe Lake

54 L/14 Tambanay Rapids

54 M/2 Point of the Woods

54 L/15 Knife Delta (West & East)

54 L/16 Churchill

54 L/9 Button Bay

1:250,000

64 J Tadoule Lake

64 I Shethanei Lake

54 L Churchill

54 M Caribou River

CHAPTER 4

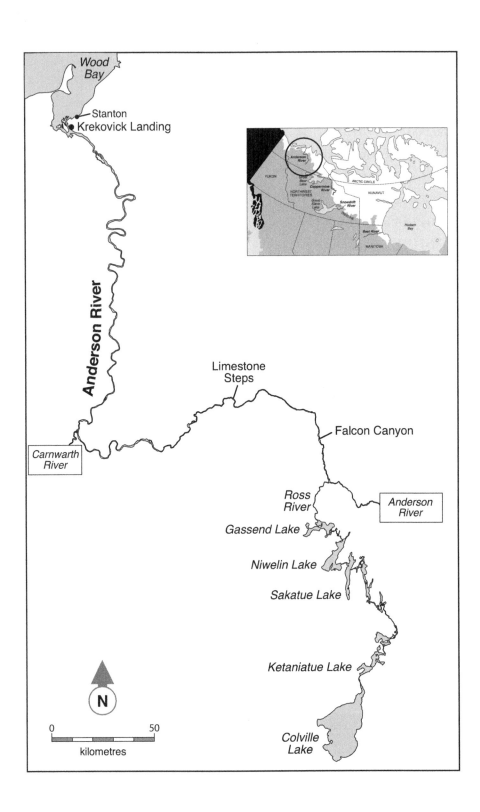

THE ANDERSON RIVER

Paddling Northern Neighbourhoods

K athleen and I began our Anderson River trip hunkered down on the frozen shores of Colville Lake, 100 km north of the Arctic Circle. We had arrived by Twin Otter on January 31, flying out of Inuvik, Northwest Territories, at -40°. We unloaded our gear and supplies onto the metre-thick ice just 100 m from the one-room cabin that would be our home until the ice went out of the lake in mid-June.

[Note: -40°C exactly equals -40°F. How beautiful is that?]

We had come to escape the crush of urban noise, concrete and congestion. The nearest community of Colville Lake, with a population of only 90 people, lay 40 roadless km to the south. Otherwise, Kathleen and I were the only inhabitants in a 200-km-wide swath stretching 500 km north to the Arctic Ocean. This immense, silent world was ours alone to enjoy. We spent the next five, glorious months reading, sipping tea by the wood stove, snow-shoeing, and revelling in the beauty of the unbounded boreal forest. We also looked forward to being the first people to paddle down the Anderson River that year.

Eventually, as the sun's warmth returned, the snowpack began to shrink. On June 11, we paddled to town through shifting pack ice to make final arrangements for shipping our winter gear back to Inuvik. Near the north end of Colville Lake, we encountered a summer camp that had just been established by the Hareskin Indians, many of whom still followed a traditional lifestyle. During the past month, we had met many Colville Lake residents during their spring hunts for ducks and geese.

On June 19, at about 11:00 p.m., Richard and Charlie Kochon stopped by our cabin, in their powerboat, on their way to Legetentue Lake, about 35 km downriver. They intended to scout the area for moose, and do a little hunting.

"Would you like some tea?"

"Yep."

They asked if we still planned to leave tomorrow, and wondered where we intended to camp. I spread out the topographic maps and pointed out the places on our intended itinerary, including our first camp in the "narrows" at Ketaniatue Lake. In fact, "Ketaniatue" means "Narrows Lake" in the local language.

"That's not a good place for camping," Richard said. "Willows too dense and tall."

Richard pointed to another spot, on a point about 4 km beyond the narrows. "This is the first good spot for camping. You should camp here."

We drank a few more cups of tea, and said goodbye to Charlie and Richard just after midnight.

I stood alone and silently as their boat vanished into the golden glow of a buoyant sun that floated softly on the northern horizon. A Bald Eagle soared majestically above Colville Lake. A beaver swam confidently through the narrows of the outlet. A northern pike broke water aggressively in the shallow warmth off our north dock.

June 20. I woke at 9:00 a.m. and strolled up to the storage cabin to start bringing our canoe packs down to the water. Suddenly, a voice rang out, "Hi!"

Charlie was calling out to me from what we called Flagpole Hill, and soon stood beside me, out of breath. *[Note: We called it Flagpole Hill because our landlord, Bern Will Brown, had placed a flagpole, complete with Canadian flag, at the top of this hill.]*

Charlie continued his story. "We broke down. Kicker stopped working. Been running all night. Bugs real bad."

"Come on in for pancakes and coffee."

A few minutes later, Richard joined us for a full breakfast in a crowded, happy cabin. I wondered how they planned to get back to their camp, located on what was locally called the Big Island, about 6 km south of our cabin.

"How are you getting back to your camp?"

"By boat."

"I don't think you can take Bern's boat (which was stored near the water's edge). He says he has no gas. You should take our canoe. Are you comfortable paddling a canoe?"

Charlie and Richard both nodded yes, and moments later they paddled away, Richard in the stern, stroking hard. Kathleen and I felt a little vulnerable watching our canoe disappear up Colville Lake. If something happened to it, we couldn't paddle down the Anderson River. What then? We were all packed up and ready to go on our canoe trip. We hadn't discussed with Charlie and Richard about how we would get our canoe back, or even when we might expect it back. It would be OK to wait a day, or two, or three. But the uncertainty would definitely be unpleasant. We returned to the cabin, boiled some tea water, and sat down to wait.

At 12:30, an aluminum boat approached, towing our canoe behind. Two older men that we had never met before stepped out onto the dock and began tying up. I waited until they finished.

"Would you like to come in for coffee?"

"Yep."

Our visitors sat down at the table while Kathleen brewed up more coffee. We talked of our trip down the Anderson River.

"Lots of bears on the river. You have a gun?"

I showed them my Browning .308. They nodded in approval.

"Lots of bears on the river. Be careful."

Finally, at 2:30 p.m., our gear was packed, and both cabins were locked and shuttered—just like we found them last January 31. Kathleen and I wandered one more time around the compound. We walked along what we called Laundry Lane and Lower Cabin Crescent. We sat below the flagpole and looked south across the wind-rippled surface of Colville Lake. We continued down the hill to our loaded canoe, which bobbed slightly in the afternoon breeze.

Change had been occurring all over the north, from the boreal forest, and beyond, out onto the tundra. During the first two weeks of June, blocks of ice and torrents of water had burst across the land. By the middle of June, the tumult and carnage of spring renewal had subsided. The grand rivers once again flowed stately between majestic banks. Like the seductive Siren of Greek mythology, the immortal Arctic summer called out to us. We could do nothing else than answer the sweet summons. Kathleen and I stepped into our canoe and paddled away from Colville Lake, down the Ross River towards its confluence with the Anderson River, which would take us north to the Arctic Ocean.

We soon reached swiftly flowing water with two shallow rapids.

"I think we should head right, to the outside bend, where the deep water is."

"Me too. How far right?"

"All the way up against the bank."

"Well done. Now let's head back left."

Not bad for our first moving water since last September. It was nice to warm up with some easy Class I.

We rounded a point into Ketaniatue Lake, directly into the northeast wind, perfectly aligned with our route. Why do all northern canoe trips seem invariably to begin with a strong headwind? We paddled hard along the southeast shore, confirming Richard's advice about the lack of camping. Willows grew thickly right from the water's edge to the very top of the low ridge.

We drifted through the narrows, where a moose browsed nonchalantly, unaware of our downwind approach. Nearly 4 km later, on the first point of a horseshoe bay, we finally found a good camping spot, just where Richard said it would be. We dragged our gear up onto a peaty, tundra ridge. The continuing wind had now become our ally, as it kept all the bugs grounded. We gathered a few sticks of willow and birch for firewood to boil tea water, and to cook our pasta supper.

At 11:30 p.m. we lay in the tent, with a splendid view south, back up the lake. White blooms of Labrador Tea dominated the foreground tussocks, interspersed with pink splashes of Bog Rosemary. The showy white flowers of Cloudberry emerged from moist crevices. It had been a very satisfying day. Up late. A lingering breakfast shared with good friends who appreciated being on the land. We were 4 km ahead of schedule, snug in our tent, looking forward to the constant light that would accompany us for the next four weeks. In some sense, I felt that I was paddling and camping in my own backyard. We had lived in this country for nearly five months. Its vast horizons and endless purity made me happy just to be alive. Kathleen and I drifted to sleep, listening to the wind, and enjoying the sweet scent of Labrador Tea.

June 21. Up late at 10:30 a.m., which is almost like a rest day. We put on the water at 12:45, once again heading into a strong wind. We soon gained the lee protection of the north shore, and headed east, calmly and serenely down the picturesque outlet of Ketaniatue Lake. Up ahead, riffles marked a drop into the last small bay, and we exchanged our wooden paddles for our whitewater paddles.

We turned north, following two Common Mergansers into the shallow, rocky riffles leading to Legetentue Lake (Frozen Fish Lake). Four kilometres of sun-drenched Class I. We enjoyed a nearly bucolic landscape as streamside willows and spruce slipped serenely behind us.

"Just keep to the outside bend," Kathleen advised. "We need the deeper water, and there's no sweepers. It's beautiful to be paddling again."

All too soon, though, the current slowed as the narrow channel opened wide to where hundreds of Bonaparte's Gulls alternately soared, floated and dove, feasting on small fish and insects.

We paddled east along a peninsula, rounded its point and turned west, heading toward a narrow opening between two opposing projections of land extending several kilometres into the lake. Thirty minutes later we set up camp on a small island that featured a narrow, index-like finger of land pointing toward an esker ridge. An extraordinarily beautiful spot—such a contrast to the mud and dense brush that we had paddled past throughout the day. Our evening home was open and park-like. Dry and sheltered. Almost no bugs, even though the air was calm. Plenty of firewood. A gentle breeze drifted through the treetops. Robins chirped, creating a feeling of backyard suburbia. We set up our tent on a soft carpet of Crowberry and Rock Cranberry. We expected to sleep very well that night.

As I have mentioned before, Kathleen and I much prefer to paddle wilderness rivers alone. We could get up late if we wish. Or, if we so desired, we could paddle late in the never ending light. We were living emancipated from anyone else's time. We could ignore even our own schedule if we wished.

June 22. We woke at 9:00 a.m. The Yellow-rumped Warblers fluttering above us sounded so very much like little wristwatch alarms. The Robins were still singing, as they had throughout the sunlit night. We slowly cooked a hot bannock for breakfast over our morning campfire. A family of Yellow-shafted Flickers followed our movements from the safety of their cavity in a camp-side dead spruce tree. A single Tundra Swan broke the morning silence with deep, bold wing beats.

"So what do you want to do, Kathleen? Our itinerary calls for a rest day. But this is only our second morning on the river. Do you want to paddle or stay?"

"I like it here. Let's just stay."

The day was, indeed, marvellously relaxing—sunny and warm at 24°. Although the air hummed with mosquitoes, we were generally comfortable without bug jackets and with only a little repellant dabbed on our hands and faces. We were alone and happy on our island, in the midst of what might as well be considered our very own land. Kathleen and I are so fortunate to have such easy access to this incredible beauty, isolation and serenity.

June 23. We put on the water at 8:30 a.m. Another sunny morning, although the mosquitoes forced us to put on our bug jackets as soon as we crept out of the tent. The river was again bucolic as we ran from outside bend to outside bend. All Class I, and very shallow. Because we were paddling so soon after spring breakup, we had expected deeper, swifter water. The river corridor teamed with birds, including Mallards, Long-tailed Ducks, Tundra Swans and Scaups. A Canada Goose encouraged us to chase, to lure us away from its mate and goslings snugged up tightly against the shore. Bohemian Waxwings darted from both sides of the river as they hawked for insects just above our heads.

We had planned to paddle only about 19 km today, intending to set up camp about halfway down the narrow, winding river flowing out of Legetentue Lake. The river, however, meandered as though through an estuary—slow, buggy and very boggy. Except for a few scattered spruce trees, dense willows covered the riverbanks. Although we occasionally beached the canoe to search, we found no suitable campsites. We paddled on.

After the next lake (unnamed), we paddled south nearly five more kilometres to another unnamed lake, where the topographic map suggested we should encounter rapids. There were no rapids, though, and still nowhere to camp. We paddled on.

Finally, after paddling about 48 km, we set up camp at 7:30 p.m. on a burned-over island at the south end of the unnamed lake east of Sakatue Lake. Despite a landscape of charred peat, blackened spruce stems and hordes of bugs, the site offered the best camping we had seen all day.

We thought we saw three seals today. They briefly lifted their heads out of the river, and then immediately submerged when they saw us. This sighting seemed so very unlikely to us. Bearded seals and ringed seals occur in the Anderson River delta, but we were such a long way (450 km by river) from the ocean. Moreover, we had not heard or read of any reports of seals on the Anderson River. We were not paying very much attention at the time, just paddling in the heat of the day. Almost dozing, really. Perhaps we were mistaken. Maybe we hadn't really seen seals. But they looked like seals. They acted like seals. What else could they have been other than seals? We know seals when we see them. Still, though. We were such a long way from the ocean.

[Note: When we returned to Inuvik, our friend Alan Fehr said that we should report this sighting of seals to Parks Canada or to regional biologists. I didn't want to do that, though. What if they said I must have been mistaken? What if they said I couldn't have seen seals? What if they said, "You were 450 km from the ocean. What are you, crazy?" I couldn't take that chance.]

We finished today way ahead of our itinerary. Even though we didn't intend to be way ahead of schedule, we now had a cushion. Cushions are good. You never know when you might need a cushion. You can always go slower if you want. But, you can't always go faster whenever you might want to.

June 24. Up at 9:00 a.m., on the water at noon. A perfect headwind. Not too strong to make paddling difficult but strong enough to force the mosquitoes out of our faces and into the lee of our backs. The land was so empty of people—the Common Loons, Tundra Swans, White-winged Scoters and Mallards seemed completely at ease.

Kathleen and I paddled silently, thrilled with the beauty that surrounded us, but still concerned about the lack of suitable campsites. How far would we be forced to paddle today? So much water. Amazing to contemplate that this complex, interconnected, serpentine route will eventually become the Anderson River that will carry us swiftly to the Arctic Ocean.

Late in the afternoon, a quick current carried us the last 2 km into Sakatue Lake. Quite surprising to find this quick current, as the topographic map indicated that Sakatue and the previous lake both lay at 216 m above sea level. Two lakes at the same elevation should have no current between them. Yet there was more current between these two lakes than what we found yesterday where the topographic map showed four rapids. I love topographic maps, but their accuracy can change over time and with water levels. The rapid into Sakatue Lake was an easy Class I. Only riffles, but very welcome.

We found some sandy beaches just south and north of the inlet into Sakatue Lake. Both beaches were small, surrounded by dense willows, and not inviting enough to camp. Anyway, it was only a little after 5:00 p.m., and we weren't tired. We paddled out of Sakatue into the river leading west to Niwelin Lake. A lone moose on the south bank stood staring at us. We pulled our canoe out of the water on the north bank to hike 1 km to the Dene village of Soka, where we found only decaying log cabins.

The location of this village, so far from the river, initially seemed incongruous to us. Why wouldn't the village be on the banks of the river? After we thought about it for a few minutes, it occurred to us that there was no need for the village to be on the banks of the river. For most of the year, the river was frozen. In fact, all of the countryside remained frozen for more than half of the year. The village of Soka was likely in the best location for hunting and trapping. Proximity to the river would be only a secondary consideration, or so it seemed to us.

Back on the river, Kathleen and I paddled on a gentle current, looking forward to camping on one of the sandy beaches on Niwelin Lake, which are described in *Canoeing Canada's Northwest Territories: A Paddler's Guide.* *[Note: For the rest of this chapter, I will refer to this guide as simply the* Paddler's Guide.*]*

The *Paddler's Guide* gave no information on exactly where these sandy beaches were, however. Perhaps there would be a sandy beach right where the river flowed into Niwelin Lake. That would be convenient, as we could enjoy a relatively early end to our paddling day. We found no sandy beach there, though—just dense brush.

As we paddled west, down Niwelin Lake, the wind intensified and soon brought rain. We stopped to put on our rain gear before rounding a point, heading north. Every once in a while, we stopped to look for the promised sandy beaches but only ever found dense willows, bogs and bugs. We began to regret that we had rejected the sandy beaches on the east shore of Sakatue Lake. Sure, those Sakatue Lake beaches were small and not overly inviting. But they were camp-able. We'd take them now.

Somewhat discouraged, we continued to paddle north, stopping in a clump of reeds at 8:00 p.m. for a gorp break. We assured ourselves that this day would eventually end. We would, at some point, be in our tent resting. We just sucked it up and paddled on.

We coasted northeast along the lake's eastern shore, and finally spotted a 2-m strip of sand. This was it. Good enough. Sixty minutes later, we sat in front of our fire, sipping tea, and stirring a bubbling pot of Spanish rice. A Common Loon yodelled only a few metres away. The sky cleared. The sun shone. We felt calm and so content to sit on the shore of this pristine lake. So far from everywhere—yet we felt very much at home.

June 25. We woke at 10:00 a.m. to a mid-morning serenade of White-crowned Sparrows. Alarm calls of Lesser Yellowlegs rolled down the beach to envelop our tent in fluid, piccolo-like tremolos.

A beautiful, clear, calm, sunny morning. Six American Widgeons landed only 1 m off the beach in front of our campfire. We leisurely sipped tea, followed by a steaming bannock smothered in margarine and jam. Overhead, Arctic Terns soared and dove for insects. We appreciated any effort on their part to keep our camp nearly bug-free. Because we paddled so late yesterday and were ahead of schedule, we decided to take our tentative rest day two days early.

Just before noon, the bugs returned in swarms, which often indicates an approaching storm. Moments later the sky turned grey. With tea cups in hand, Kathleen and I retreated to the tent, where, an hour later, we lay listening to the soft, pleasant patter of large raindrops on the nylon tent fly.

After the brief storm, we heated water for laundry and bathing. An evening offshore breeze drove the mosquitoes to cover, and we relaxed in front of the fire, on the east shore of Niwelin Lake, until retiring to the tent at 10:30 p.m.

June 26. Up at 9:00 a.m. Once again, we began our day with bannock— sweet, sweet bannock. At 11:00, we set off on a placid lake, with a gentle headwind. We stopped a few kilometres later to inspect a fine sandy beach on the east shore, where the lake narrowed. So. Good camping does indeed exist on Niwelin Lake, just like the *Paddler's Guide* claimed. We spotted another beach just north of Niwelin Lake's outlet on the west shore. If you ever paddle the Anderson River, you might want to keep these potential campsites in mind.

We entered the outlet of Niwelin Lake and paddled casually down the winding river approximately 1 km to the rapid marked by only a single line on the 1:50,000 map. The *Paddler's Guide* advised that "the rapids/falls should be portaged."

Now, when I see the word "should," I assume there is some leeway in the recommendation. "Should portage" means that some paddlers might portage, while other paddlers might run. "Should" means strong consideration rather than a command. You might remember the *Paddler's Guide* description for the Rocky Defile on the Coppermine River: "Paddlers should pull out...well above the entrance. Only expert paddlers should attempt this canyon."

The word "should" for the Rocky Defile implied ambiguity. It suggested uncertainty. Some paddlers would portage, while others would run. Kathleen and I would not likely be classified as "expert" paddlers, but we did run the Rocky Defile. So, when I read the recommendation that these rapids/ falls west of Niwelin Lake "should" be portaged, I naturally concluded that it might be possible to run them. Not a chance of that, though. Boulders guarded the entrance, with large standing waves and reversals at the bottom of the drop. We packed our gear along a well-defined trail on river left and completed what I considered a "must portage" by 3:30 p.m. We then enjoyed lunch perched on the rocks above the falls. Squadrons of Cliff Swallows feasted on swarms of bugs. We wished the birds much success in their hunt.

We put back on the fast-flowing water and headed downriver, admonished by a Peregrine Falcon who strongly objected to us entering its territory. Suddenly, whitewater, completely unexpected, appeared ahead. We enjoyed 2 to 3 km of Class II water, with boulders and rock gardens that required some manoeuvring—more than just running from inside bend to inside bend. We actually had to make collective decisions about the best route. A very pleasant surprise, as this entire stretch, like the "rapids/falls," was marked by only a single line on the topographic map. The *Paddler's Guide* made no mention of these rapids.

All too soon, the fun ended as we floated into an evening of pure magic on Gassend Lake. The water's surface was like glass. Or perhaps it was like a millpond. Or perhaps it was like polished marble. You know what I mean, so feel free to choose your own favourite simile or metaphor. Just make sure your selection indicates a lake that is absolutely still. Common Loons dove, surfaced and called all around us.

We finally beached the canoe at 10:00 p.m. on a beautiful sandy shore at the end of the peninsula pointing northwest toward Gassend Lake's outlet. As we strode up the beach looking for a campsite, an outraged Arctic Tern immediately dove, landed on my head, and started pecking away. What the heck was this all about? I swatted at the tern with my hat, and it flew up just out of my reach—still very angry and still threatening more aerial strikes. The tern circled and swooped, while I crouched and swatted. It was then that I noticed the tern's nest excavated in the sand only 1 m from the water's edge. The small, obscure depression contained two dark eggs that I had so nearly trampled. I quickly moved away, and the tern quit attacking me.

Each year, the robin-sized Arctic Tern travels up to 35,000 km (20,000 miles) from the Arctic to the Antarctic and back again. The feat is even more remarkable, researchers say, because the bird almost never rests. It is constantly either in the air, diving for fish, or bringing food to its nestlings.

As Kathleen and I searched for the perfect campsite, we discovered footprints in the sand. People had been here before us! How could that be? These intruders, these cheaters, must have flown directly to Gassend Lake from the south. This was highly unfair. Surely Kathleen and I, after spending five winter months on the shores of Colville Lake, had earned the privilege of the year's first descent. Oh well. Maybe we won't see these interlopers. They might have left Gassend Lake days ago. If so, it was not likely we would catch them. Good. We didn't really want to see anyone else on our wilderness river adventure, anyway.

The midnight sun glowed warmly. Light and isolation surrounded us. We remained content despite the proximity of other people.

Kathleen and I stayed up late, sitting in front of our midnight campfire, sipping tea and watching a moose browsing in the shallows at the end of the peninsula. Arctic Terns flew sorties to repel Mew Gulls seeking to plunder their eggs. These terns never get to rest.

June 27. We woke at 10:00 a.m. to the sound of surf running swiftly up onto the beach. A strong wind blew toward us from the northwest. Not a good day for paddling. Sunny and warm, with no bugs, however. Absolutely perfect conditions to strip off our clothes for bathing, which we did.

Following a breakfast of …?

Well, what do you think we had for breakfast? Take a guess. You're right! Bannock. Following a breakfast of bannock, Kathleen photographed a Large-flowered Wintergreen. The leaves of the Large-flowered Wintergreen remain green all winter. That's why they call it wintergreen. This adaptation allows last year's leaves to photosynthesize with the first warm weather in spring, before the new year's leaves have had time to develop.

Kathleen then strolled down the beach to take pictures of the Arctic Tern sitting on its nest. I ambled in the opposite direction with my fishing rod. After only a few casts I returned to camp with a 60-cm (25-inch) northern pike. The pike is a voracious fish, which can feed on other fish fully half its size, and has been known to hunt ducklings and lemmings. This was the first pike I had ever caught. I was curious about how sharp its teeth were. I learned

Bannock is one of the major reasons why Kathleen and I go on canoe trips.

an important lesson that morning—never stick your fingers in a pike's mouth, even if you do want to see how sharp its teeth are. I discovered that its teeth are very sharp. Kathleen took pictures of my bloodied fingers just to prove it.

By mid-afternoon the sky darkened, and we retreated from the developing storm to the haven of our tent. A few minutes later the rain began, and we spent the rest of the afternoon dozing and reading.

The wind and sporadic rain persisted into the evening. At 8:00 p.m. we concluded that we would postpone supper for better weather. After all, we would have enough light for cooking for at least another month no matter what time of day or night. At 9:30, the rain stopped, and we moved our cooking area to the shelter of a clump of spruce trees. Thirty minutes later, we had fried the pike to a golden brown on our small, backpacking stove.

Despite all the negative rumours about pike, we thoroughly enjoyed this fish—large, chunky fillets of firm flesh with the consistency of tuna. We had heard that pike are full of small bones, but the people of Colville Lake had taught me how to properly fillet a large fish to easily remove all the bones. Kathleen and I very much enjoyed eating our first northern pike. We liked it so much that we ate it all in one sitting. We looked forward to eating more northern pike.

I also looked forward to tomorrow. Only 2 km remained between us and the outlet of Gassend Lake. In only 2 km we could escape the winds that make lake travel so challenging. In only 2 km we could enjoy moving water for the remaining 420 km to the Arctic coast.

June 28. The storm persisted, unabated, throughout the night. We decided against paddling in the morning, hoping for more comfortable weather. We breakfasted late (11:00 a.m.), squatting before the heat of our fire on the beach. We then returned to the shelter of our tent to read and play a few games of cribbage.

Wind, waves and a very dark sky met our eyes when we peered out at 4:30 p.m. The northwest horizon showed no relief from the storm. All northern canoe trips include days when the wind blows relentlessly, confining canoeists to the small sanctuary of a nylon tent or tarp. Kathleen and I now felt little hope that we would ever paddle again. I know this sounds extreme, but we had been trapped at Gassend Lake for two full days. Despair naturally creeps in.

We knew, in our minds, if not in our spirits, that this wind would stop one day. The sun would, one day, shine again. We would someday pack up and head downriver. Golden sunlight would, one day, once again, drip from our paddles. Our arms, shoulders and backs would one day, once again, eagerly lean into the paddling stroke. Until then, we must be patient. Surely this wind would eventually stop. A slight respite at 7:30 p.m. permitted a quick supper of hot minestrone soup, salami, crackers and tea.

Bern Will Brown had told us that he likes to fly out over the Anderson River to visit with canoeists, and perhaps bring fresh fruit. You remember Bern Will Brown. It was Bern's cabin that we had rented to overwinter at the north end of Colville Lake—the cabin from where Kathleen and I began this canoe trip down the Anderson River. Before we left Colville Lake, Bern promised to bring us any mail that arrived for us after our departure. Bern's

Cessna passed over our camp twice during the day, but he didn't see our canoe stowed against the storm in a clump of spruce. Too bad. Although we had come to escape modern technology and comforts, it would have been very novel, even fantastic, to have received airmail delivery of gifts and letters.

At 8:15 p.m., a strong wind driving a cold (8°) rain sent us back to the comfort and warmth of our tent. We fell asleep listening to the surf pounding on the beach, pounding our spirits, pounding down our hopes of paddling tomorrow. Despite the imposed two-day layover, though, we remained almost exactly on schedule. The "cushion" we enjoyed only a few days ago had already turned out to be useful. I told you it might.

June 29. I lay awake most of the night, listening to the wind, listening to the surf. Most of all, though, I lay awake worrying. Worrying about the weather and if we'd ever get off this beach. Worrying about my academic career and the research funding I would need when I returned to UBC in August. Even the birds annoyed me. Lesser Yellowlegs rattled away all night, and a White-crowned Sparrow practiced seemingly infinite variations of its song just outside the tent. I finally fell asleep around 5:00 a.m.

We woke at 8:00 a.m. Grey sky. Cold. Threatening clouds. Persistent wind. Pounding surf. But no rain. "We gotta get out of here, Kathleen. Let's cook breakfast and pack up."

We shoved into the surf at 10:15. Only 2 km to the outlet of Gassend Lake. Only 2 km to moving water. Despite the last two days, I had enjoyed paddling on this series of small lakes. But I looked forward to a wide river, with a strong current, to carry me to the Arctic coast.

We struggled against the wind and breaking waves but managed to reach the outlet of Gassend Lake, where we glided, almost effortlessly, onto the current of the Ross River. More Cliff Swallows darted out from riverside limestone ledges. Rain soon began, and we stopped briefly to don our sou'wester rain hats, and to fit our spray skirts snugly over the coaming of the spray deck.

The Ross River carried us quickly to the Anderson River—approximately

25 km in less than four hours, with very little paddling on our part. In addition to the three rapids marked on the topographic maps, several more rapids made our descent quite enjoyable. All the rapids were fairly easy and straightforward. None required scouting, and none exceeded Class II. Most rapids consisted of standing waves created either by the river deflecting off points or the current spilling into calmer water. A few rapids provided fast, shallow, braided sections. Kathleen and I worked well together. Certainly one of life's greatest pleasures is for you and your life's partner to share the thrill and satisfaction of paddling rapids together, confidently and successfully. Fish continually jumped and surfaced during our descent.

Several kilometres upstream from the confluence with the Anderson River, the riverside ridges became drier and less overgrown. Splotches of Shrubby Cinquefoil, Bear Root and Northern Sweet-vetch adorned the open stands of spruce. Nevertheless, no suitable campsites induced us to stop. "Suitable," when one first starts looking for camp near the end of a paddling day, means sandy beach, open tundra ridge, and easy access.

Besides, we wouldn't have wanted to camp with Bear Root, which is a favourite food of grizzly bears. On our Thelon River trip in 1993, Kathleen and I saw large patches of Bear Root that had been dug up for its edible and apparently very tasty roots.

We reached the Anderson River at 2:30 p.m. and set up camp on the first large island just downstream from its confluence with the Ross River. We had found our suitable camp on a level, open terrace just above the water. The rain had stopped, and we took advantage of the interlude to put up the tent dry. The wind finally quit blowing at about 7:00 p.m., and the sky showed thin patches of blue at 9:30. We were finally on the Anderson River itself, which, at this point, had a strong, shallow current. We now expected short, easy, unhurried paddling days. The water level had obviously been dropping quickly on the Anderson River, as the exposed mud and sand were still wet a full 1.5 m above the present waterline.

We hiked briefly around our island, which showed obvious signs of moose browsing on the willows. Spring blooms adorned many plants, including Mountain Avens, Lapland Rosebay and Common Butterwort. As presented in Johnson et al. (1995), Common Butterwort, only 4–12 cm (2–5 inches) tall, consumes insects by trapping them in the greasy surface of its leaves, which are covered with small glands. The insects become stuck and are digested by acidic mucilage and enzymes.

June 30. We rose at 9:00 a.m. and put on the water just before noon. The Anderson River was moving very quickly, and almost immediately we arrived at a ledge extending out from the west bank on an outside bend. Plenty of room, though, on the inside bend.

About an hour after leaving camp, we reached the first rapid marked on the topographic map, and sauntered downstream to reconnoiter.

"Look, Michael. Footprints in the mud. Must be the same people whose prints we saw at Gassend Lake."

"I hope they're the same people. I wouldn't like to think that we're trailing two or more groups of paddlers down the Anderson River."

The rapid swept sharply right—around a bend—and disappeared from our view. Kathleen and I are very cautious wilderness paddlers. We generally don't paddle down rapids that disappear from our view. So we climbed back into the canoe and ferried over to the left bank where we could more easily peer around the corner. We were surprised to discover footprints again, plus the bow marks of three canoes. Obviously, these Anderson River interlopers were also cautious wilderness river runners, just like us. Maybe they were not truly horrible people after all.

We "lifted over" the entry ledge to the rapid, a short portage of only 40 steps. We then ferried over to an island and hugged its west bank toward a 2-metre gap that took us by the next ledge. We then powered left to avoid the haystacks in river centre, making sure to stay river right of two more ledges extending out from the west bank.

Did you follow all that? You might want to read it again. That was an interesting run—certainly the most complicated and challenging rapid so far. Wait, I'll play it back for you in slow motion:

- We lifted over the entry ledge to the rapid, a short portage of only 40 steps.
- We then ferried over to an island and hugged its west bank toward a 2-m gap that took us by the next ledge.
- We then powered left to avoid the haystacks in river centre, making sure to stay river right of two more ledges extending out from the west bank.

We reached the next serious rapid only 10 minutes later, and first scouted on river left, where again we saw footprints in the sand. Ledges and pour-overs clogged the run on river left, so we ferried over to scout on river right, which seemed runnable. Back in the canoe, we ferried out to river centre to hit a 2-m wide tongue of water that flowed between a threatening, dropping trough of water pounding by an island on river left and a ledge on river right. After blasting by the ledge, we powered closer toward river left to bypass a second ledge projecting even farther out from the right bank.

We camped on the east shore, above the narrow entry just above Falcon Canyon. Very serious whitewater cascaded away immediately below our camp. The *Paddler's Guide* said that the Anderson "is not a river for paddlers seeking a wild whitewater experience." Maybe not. Even so, moving-water skills, or a passion for portaging, were essential for this section of the Anderson. Indeed, the *Paddler's Guide* also indicated that "there are major rapids along the way." These two statements in the Guide stuck me as somewhat contradictory.

The two rapids we scouted and ran today might not be considered major by the *Paddler's Guide*, but both featured ledges, powerful hydraulics and high standing waves. The best route through, I believed, required scouting from shore. The rapid below our camp, with even more powerful water, showed no obvious route through—I would rate it as a high Class III. Kathleen and I would be on the portage trail tomorrow morning.

July 1 – *Canada Day*. We celebrated with an extra cup of tea before carrying our canoe and gear 250 m along a fairly well-marked portage trail. Footprints in the mud indicated that our fellow paddlers had also chosen not to run this rapid. The footprints seemed fresh. I wondered if we would ever see these people.

We loaded the canoe and paddled downriver just after 1:00 p.m. Only a few minutes later, we arrived at what we concluded was the "official" entry to Falcon Canyon. We beached the canoe and sauntered downstream to scout the entry rapid. Our initial impression had been that this rapid would be un-runnable. Although formidable, we did find a route and ran down.

We celebrated the rest of Canada Day by running down Falcon Canyon in big, pushy water, all the while avoiding ledges, and then eddying out to scout the next bend and drop. We sometimes walked both banks to gain better views, and found footprints wherever we stopped. These people run the river just like us. It might even be nice to meet them, to compare our experiences.

At lunch, Kathleen and I climbed to the top of a ridge to enjoy a very scenic view of the canyon. We hiked through an open, dry forest, similar to an alpine environment, including botanical features such as the ground-hugging, pincushion-like Moss Campion. Interestingly, we spent only 40 minutes on the water to cover approximately 8 km. Yet, because of all the time scouting from shore, we didn't approach the exit rapid of Falcon Canyon until the end of the day. Despite the challenges, though, we had run all the rapids so far.

Kathleen and I were now camped on the island where the 1:250,000 topographic map (Simpson Lake) showed two rapid symbols. Just this one rapid to go and we would be out of Falcon Canyon. We decided to stop for the day, though, before dealing with this very difficult rapid. We had pulled out, just above the rapid, in a small cove on river left, exactly where the bow marks of three canoes were clearly etched in the mud. Many footprints indicated that this group of paddlers had camped here, likely only a couple of days ago.

"I hope we get to see these people, Michael. It's like we're travelling together."

I have to admit that I too kind of hoped that we would get to see them. I

Lunch in Falcon Canyon.

was curious to know what they thought about the Anderson River, which, you remember "is not a river for paddlers seeking a wild whitewater experience."

So, let me describe this last rapid in Falcon Canyon. The main channel offered 1.5 to 2.0-m diagonal, curling waves in the centre, with ledges extending out from both banks. A total run of about 500 m. We considered scrambling downstream along the canyon wall to lower our canoe and gear with ropes over a 5-m cliff, just below the first two ledges on river left. We could then run down the left bank to more easily avoid most of the biggest water in river centre.

Lowering gear and canoe by ropes seemed like a lot of work, though. The alternative, to portage along the left bank, would be extremely difficult as the high canyon walls climbed straight up out of the surging river. What to do? We were already tired and didn't want to make any rash decisions.

So we set up camp and postponed our decision till morning. Perhaps the best choice would be more obvious after we were well rested. Following supper, I strolled west, away from camp, into the side channel around the island.

Last rapid in Falcon Canyon.

I felt somewhat depressed. I didn't relish portaging along the canyon wall, and the rapid seemed beyond our skills to run successfully.

The side channel was mostly dry. Too bad, I thought. If the channel had water, we could paddle around the island and avoid portaging along the cliff or paddling the rapid. I fretted for a few moments before my mind stumbled upon the obvious. This was a side channel, Mike, you dimwit. The topographic map indicated that the channel circled around the island, on the back side of the cliffs. I fairly skipped back to camp to get Kathleen, and together we followed footprints down the curved channel 750 m to where it re-entered the Anderson River only a few metres below the end of the rapid. What good luck—a convenient and easy portage around a very difficult rapid.

July 2. The day began cold, windy and overcast, with snowflakes early in the morning. We lingered in our sleeping bags. After breakfast, we completed the portage quickly and efficiently—three loads for me, only two for Kathleen. Normally, we both carry three loads on all portage trails.

We put on the water just as the sun burst through the gloom, as though it was happy and pleased that we had finally exited Falcon Canyon safely. Soon, though, the sky darkened and the northwest wind blew coldly, as it had for nearly a week now.

An hour later, on the right bank, we spotted our first grizzly bear of the trip. Even at 200 m, through binoculars, the grizzly looked darned impressive and formidable.

We soon reached the limestone outcropping of Air Weave Canyon and stopped for lunch and to scout the first of four marked rapids. We also found 50 m of brand new rope. Must have been dropped by the footprint people. Perhaps they wished to befriend us. I know what you're saying. Of course, that was absurd. The footprint people didn't even know we were on the river. Even if they did know, they likely would not purposefully leave brand new rope on the bank of the river, hoping that we would find it and appreciate their gift.

Just after pouring hot water into our cups of noodle soup, a second grizzly bear approached from about 250 m upstream, on river right, the same bank where we now sat. We gulped our soup, quickly stepped into the canoe, paddled down the right bank, and ferried across a small tributary that flowed into the Anderson River from the east. We then ferried over to the left bank of the Anderson River. That grizzly would never find us over here. Pretty clever and tricky, don't you think?

A brief scouting downstream confirmed a safe route through the first part of Air Weave Canyon right up against the left bank, adjacent to some very serious ledges. Very shallow water, however, prevented us from just paddling down the left bank from our current position. To get into water deep enough to float our canoe would require paddling out, and then downriver very near to a large hydraulic reversal. We would then have to quickly turn back and power hard to river left.

Kathleen and I could almost certainly make this move—almost certainly. But a mistake and capsize on the approach could have serious consequences, and would possibly send us capsizing over the ledges. We lined by.

We then ferried back over toward river right to get a better view of what lay around the bend. We made our decision even before reaching the opposite shore.

"What do you think, Kathleen?"

"We can run this. Let's go."

We turned downriver, running slightly back toward river left and paddled out of Air Weave Canyon. We pulled out to congratulate ourselves, to let our adrenaline subside, and to enjoy the rest of our lunch. Hopefully, the grizzly wouldn't show up, demanding a share of our peanut butter on crackers.

The sun reappeared, like this morning at Falcon Canyon, as though pleased with our success. We paddled and drifted a couple more hours in calm light before setting up camp a little more than 30 km upstream from the Limestone Steps, our original destination for tonight. Although behind schedule, we felt content to be beyond the canyons. We looked forward to a relaxing paddle tomorrow. The terrain and character of the Anderson River had changed completely since this morning. Mud banks had replaced sandstone cliffs. Bank Swallows had replaced Cliff Swallows.

We were settled in a beautiful riverside camp, with Wild Chives blooming all along the ice-scoured beach. Wild Chives have a slight onion smell and taste very much like the commercial green onions. They certainly added a pleasant seasoning to camp stew.

July 3. Up at 10:50 a.m. and on the water at 1:20 p.m. to face a strong northeast wind. Only 8° during breakfast. Throughout the day, clouds raced toward us from beyond the horizon. We endured splatterings of rain, with only brief, periodic moments of sunshine and warmth.

We reached the Limestone Steps at 6:30—a very menacing stretch of water. The Anderson River disappeared into a grey, jagged maw, turned left, and then dropped over a ledge, gaining speed all the way. It then squeezed through a narrow gash before plummeting over two more river-wide ledges, both with 3-m drops ending in magnificent, curling waves. The *Paddler's*

The Limestone Steps.

Guide warned, in capital letters, that the Limestone Steps "MUST BE PORTAGED." We agreed completely.

The portage trail on river left was fairly evident, although sometimes faint and indistinct. Most people obviously began their portage about 500 m upriver from a very nice campsite overlooking river left. You could, I think, avoid this part of the portage by running three smaller ledges with fairly paddle-able water in between. Kathleen and I decided against this, however, as there was no margin for misjudgment or error. All the water thundered toward river centre. Unfortunate canoeists, those canoeists who had made a mistake, would plunge over the ledge and likely die in the recirculating water below. Kathleen and I would begin our portage tomorrow where most others had also begun.

Our campsite that night was very nice. We enjoyed a stunning view over the river. Moss Campion and Mountain Avens surrounded us. You might know that Mountain Avens is the floral emblem of the Northwest Territories. I have always known this plant species to be called Mountain Avens. In the mid-1990s, Kathleen and I gave our Thelon River slide show to the Vancouver Natural History Society, at the Vancouver Planetarium. Unbeknownst to us, E. C. Pielou, author of *A Naturalist's Guide to the Arctic*, sat in the audience. During the presentation, I referred to a plant on the screen as Mountain Avens. Afterwards, during the question period, Ms. Pielou raised her hand and chastised me for calling the plant Mountain Avens. As she correctly pointed out, the genus for the group of plants called avens is *Geum*. The genus of the plant I had been calling Mountain Avens was *Dryas*. So it couldn't truly be called an avens. From now on, she recommended, perhaps even demanded, that I refer to the plant as Arctic Dryad, as she had in her book.

I have a great deal of respect for E. C. Pielou, her taxonomic knowledge, and her extraordinary book. I have, however, always called the plant in question Mountain Avens. The Northwest Territories still calls their floral emblem Mountain Avens. I cannot change my ways, even though I would be correct to do so. *[Note: I recently learned that NatureServe, an organization that many people consider to be the authority on accepted/official common and scientific names of plants refers to Mountain Avens as Entireleaf Mountain-avens, with a hyphen. The hyphen indicates that the plant is not a true avens. So you can see that NatureServe still uses the words 'Mountain' and 'Avens,' not 'Arctic' and 'Dryad.' I feel somewhat vindicated.]*

Kathleen and I were now halfway (14 days) through our trip, exactly on schedule. All of the lake water, most of the rapids, and the longest paddling day on our tentative itinerary lay behind us. Things were going very well. I hoped that tomorrow would bring sun, warmth and calm conditions.

One of my favourite parts of all canoeing days is when Kathleen and I crawl into the tent to drink tea, to study our plant books and maps, and to review tomorrow's course down the river. We often don't stay up much after supper is over, but retire to the tent right after the dishes have been washed and our gear has been organized for the night.

July 4. We rose at 9:00 a.m. and finished the portage past the Limestone Steps at 1:30 p.m. We found the portage relaxing, actually, interrupted by tea breaks and photography. We then drifted downriver, ran a ledge, and then eddied out on river right to scout Flat Rock Rapids. The *Paddler's Guide* suggested that this rapid "can be paddled or easily portaged." Kathleen and I naturally discussed these two options. After all, there are never any more nor any less than these two options. We hemmed and hawed, and nearly decided to run. There was just a little too much pushy water, though, ending in a ledge. We portaged about 200 m.

We put back on the water, looking forward to some leisurely drifting, not expecting any rapids until those marked on the map about 10 km away. We paddled nonchalantly, slightly southwest, enjoying the scenery. We turned a bend heading back northwest and saw a line of white up ahead.

"What's that, Michael. Have we reached the rapids already?"

"No, it can't be. They're still about 5 km away."

I continued paddling.

Kathleen turned to look back at me. "I think we should get out. The white line goes all the way across the river."

"I think it's OK, Kathleen. Let's just paddle down and have a look."

"No. I want to get out now. It looks like a ledge to me."

We paddled over to river right, tied the canoe to a shrub, and walked down to have a look. Yep. As always, Kathleen was right. A serious ledge stretched all the way across the river. Unmarked and un-runnable. We unloaded the canoe and headed down the portage trail. We found this portage, even though short, very unpleasant. No one likes to portage rapids that, according to the map, don't even exist.

By comparison, we easily ran the three marked rapids 5 km farther downriver, even without scouting. We remained exactly on schedule and were pleased to have completed the longest portage of the trip, a distance of 1 km past the Limestone Steps. At least we think we had completed the longest portage of the trip. You never know when unmarked rapids might suddenly appear again.

Only 25 km to Juniper Rapids, tomorrow's goal. The sun shone brightly at 11:00 p.m. No wind disturbed the evening quiet. We felt as though we had entered a new space, both physically and emotionally. We felt as though we had gotten somewhere today. In celebration, after our chill supper, I even brushed my teeth and shaved before retiring to the tent.

July 5. Loud splashing in the river startled us awake at 1:00 a.m. Kathleen and I instantly thought the same thing—must be a bear. I grabbed for my rifle, and Kathleen reached for the pepper spray. We peered out cautiously to see a moose, knee deep in the river, wading along the opposite shore. Sensing our presence, he turned abruptly up the bank and disappeared into the willow and spruce. Glad it wasn't a bear—it would have been hard to sleep afterwards. Even so, just the thought of a bear perhaps passing by while we slept made us uneasy as we lay in our sleeping bags—eyes closed but ears wide open.

Up at 9:30. On the water just before noon. We paddled into a day of sunshine, warmth, and a gentle breeze wafting up from the south. We drifted lazily toward Juniper Rapids. A Peregrine Falcon sat on the shore, tearing at the flesh of a gosling while its parents stood stoically nearby. A Bald Eagle sat elegantly on a riverside snag, ignoring us disdainfully as we floated by.

We reached Juniper Rapids shortly after 4:00 p.m. We scouted and then ran the ledges in the upper portion of the rapid, and set up camp on the right bank. Our footprint friends had similarly scouted the upper ledges and had also camped in the same spot, perhaps as recently as last night. Another gift had been left behind for us—a highly useful butane lighter. I wondered what more prizes waited to be discovered.

The early evening remained very warm at 23°. Surprisingly, there were nearly no mosquitoes, so we boiled three pots of water for bathing and laundry. Afterwards, Kathleen and I stood innocently naked, fresh and clean beneath the Arctic sun. We had paddled nearly 300 km since leaving our cabin at Colville Lake and were more than halfway to the Arctic coast. We sat before the evening campfire, feeling very content. Both of us had our own "pokey stick" to rearrange the coals "just so." Both of us poked silently—lost in our own thoughts of previous challenges, obstacles and accomplishments.

Both of us wondered about the unknown adventures that surely still lay before us, somewhere down the Anderson River.

The day had been idyllic and relaxing. We had pitched our tent on a rocky outcrop about 100 m from the water, in an open, park-like setting. We enjoyed a commanding view out over the Anderson River. We rested in our most beautiful campsite of the trip, which we were actually quite surprised to find. For most of the day, we had paddled past mud and willow flats with very poor camping conditions. As you remember, we left Colville Lake soon after breakup. We were early in the season. Water levels on the Anderson River were still receding, and the banks had recently been submerged. Mud dominated the landscape. Looking for campsites had been discouraging. Still, though, we needed only one good camping spot at the end of the day, and we had certainly found it.

July 6. Up at 9:00 a.m. for breakfast and to break camp. We carried our canoe and gear 200 m past some pushy water and then ran by the last three ledges of Juniper Rapids. Based on our information, all the whitewater was now behind us. A few minutes later, we climbed a steep, muddy bank to an old, and apparently abandoned, trapper's cabin. According to the *Paddler's Guide*, approximately 20 trappers lived and worked along the Anderson River in the first half of the 20th century until the last one abandoned his lines in 1956. We seemed to be gaining on our footprint friends, who had now increased in number. We found four very fresh bow marks on the muddy bank below the cabin.

"Maybe we'll see them soon, Kathleen. I kind of hope so, although I have grown somewhat fond of my new butane lighter, and I can always use more rope." I often say that "you can never have too much rope on a wilderness canoe trip."

Soon after heading downstream, the sky began to spill rain, and mud surrounded us. The Anderson River now flowed shallowly, less than 25 cm (10 inches) deep, through a delta-like complex of gravel bars and wooded islands. Trees lay lacerated and uprooted from ice muscling its way downriver during breakup. We ran from outside bend to outside bend, trying to keep water deep enough to float the canoe.

Common Loons, Lesser Yellowlegs, Surf Scoters, Tundra Swans and Arctic Terns appeared in large numbers. Mud everywhere. Finally, on the south bend of the river before the confluence with the Carnwath River, we set up camp at 6:40 p.m. in a relatively drier mire of mud.

A successful day, as we were now 38 km closer to the Arctic coast. We had portaged our last un-runnable rapid. We had paddled through our last known rapid. The longest day left on our tentative itinerary was only 30 km. All days from now on would be easier and shorter. If only we could find camps that weren't so horribly muddy.

July 7. Another grey, sodden day. Tundra Swans flew before us—at first, so elegantly cumbersome as they lifted off. Eventually, so pleasingly graceful as they finally gained altitude. Pure white bodies and wings contrasting so beautifully against the dull background of grey sky.

For lunch, we stopped at an old trapper's cabin at "Shantyville," just upstream from the Carnwath River. As reported by John Stager in his article about Fort Anderson, most of the wood for Fort Anderson was cut at Shantyville and then rafted downstream to the fort on June 9, 1861.

For dessert after lunch, I sat munching on dried pineapple rings. I love these special treats on canoe trips and could easily dispatch a whole bag in a single sitting. This meal ended disastrously, however, as a particularly chewy and sticky ring of pineapple inexplicably extracted my brand new gold inlay.

"This is not good, Kathleen. I can fit my entire tongue in the hole. What's the chance of finding a dentist out here?"

"Maybe one of our footprint friends is a dentist," she suggested.

"Maybe. It doesn't hurt, though. I'll just chew on the other side of my mouth and hope for the best."

It didn't seem possible, but the banks of the Anderson River became muddier, seemingly with each bend in the river. When we pulled out at the end of this paddling day, we spent about 30 minutes walking up and down the beach looking for a non-muddy spot to pitch the tent. We finally came to the conclusion that we should just pitch it. No need to be picky—we're already covered in mud. It doesn't make any difference where we camp.

While I began arranging rocks for a cooking fire, Kathleen was at the canoe, bending over a large pack. As she pulled on the straps to lift it out of the canoe, she slipped in the mud and fell flat on her back. I have learned not to laugh at situations like these, even though they are pretty darn funny.

"Are you all right?" I asked, with just the right amount of concern in my voice.

"You know," she said, "I imagine everyone at home would think I was crazy, but I'm actually enjoying this trip."

Despite my amusement and Kathleen's apparent joy at lying flat on her back in the mud, today was generally unpleasant.

July 8. Hooray—a very pleasant and memorable day. Up at 9:00 a.m. Grey sky, but no rain. Strong, blustery wind. We opted for a quick breakfast of granola, which is when we learned our second lesson of the trip. Do you remember our first lesson of the trip? Yep. You're right. "Never put your fingers in the mouth of a northern pike, even if you do want to see how sharp its teeth are."

This morning's lesson was: "Never put your fuel bottle in the same pack as your food, even if the food is bagged and the fuel bottle is apparently tightly closed."

Now, I should tell you that we have packed fuel bottles in with food on all of our wilderness canoe trips. In fact, we had done so throughout this Anderson River expedition. Until now, there had never been a problem. I have no explanation for what happened this time.

Let me tell you, though, that granola, flavoured with white-gas fumes, is not the best way to begin a paddling day. You should have seen the look on Kathleen's face. Until then, I had no idea that a human face could become so incredibly distorted. It was darned funny. Just like when Kathleen lay sprawled on her back in the mud yesterday. Even so, I chose not to laugh—at least not out loud. Good move on my part, I am sure. We ate quickly and put on the water just before 11:00. We gotta get going. I hate this mud.

The sky continued to clear throughout the day, and the strong current pulled us forward, against an ever stronger wind. In the early afternoon, we spotted a wolverine, loping, seemingly tirelessly, along the opposite bank. I had never seen a wolverine before. It's gait and stance exuded pugnacious power and confidence. It moved with its head down, swaggering from side to side, so very much in character for this elusive, fearless menace of bush cabins and camps. It seemed to be spoiling for a fight.

In mid-afternoon, we noticed large splotches of brightly coloured objects—red and yellow and purple—on the beach up ahead. What could this be? Why would there be bright colours on the beach? We stared downriver. Some of the colours moved. It must be people down there. Gotta be our footprint friends!

We paddled harder and pulled out on river right to visit eight young people from Denmark—six men and two women. Kathleen and I were treated like welcome royalty. We shared animated, excited conversation. They gave us pancakes, coffee, whisky, popcorn, salami and fresh bread. Did I mention the whisky? This was their takeout. Their plane was a day late and their radio wasn't working. Even so, they were trying as best as they could to use up all of their remaining food and whisky. Kathleen and I were delighted to assist. Our new companions were equally pleased to recover their butane lighter and 50 m of brand new rope.

"Just out of curiosity," I asked. "Do any of you happen to be a dentist?" They all shook their heads no, but commiserated with my predicament.

Their group leader, Joachim, said he has paddled *most* rivers in northern Canada, some of them several times. Note my emphasis on the word most. Joachim didn't articulate what he meant by northern Canada. But let's assume he means the rivers north of 60°, other than those on the High Arctic islands. Let's also assume that Joachim means "major" rivers and not just any old short river that would not be attractive for extended wilderness canoe trips. The *Paddler's Guide* includes 19 such rivers. Madsen and Wilson's book on *Rivers of the Yukon* lists 52 rivers, many of which are major, such as the Yukon itself. That brings us to 71 rivers. The Seal River in Manitoba lies just south of 60°, but I would consider it to be a major northern river. That brings the total to at least 72 major northern Canadian Rivers.

Joachim was a fairly young man at the time, likely no more than 40 years old. Let's say he started paddling northern Canadian rivers at the age of 20. Remember, he's Danish and does not have easy or inexpensive access to northern Canada. Let's say he has paddled one river per year. That gives him 20 northern Canadian rivers under his belt (or under his PFD, perhaps). Remember also, that he has paddled several of them more than once, bringing the total to something less than 20. Joachim also talked about the Siberian rivers he has descended, further reducing the time available for him to paddle northern Canadian rivers. Even if he sometimes paddled more than one river per year, which would be unusual, I estimate that he has paddled only 15 northern Canadian rivers. This total falls far below 37, the minimum number of rivers needed to have paddled most of 72. I'm not trying to be contrary. I'm just taking this opportunity to illustrate that there are a lot of major, northern Canadian rivers for you to paddle. If you want to paddle most of them, you better start early in your life.

I also wanted to illustrate that Joachim is certainly an experienced, skilled canoeist. He said that on a day trip, he would paddle the Limestone Steps. Now that is very impressive. I would definitely like to see anyone run the Limestone Steps in a canoe. So, Joachim definitely had paddling credentials, and he considered the Anderson River, especially Falcon Canyon, to be one of the most dangerous rivers he has ever paddled, particularly for novice groups. At least two people had died in Falcon Canyon in the previous seven years. Joachim believed, as I do, that someone on a later season trip likely prepared the *Paddler's Guide* report for the Anderson River. As such, the report can be very misleading.

For example, according to data from the Water Survey of Canada, the water flow on the Anderson River when we entered Falcon Canyon on June 30, soon after breakup, was 241 m³/s (8,500 ft³/s), as measured just below the Carnwath River. One month later, it had dropped to less than half, at 115 m³/s, and by August 15, it was only 80 m³/s. Joachim said that he had paddled the Anderson River twice before, in August, and simply drifted through Falcon Canyon without getting out of the canoe to scout even once.

Allan, a member of the Danish military, asked Kathleen if we had been surprised by the ledge that didn't appear on the topographic maps. Apparently, none of us liked the surprise ledge at all. After hearing our story of overwintering at Colville Lake, one of the women told Kathleen that she was inspirational. It must be nice to hear one's peers refer to you as inspirational. I wouldn't know, though. I've never been called inspirational.

I very much enjoyed being with the Danish group. I wondered if next time Kathleen and I should paddle with other people, to share the camaraderie and collective confidence and skills. Perhaps my perspective on wilderness canoeing was changing. These people all seemed so very nice. I thought it would have been a pleasure to have travelled in their company. Of course, one evening is not the same as four weeks. And it's likely, perhaps probable, that even I am not very likeable after four weeks of daily contact.

July 9. Kathleen and I slept soundly and late, followed by a relaxing bannock breakfast with our footprint friends, who filed by in a line to shake our hands and wish us well as we pushed off from the beach a few minutes after noon. We paddled beneath a nearly cloudless sky, with almost no wind— warm at 22°. A perfect canoeing day. This good weather should also allow the Danes to be picked up. Most of them had connections that they needed to make within the next 24 hours.

We stopped around the next bend to visit an abandoned trapper's cabin, and stopped again a few kilometres later to stroll around the site of old Fort Anderson. Built in 1861 and named for a chief factor of the Hudson Bay Company, Fort Anderson intended to take away the fur trading business that the American whalers enjoyed with the Inuit along the Alaska coast. Up to 600 Inuit and Dene lived in the Anderson River area before European exploration. The business venture quickly failed, however. The death of 64 sled dogs in 1864 due to distemper, and a scarlet fever/measles epidemic in 1865, in which many Inuit hunters and traders died, caused Fort Anderson to close in 1866.

John Stager's article provides the latitude and pictures of the site of Fort Anderson. He also indicates that virtually nothing of Fort Anderson remained when he published his article in 1967. Kathleen and I found no certain remains of the fort. Just an obvious clearing in the surrounding forest of spruce. I was disappointed about not finding tangible evidence of Fort Anderson, but was also pleased to see that the forest was gradually reclaiming its domain. I was satisfied to simply absorb the ambience and essence of what certainly was an active fur trading post, even if only for a few years. At one time, so very much an integral part of Canada's European history in the far north, and now simply so much Labrador Tea and Crowberry.

Kathleen and I paddled downriver, enjoying the current and the scenic hillsides, which had become increasingly more open and bare during the past two days. A white wolf trotted along the right bank.

At about 7:30 p.m., I faintly heard the sound of a distant motor.

"Say, Kathleen. I think I hear a motor boat coming."

"No way."

"Well, there it is, nevertheless."

An Inuit man with two younger women pulled up alongside our canoe to say hello.

"Are you staying at our place?" the man asked.

"We didn't even know you had a place, or where your place is."

"Where's your map? I'll show you. Make yourselves at home. We'll be back later. You'll see a boat on the shore. The cabin's about a kilometre into the bush."

"Thanks. We'd like to do that. There's a group of eight Danes up the river. Just south of old Fort Anderson. Their radio is broken. Could you check to see if they got out today? If not, perhaps you could radio for them."

"OK. We'll be back in four to five hours. Just make yourself comfortable."

Our new friends powered upriver, while Kathleen and I paddled down.

At 11:45 p.m., Kathleen and I sat at a table, eating cheese and crackers, wondering when our gracious hosts would be returning.

We crawled into our sleeping bags at 1:00 a.m., with still no sign of our powerboat friends. They finally arrived home at 4:00 a.m.—very tired and covered in mosquito bites. Kathleen and I got up to ask about the Danes.

"We found their camp. They were still there. We called Inuvik. Two planes will be coming first thing tomorrow morning to pick them up."

"So what took you so long getting back?"

"Well, until we met you, we didn't plan on going so far up the river tonight. On the way back, we ran out of gas."

Our Good Samaritan hosts had spent much of the night hauling, lining and dragging their powerboat back downriver, thereby illustrating one of the many advantages of a canoe. Most important among these advantages? A canoe never runs out of gas.

July 10. The next morning, Jorgan Elias introduced himself, his daughter Roseanne, and Roseanne's friend, Mary Gruben. All three lived in Tuktoyaktuk, on the Arctic coast, but were spending time at Jorgan's hunting and fishing camp. Surprisingly, Jorgan, Kathleen and I shared a common acquaintance. You remember Bern Will Brown, our landlord at Colville Lake? Well, Bern's wife Margaret and Jorgan are cousins. Small world, as they say.

In the afternoon, we hiked to the top of the ridge above Jorgan's camp to enjoy a spectacular view overlooking the Anderson River valley. Just to make casual conversation, I pointed toward a dark object on the right bank, perhaps 2 to 3 km downriver. "Perhaps that's a bear," I said.

"No," replied Jorgan, "that's a stump that washed up about a week ago."

Jorgan did seem to know everything about the region, and shared his obvious affection for the Anderson River.

"God must have made Tuktoyaktuk on Saturday when he was tired. He made the Anderson River on Monday, when he was fresh and eager."

I'm sure you know that God began his work of creation on Monday—fresh and eager. Saturday was his last day of work before resting on Sunday.

This explains only part of Jorgan's statement, however. You also need to know that Jorgan's hometown of Tuktoyaktuk suffers from crime and alcoholism. In stark contrast, the Anderson River flowed so very strongly and nobly—north to the Arctic coast.

Kathleen and I normally don't hike to ridge tops on our wilderness canoe trips. We paddle on wilderness canoe trips. At the end of the day, we rest in our riverside camp. On layover days, we sleep late, fish, wash and rest in our riverside camp. You already know this if you've been reading these stories in order. This afternoon, however, Kathleen suggested hiking to the top of the ridge to commemorate her parents' 75th year.

Joe and Terry, Kathleen's parents, regularly sent us letters while we were at our cabin at the north end of Colville Lake. An April letter indicated that "both your mother and father are now 74 years old, and in their 75th year, sort of a milestone, which the dictionary describes as 'an important event' Observance of 75 years is often called a jubilee or an anniversary thought of as a time for rejoicing."

A subsequent April letter explained that "The Bible describes how the ancient Jews forgave debts in the Jubilee Years. We think that it is a good idea that all debts owed us by our (eight) children are hereby cancelled."

Now Kathleen and I didn't owe any money to her parents. So there was no loan to forgive. But in early February, we had accidentally knocked Bern Will Brown's barometer off our cabin wall onto the floor. It never worked again. And, before renting the cabin, we had accepted Bern's condition that we would replace anything that we broke. Kathleen had written her parents asking them to please send a new barometer as soon as possible. The barometer arrived just before we left Colville Lake, and looked great hanging on the cabin wall. Terry and Joe cancelled our debt of one barometer.

I should emphasize that Kathleen wanted to hike to the top of the ridge to truly honour her parents' 75th year by standing at the highest point, surrounded by magnificent grandeur. The barometer story was purely incidental. I hope you found it somewhat entertaining.

In the early evening, Jorgan asked, "Would you like to have a fish barbecue for supper?"

"Sure. That would be great." Who wouldn't want a fish barbecue for supper?

Roseanne set out the nets and only a few minutes later had caught several fish, including a 100-cm (3-foot) "conny." This seemed like a very big fish to me, but Jorgan said, "This is just a small conny."

The conny (*Stendous leucichthys*) occurs only a short distance east of the Mackenzie River delta. Alexander Mackenzie and his French voyageurs were the first Europeans to see this species of fish in 1789. The voyageurs called the fish "inconnu," which is French for "unknown."

Roseanne cleaned and prepared the conny for supper. Jorgan piled wood on the beach, placed a grate on top of the wood, sprinkled on some gas and threw on a match. Flames leaped upward. (Of course they leaped upward. Flames never leap downward, do they?) After the flames died down, Jorgan set the conny fillets on the grate, which lay right on top of the embers and coals. "One" would have thought that this approach would produce burned fish. That's what I thought, anyway. Well, "one" and I were both wrong. The conny was absolutely delicious.

During the banquet, Bern Will Brown flew low overhead, still trying to deliver our fresh fruit and mail. Disappointingly, he again failed to see our red canoe, which, as always, had been pulled up and tied in the bush.

At around 10:00 p.m., Jorgan asked us if we would like to share a glass of whisky with him.

"Of course." Who wouldn't like to share a glass of whisky at the end of such an enjoyable day? We drank that glass.

"Would you like another one?"

"Sure."

We drank that glass.

"Would you like another one?"

"If you're pourin', I'm drinkin'."

This went on for a quite a while. Well, it went on and on and on for a very long time. By 4:00 a.m., Jorgan and I were pretty darn drunk. Kathleen and I excused ourselves from the party and crawled into our sleeping bags. Well, Kathleen crawled in. I sort of oozed in. I certainly enjoyed the first few glasses of whisky. Getting plastered, however, is not why I paddle wilderness rivers. Getting hammered is not fun. "Why did you do it, then?" you might ask. Fair question.

In some sense, I was trying to be gracious. After all, a good guest doesn't

Jorgan said this was a small conny.

offend an eager host by declining his generosity. Also, Kathleen and I hadn't brought any alcohol with us to our cabin at Colville Lake, and I was enjoying the whisky after a long period of abstinence. Anyway, whatever the reasons, drinking until 4:00 a.m. proved to be an unpleasant end to what had been a very enjoyable day.

You might be wondering about my spelling of whisky, without an "e." I was wondering that myself. Shouldn't it have an "e"? My spell checker didn't indicate a misspelling. I inserted an "e" just to see what would happen. My spell checker was happy with that spelling too. Odd, I thought. How could both spellings be correct? An Internet search indicated that whisky is the proper spelling in Canada, Scotland and Japan. Whiskey is the proper spelling in the United States. A trip to the liquor store confirmed this. Whiskey bottles from the United States had an "e." Whisky bottles from Canada and Scotland did not. Thought you would like to know, if you didn't happen to know that already.

July 11. Sounds of the ongoing, now very raucous party woke Kathleen and me at 8:00 a.m. After hot coffee and cold pancakes, we put on the water at noon. That afternoon we camped on a pleasant, sandy beach about 30 km downstream from Jorgan's camp. Only 100 km to go. Maybe we could reach Krekovick Landing, at the coast, in two days. I was kind of eager to get there. Getting there in two days would mean we would arrive on July 13, three days ahead of schedule. This would give us five days at Krekovick Landing before our chartered plane came to take us back to Inuvik. Five days is a lot of time to spend in one spot. But we could stay in the abandoned Canadian Wildlife Service cabin, which might be comfortable. We could enjoy day trips, fishing, botanizing, birdwatching, and just hanging out. Who knows, we might even do some hiking.

Anyway, for the first time on any wilderness canoe trip, I was ready to reach the end. Perhaps all that drinking and partying last night soured my enthusiasm for being here. I was ready to reach the Arctic coast. One hundred kilometres was not so far. We had a strong current. We could very easily get there in two days. On the Thelon River in 1993, we once paddled 80 km in one day. On the South Nahanni River in 1990, we paddled from Kraus Hot Springs to Blackstone Landing in one day—a distance of 102 km. One hundred kilometres was not so far.

After supper, Kathleen and I snacked on popcorn, a farewell gift from our footprint friends. I hoped that we would have good paddling conditions tomorrow. I wanted to get to the coast.

July 12. We put on the water at 9:00 a.m. and spent much of the day paddling down long, seemingly unending stretches of the Anderson River. I never like it when I can see several kilometres downriver. It seems like you're never making any progress, particularly on a big river like the Anderson. Throughout the morning, we startled hundreds of Tundra Swans, most of them young, flightless cygnets, which fled on foot from our canoe, along the banks, often for more than 1 km at a time.

We stopped for lunch on a very wet, muddy shoreline. Camping seemed to be getting worse. I looked forward to reaching Krekovick Landing at the coast.

A strong, northwest headwind battered us for most of the day. We paddled hard, heads down, not saying much, just trying to paddle as many kilometres as possible. At least there were no bugs. We had to thank the wind for that.

At 7:00 p.m., Kathleen and I agreed to stop and look for a campsite. Nearly 10 hours on the water—battling the wind. We were both tired. We trudged up and down the gravel beach, looking for even a small flat spot. Trudge forth. Trudge back. Trudge forth again. Trudge back again. You can trudge back and forth only so many times before you finally realize that there are no flat spots. We gave up and pitched our tent on a muddy, rocky, sloping site.

We were camped in what we believed to be Jorgan Elias' Windy Bend. According to a paper by J. Ross Mackay, Windy Bend is the first of two very large east-trending bends in the Anderson River north of treeline. Husky Bend lies about 20 km farther downriver from Mackay's Windy Bend.

Mackay reported that both names are local terms. In fact, they do not appear on topographic maps or in the *Paddler's Guide*. When we mentioned this to Jorgan, he asked to see our topographic map, and said that Mackay was incorrect. The "real" Windy Bend, according to Jorgan, is the first large bend to the west—just a little bit north of Mackay's Windy Bend. Who to believe? Well, Windy Bend is a local name. Jorgan is local. I'm putting my money on Jorgan. We were camped in Jorgan Elias' Windy Bend—the real Windy Bend.

For the first time on this trip, firewood was becoming hard to find. In fact, there was no firewood on our muddy, gravel beach. So, after organizing our gear for the evening, I climbed up onto the ridge to look for driftwood. What, I hear some of you saying. Why would you go up onto a ridge to look for driftwood? Well, during spring runoff, the Anderson River certainly ran much higher up the bank than it did now. After reaching peak volumes, the river dropped quickly, leaving the driftwood in long lines up above the shore. So there I was, up on the ridge, looking for driftwood for our campfire.

I quickly gathered several armloads and looked up from my mundane task to see if Kathleen was close to having her "kitchen area" ready to prepare supper. The entire scene fell away before me, and I was stunned by its beauty and romance. The Anderson River flowed confidently north to the Arctic Ocean. Broad, undulating tundra stretched endlessly eastward. And there was my tent and my canoe in that pristine vastness. And there was Kathleen, my life's partner, waiting patiently for me to return with firewood. Could this really be my life? I am so very lucky. Kathleen and I are so very fortunate to have this opportunity to live—free and open—on the Anderson River.

After supper, Kathleen and I once again enjoyed footprint friend popcorn for dessert. We sat before our campfire watching the midnight sun arcing toward the northern horizon. Beneath its soft light, the Windy Bend cliffs, composed of iron and sulphur oxides, glowed magnificently red and yellow. Beautiful, indeed. Even so, our campsite remained very muddy. The wind still blustered away.

Good campsites were sometimes hard to find: there was a lot of mud.

We had put in a long day for comparatively little progress—only about 33 km gained. We felt rested and hoped for calmer conditions tomorrow. It was still about 67 km to the coast. Probably still two more days to reach the coast if this wind keeps up.

July 13. The day began cold (5°), wet and rainy. We lay in our tent, waiting for better weather. Today was listed as a rest day anyway, and we were already ahead of our proposed itinerary. Plenty of time to reach the Arctic coast. No need to rush. We could wait for better paddling weather.

The mist cleared and the sky lifted slightly at 10:00 a.m. We hurried through our breakfast of bannock and tea, broke camp, and put on the water at half past noon.

"Only 67 km to the coast, Kathleen. With good weather and a strong current, we could get there today."

The northwest wind continued, driving the damp, 5° temperature into our unwilling bodies. Heads down, we concentrated on the immediate task of paddling.

We stopped only once, and very briefly, to collect broken fragments of red, yellow and pink ochre, the material that caused the Windy Bend cliffs to glow so magnificently last night. At approximately 5:00 p.m. we passed a sign that indicated we had reached the southern boundary of the Anderson River Delta Bird Sanctuary. After seeing multitudes of geese and swans during the past week, the sanctuary, for some reason, was nearly empty of birds. In the next hour, we saw just a few Tundra Swans, one Mew Gull, a couple of Arctic Terns, several Bank Swallows and one caribou.

The wind intensified. We paddled on, still with our heads down, mostly in silence. Finally, after much prodding by Kathleen, I agreed to head for shore at 6:00 p.m. It went something like this.

"Aren't you tired of this, Michael?"

"No. I'd like to get to Krekovick today."

"How far is it?"

"Looking at the map, it seems to be less than 40 km."

"That's way too far. We started out this morning with 67 km to go. Are you telling me we haven't even gone halfway? And we've been paddling for six hours? I'm going to shore to have some tea and warm up in the tent."

Of course she was right. But I would have paddled on. We did have constant daylight, after all. And it would have been nice to spend the night in the cabin at Krekovick Landing.

We pulled out on river left and set up camp on a muddy bank. Beef stroganoff, tea, and then to the tent for gorp and more tea. I have to admit that I felt content to rest. It was also good to be warm after our cold day. As always, when I lay in the tent, I studied the maps to determine how far we had come during the day and how far we needed to go tomorrow. I turned toward Kathleen, who was reading the bird book as she lay snuggled in her sleeping bag.

"Only 38 km to Krekovick Landing, Kathleen. Just one good day's paddling."

July 14. Up at 6:30. Still cold at 6°. Still misty, but a trifle calmer. On the water at 8:30, hoping for fair weather. Hoping to reach Krekovick Landing today.

The sky lifted and cleared by noon, but the headwind continued, blowing directly into our faces. Despite paddling hard, we were making very little progress. The cute little Arctic ground squirrels, known by the Inuit as *sik-siks*, seemed amused by our struggles, as they scurried along beside us, darting in and out of their bank-side burrows. Red-breasted Mergansers flew away from our canoe. Tundra Swans bugled in the distance. Arctic Terns and Glaucous Gulls soared overhead. Northern Harriers glided low across the tundra.

By mid-afternoon, the wind blew even stronger, and we stopped at 5:00 p.m., still 15 km short of our destination. In the far distance, though, we could see the point of Krekovick Landing.

We set up camp in a beautiful meadow carpeted with wild flowers, including Sea-shore Chamomile, Tall Jacob's-Ladder and Black-tipped Groundsel. The scientific name for Black-tipped Groundsel is *Senecio lugens*. I know some of you are likely thinking, so what? Why should I care about the scientific name of Black-tipped Groundsel? Well, it's interesting, that's why. Let me explain. Sir John Richardson, with the Franklin expedition, was the first European to describe this plant species, which he discovered at Bloody Falls on the Coppermine River in 1821. Page Burt, in her book *Barrenland Beauties*, reports that "the black tips of the involucral bracts inspired the specific name (*lugens*) from the Latin *lugeo* (to mourn)," and refers to the massacre of Inuit at Bloody Falls by Samuel Hearne's guides and hunters in 1771. See. I told you it was interesting.

As always, I organized our campfire for supper down near the water's edge. I prefer to cook on sand or gravel. That way I don't damage plants, and afterwards, there's no blackened soil. It's a very good approach, except of course, when camped only 15 km from the Arctic coast. During supper, the incoming tide flowed up the Anderson River, crept 3 m up the bank and completely flooded out our campfire. Now this didn't happen all at once. We could see the river rising. Every few minutes we would reassure ourselves that "It can't come much higher. It's bound to stop rising soon. After all, we're 15 km from the coast. How much farther up the bank can it come?"

Far enough to force us to abandon our campfire—that's how far. At least now, though, we knew when high tide would occur tomorrow morning. That would be approximately 12 hours and 15 minutes from now. We would be ready to leave tomorrow on the falling tide and just ride the current down to Krekovick Landing. *[Note: I've just reread Mackay's paper on the Anderson River, and he wrote that "the tidal effects are said to be felt as far as Husky Bend," which is about 50 km upriver.]*

At 9:00 p.m. we heard the sound of a motor coming down the Anderson River. A few minutes later Jorgan Elias stepped out of his boat.

"We're going down to the cabin at Schooner Landing for a few days. You should join us there tomorrow." *[Note: Schooner Landing is the local name for Krekovick Landing.]*

"Sure, Jorgan. That would be great."

I hoped we could make it tomorrow, I thought to myself. It's only 15 km. We'll have a falling tide plus the river's current. We should be able to make it, even with a headwind.

"On the way down here from my camp," Jorgan reported, "I passed three groups of canoeists. One couple is about two days from here. Two more groups of four are behind them."

The Anderson River seemed to be getting crowded. Time to get to the coast. Only 15 km to go. We should make it tomorrow, one day ahead of schedule.

July 15. I slept soundly until 8:00 a.m. Kathleen and I enjoyed a leisurely breakfast in a warm, calm morning. We waited for the ebb tide to flow down-river, and headed off to Krekovick Landing. We drifted past low, gentle verdant hills looking almost manicured—stretching out endlessly away from the river.

In the early afternoon, 27 days after leaving our cabin at the north end of Colville Lake, we finally arrived at Krekovick Landing, where Jorgan, Roseanne and Mary greeted us with warm hospitality and hot coffee. Soon afterward, we headed 6 km back up the Anderson River in Jorgan's power-boat to collect fresh water from a small lake at the head of a barely navigable tributary. You should remember this if you ever paddle the Anderson River. You might want to take fresh water with you to Krekovick Landing.

After supper, we chatted in the cabin until 1:30 a.m., stepping outside frequently to admire the midnight sun. A whaler originally built this Canadian Wildlife Service cabin in the 1960s. He intended to establish a trading post here but drowned before completing construction. The Canadian Wildlife Service abandoned the cabin around 1990, and it is now used primarily by native hunters.

After saying good night to our hosts, Kathleen and I crawled into our sleeping bags that were spread out on a bedroom floor. Nice not to have to make or break camp. Good to be out of the wind. Good to be out of the

We drifted past gentle verdant hills looking almost manicured—stretching out endlessly away from the Anderson River.

mud. We intended to sleep late. Our Anderson River paddling adventure had ended. Zero kilometres to go.

July 16. The following afternoon, we motored off in Jorgan's boat approximately 8 km east along the Arctic coast to the site of Stanton, which was established in 1937 as a Roman Catholic mission. Several small cabins were built of driftwood at the mouth of a small stream. Originally, only one white trapper and his family lived there, but later, about five Inuit families also came to live at or near Stanton.

Margaret Brown's father was a whaler from Texas, and she was born here to an Inuit mother. You remember Margaret. She is the wife of Bern Will Brown, our landlord at Colville Lake. Our host Jorgan was also born here at Stanton. Nothing now exists of the small community except for the church and two graveyards, slowly deteriorating on a bleak and desolate beach at the edge of the polar sea.

The site for Stanton was chosen partly because of plentiful nearby driftwood and good fishing, which remains excellent to this day. In only minutes, Roseanne's nets teemed with whitefish, and we headed back to Krekovick Landing. *[Note: According to the 1:250,000 map, Stanton appears to be approximately 8 km east of Krekovick Landing. According to the 1:1,000,000 map, the distance appears to be approximately 18 km.]*

At 2:00 a.m. we sat on the beach enjoying barbecued fish and baked potatoes —our campfire fuelled by a forest of driftwood deposited here at the mouth of the Anderson River. The sun drifted toward the northern horizon with no intention of setting. Kathleen and I began this journey six months ago, January 31, at the north end of Colville Lake. We had come with our urban vision of wilderness as a vast, empty, unpeopled landscape. Instead, we had discovered a neighbourhood—a community of people—both past and present—sharing their journeys through time and space. We went to bed that night satisfied and content.

July 17. After breakfast, we set off down the Anderson River in Jorgan's powerboat to hunt caribou. Within minutes, we spotted a caribou on the ridge, on river right. Jorgan stood up in the boat and fired his rifle, sending up a puff of dirt at the caribou's feet. The caribou didn't move. Jorgan fired again, sending up another puff of dirt at the caribou's feet. I'm not a hunter, but I was impressed with Jorgan's marksmanship. The caribou stood a couple hundred metres away, and Jorgan was shooting from a moving, pitching boat. Even so, he came very close to hitting the unsuspecting caribou.

Jorgan fired a third time and seemed to miss completely—no puff of dirt. The caribou appeared completely unconcerned and simply turned to wander slowly over the ridge and out of view. We motored down and then back up the Anderson River for another 30 minutes or so without seeing any more caribou. We headed back to the cabin for lunch.

Back inside, Jorgan expressed surprise that he missed completely on his third shot.

"I shot higher. I should'a got 'em."

Jorgan then looked down the barrel of his rifle and saw that the third bullet had lodged just before exiting. The bullet was truly jammed. Jorgan and I worked for over an hour to get it out. I don't know why, or how commonly, bullets jam in rifle barrels. But I was very surprised. I'm also thinking that we were lucky that the caribou had wandered over the ridge. If Jorgan had fired a fourth time, with that third bullet lodged, I assume that someone could have been seriously hurt.

After lunch, we used Jorgan's radio phone to call the float plane company in Inuvik about our pickup. We had originally scheduled our pickup for the late afternoon on July 18. We had planned to reach Krekovick Landing at the end of the paddling day on July 16. A full layover day on July 17, followed by nearly another full day on July 18 gave us an ample cushion in case we had fallen behind schedule. But, Kathleen and I were at Krekovick Landing now. We were ready to go home. Might as well leave a few hours earlier—in the morning, rather than the afternoon.

Jorgan also called relatives in Inuvik, asking them to buy groceries and supplies to take to the float plane company. No sense for the plane to come out empty. Kathleen and I were paying for the flight out to Krekovick Landing, so the plane might as well bring groceries. It was the least we could do to acknowledge Jorgan's hospitality.

July 20. Our charter flight arrived in mid-morning on July 18, and we flew back to Inuvik, where last January 31, Kathleen and I lifted off the frozen runway at -40°. So different from today's warmth. Our friends Marilyn and Alan Fehr were waiting for us, with our van, at the float plane dock. After nearly six months, our northern adventure was truly over.

Inuvik's annual arts and craft fair was in full swing, and we decided to spend a few days in town before heading south, back down the Dempster Highway, toward our home in North Vancouver. Late in the afternoon, on our third and final day in Inuvik, we found a note jammed under the windshield wiper of our van. I don't have the note anymore, but it said something like this:

"We see that you have a red canoe. You are probably the people who were a day or two ahead of us on the Anderson River. Why don't you come over to the hotel pub this evening around six."

That sounded like fun. I would love talking about the river with other canoeists. So Kathleen and I showed up a few minutes before six, sat down, and watched people coming through the door. A few minutes after six, a man and a woman entered the pub, glancing around as though they were looking for someone. They sat down at an empty table, still looking around. They must be the note writers, so we walked over and introduced ourselves. I'm sorry that I can't remember their names. I should have still been keeping my journal. But the canoe trip was over. I don't keep a journal unless I'm on a canoe trip. I'll call our new friends Bob and Mary. I'll call them Bob and Mary from Toronto. The Toronto part is accurate. I remember that.

"Say, Bob. I'm curious. Why did you think that Kathleen and I were the people ahead of you on the river just because we had a red canoe on our van?"

"Well, you won't believe this, Michael, but we were sitting in camp one night when a float plane landed and a man by the name of Bern Will Brown popped out and gave us a fresh-baked pie! He said he'd been out several times looking for you and your red canoe. He spotted our red canoe and thought it was yours. 'I've landed,' he said. 'You have a red canoe. You might as well have the pie'."

"Hey, Bob. That was my pie. You don't happen to have any mail for me, do you?"

"No. But I would be honoured to buy the next round and drink a toast to all our great memories of the Anderson River."

You had to like Bob and Mary. We reminisced for a couple of hours. We shared with them our many, memorable images. Isolated lakes. Seemingly infinite boreal forest. Timeless polar ocean. Verdant tundra stretching toward the horizon. Canyons and rapids. Grizzlies and wolverines. Swans and geese. Unrelenting northwest wind. Absolute silence. Unending light. Unbounded freedom. Morning campsites adorned with wildflowers. Sunlit cliffs of ochre, glowing red and yellow. Hot bread and buttered popcorn shared with our footprint friends. Beach barbecues hosted by Jorgan, Roseanne and Mary. Bern Will Brown bearing gifts from above. It was one heck of a trip. Apparently I had already forgotten about all that mud.

PROPOSED ANDERSON RIVER ITINERARY (1999)

Date	Activity	Kilometres		Miles	
		Daily	Total	Daily	Total
June 20	Narrows in Ketaniatue Lake	13	13	8	8
June 21	Esker in Legetentue Lake	21	34	13	21
June 22	Hiking & fishing at Legetentue Lake	0	34	0	21
June 23	Bend in river N. of Legetentue Lake	19	53	12	33
June 24	South end of "this-way-that-way lake"	29	82	18	51
June 25	West shore of Sakatue Lake	20	102	12	63
June 26	Outlet of Niwelin Lake	19	121	12	75
June 27	Fishing & hiking at Niwelin Lake	0	121	0	75
June 28	South shore of Gassend Lake	12	133	7	82

June 29	West bend of Ross River	18	151	11	93
June 30	Confluence of Anderson River	16	167	10	103
July 1	Beginning of rapids at bend to west	33	200	20	123
July 2	Beginning of Limestone Steps	45	245	28	151
July 3	Resting & hiking at Limestone Steps	0	245	0	151
July 4	Bend to south	26	271	16	167
July 5	End of Juniper Rapids	25	296	16	183
July 6	South bend of river	38	334	24	207
July 7	Entering canyon N. of Carnwath River	30	364	19	226
July 8	Resting & hiking	0	364	0	226
July 9	Sandbar at west bend of river	27	391	17	243
July 10	Island nearing end of canyon	30	421	19	262
July 11	First west bend on tundra	26	447	16	278
July 12	Entering tundra cliffs	30	477	19	297
July 13	Fishing & hiking at tundra cliffs	0	477	0	297
July 14	East bend of river	30	507	19	316
July 15	Large island next to ridge entering delta	23	530	14	330
July 16	Krekovick Landing	27	557	17	347
July 17	Hiking & resting at Krekovick Landing	0	557	0	347
July 18	Fly to Inuvik				

MAPS FROM THE
CANADIAN NATIONAL TOPOGRAPHIC SYSTEM

1:50,000

    96 M/1

    96 N/4

    96 N/5

    96 N/6

    96 N/11

    96 N/12

    96 N/13

    97 B/3

1:250,000

> 96 M Aubry Lake
>
> 96 N Maunoir Lake
>
> 97 B Simpson Lake
>
> 107 A Crossley Lakes
>
> 107 D Stanton

1:1,000,000

> NR-9/10/11/12 Horton River
>
> NR-7/8/9 Firth River

The 1:50,000 maps were extremely helpful in finding our way along the complicated 140 km from Colville Lake to the outlet of Gassend Lake. The 1:250,000 maps do not provide sufficient resolution for this purpose. We had originally planned to begin our Anderson River trip at the town of Colville Lake, for which maps 96 M/1 and 96 N/4 are necessary. These two maps can be omitted for trips beginning at the outlet of Colville Lake. Maps 96 N/13 and 97 B/3 present only a portion of Gassend Lake. A full view of Gassend Lake would also require 1:50,000 maps 97 B/2 and 96 M/16. We did not take these maps, as we were able to navigate from Gassend Lake to the Anderson River with the 1:250,000 maps 96 N, 96 M and 97 B. It's hard to believe that three 1:250,000 maps would be required to contain all of one relatively small lake. It always seems to happen on every canoe trip that one topographic feature requires many maps.

The 1:1,000,000 maps covered the area from Gassend Lake to Krekovick Landing. These maps gave us a perspective of where we were in the broader landscape.

CHAPTER 5

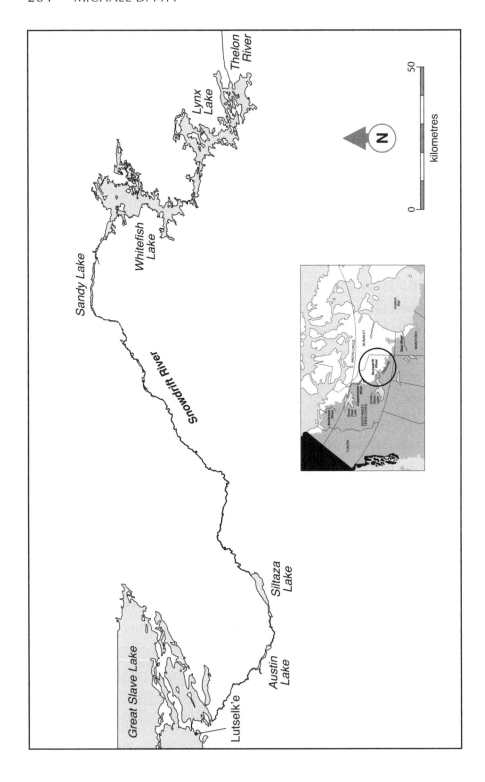

THE SNOWDRIFT RIVER

A Gentle Journey, Eventually

P eople often ask how Kathleen and I select what river to paddle. For us, the choice is often unplanned, perhaps even spontaneous. If you have been reading these chapters in order, you know that we paddled the Coppermine River in 1995 because Carey and Janice invited us. We paddled the Seal River in 1997 because I needed to attend a conference in Manitoba, and the Seal provided the most northerly and isolated experience in that province. We descended the Anderson River in 1999 because it happened to flow away from Colville Lake, where we had overwintered.

Our selection of the Snowdrift River in 2001 was a little more purposeful. First of all, we could land at the same spot at which we began our Thelon River trip in 1993, which very much appealed to us. We loved that camping spot at the east end of Lynx Lake. Secondly, instead of travelling east toward

Hudson Bay, we could paddle west toward Great Slave Lake. Starting at the same spot but ending up in completely different watersheds intrigued us. Thirdly, during the first part of the trip, we would be living on the tundra and camping on eskers, one of our favourite landscapes. And finally, during the last portion of the journey, we would enjoy the transition back to the boreal forest. There was also the strong possibility of finding Tundra Tom's eco-tourism camp at the west end of Whitefish Lake. If so, that might provide a pleasant interlude.

The only information that we could find on the Snowdrift River was a six-page summary prepared by Ed Struzik as part of the series of *Northwest Territories River Profiles*. Ed found the "upper reaches of the headwaters too shallow for canoe navigation," with water levels "less than a foot (30 cm) deep for long stretches. There were also a lot of rapids and rock gardens below Sandy Lake." As a result, Ed's group began their trip "on a small lake about 15 km below Sandy Lake."

This didn't concern us (or should I say me) too much. Kathleen and I are used to shallow, rocky rapids. And a portage or two is just part of every wilderness canoe trip. Besides, our trip would begin at Lynx Lake. We had no choice. We had to go through Sandy Lake and the shallow, turbulent water below.

The Snowdrift River ends its journey at Great Slave Lake, near the small community of Lutselk'e, which until 1992 was known as Snowdrift. Ideally, Kathleen and I would have paddled all the way to Lutselk'e. Ed's summary, though, noted that the last 50 km of the Snowdrift River below Austin Lake contained "approximately 35 rapids and waterfalls, most of (which) require portaging." As you know, I kind of like portaging, but like Ed, we decided to end our trip at Austin Lake.

As you can see from our proposed, nearly four-week itinerary, Sandy Lake was approximately 134 km and 11 days into our trip. We had allowed two days to complete the 10-km stretch of four rapids below Sandy Lake that are marked on our topographic map. Ed reported that another rapid marked on our map, about four to five days below Sandy Lake, is actually a waterfall, and is a must portage.

I allocated 26 days to paddle 330 km between Lynx Lake and Austin Lake. This would give us plenty of time to do the Snowdrift River comfortably. As I told Kathleen, "We have to average only 12 km/day to complete the trip."

By comparison, Kathleen and I did the Thelon's 950 km in 37 days, for an average of 25.7 km/day. This included nearly 200 km of tundra lakes and seven portages, one of which was 5.5 km long. Carey, Janice, Kathleen and I did the Coppermine's 645 km in 29 days, for an average of 22.3 km/day. This included four days on a large tundra lake, 15 portages totalling 9.6 km, 13 drags totalling 5.8 km, and four trackings upstream totalling 1.7 km. We did 283 km on the Seal River in 15 days, for an average of 18.9 km/day. That included a couple of portages and some scouting of the 39 rapids, 16 of which were rated Class III or IV.

Of course, starting and ending our Snowdrift River trip in two completely different watersheds meant that Kathleen and I would have to cross over the height of land. Six years had passed since our struggles on the Coppermine River, and Kathleen had apparently forgotten about the potential rigours of dragging, portaging, tracking, lining and occasionally paddling our canoe over a continental divide.

Even so, I genuinely believed the Snowdrift River would be the most gentle wilderness canoe trip we had ever attempted. As I told Kathleen, "There is only one rapid out of Whitefish Lake, and only a few rapids below Sandy Lake. We've never had a trip so easy. In fact, this will be the easiest canoe trip that we have ever done!"

I don't know why I say those things. I just do. And I don't know why Kathleen continues to believe me. She just does. I was confident, though, that the Snowdrift River would be easy. Only 12 km/day. That's doable, even if we portaged and dragged much of the way. I'm not saying that I would want to portage and drag much of the way. I'm just saying that it would be possible.

And certainly we wouldn't have to portage and drag very much of the way. Most of the first 114 km would be on Lynx and Whitefish Lakes. No portaging or dragging required on these lakes. From the east end of Whitefish Lake, it was only 20 km to Sandy Lake, just beyond the continental divide. I had allocated 12 days to reach the west end of Sandy Lake and its outlet to the Snowdrift River. Only 12 days from Lynx Lake and we would be lazily drifting the final 200 km down to Austin Lake. This would, without doubt, certainly be the easiest trip we had ever done. Just Kathleen and me. Alone on the river. Floating easily through the wilderness. A perfect canoe trip.

I don't remember if I really stressed to Kathleen the information in Ed Struzik's brief Snowdrift River report that described the "upper reaches of the (Snowdrift) headwaters (below Sandy Lake as) too shallow for canoe navigation." Maybe Ed was wrong. After all, he hadn't actually paddled that stretch of river below Sandy Lake. I'm not just being naively optimistic here. Kathleen and I have a fair amount of experience with shallow rocky rivers. We don't need much water to float our canoe. We'd be content with as much as 30 cm (1 ft).

Anyway, from the east end of Whitefish Lake, where we would begin our journey over the height of land, the tentative itinerary indicates that we would need to average only 14 km/day to reach Austin Lake in time for our pre-arranged pickup by float plane. And, if we had to, we could portage all of the approximately 10 km of marked rapids below Sandy Lake. At three loads each, it would be a total distance of only 50 km. It would be like a moderate, three-day backpacking trip. And half of that distance would just be sauntering back to pick up another load. After completing the portage, we could make up time and distance quickly by putting in long days on the flowing Snowdrift River. Piece of cake. Anyway, I never believed that we would need to portage the entire 10-km stretch.

July 1. We drove into the Queen Elizabeth Campground in Fort Smith, where we spent the evening talking canoeing and Canadian exploration history with a German couple from Leipzig. They had just paddled 600 km in 20 days, beginning on the Clearwater River in Saskatchewan. The first four of those days included the 20-km Methye Portage, which connected the Hudson Bay watershed with the Mackenzie River drainage system. They were following journals and reports of the Fur Brigade Trail dating back to Alexander Mackenzie. They planned to continue down the Slave River to access Great Slave Lake, and then down the Mackenzie River to Inuvik. Two East Germans, young and adventurous, living more Canadian history and geography than most Canadians are even aware exists.

The next morning we felt some anxiety as we stood on the float plane dock. It was a morning of transition. We were about to embark on another adventure of unknown stories. Another adventure out onto the Barren Grounds, our favourite landscape. At the last moment, on a whim, we packed the rest of our highway food (salami, pepperoni, cheese, cookies, apples and oranges) into the plane. We lifted off Four-Mile Lake into a northwest wind of 15 knots. Two hundred and eighty-eight pounds (131 kg) of gear, plus the canoe tied onto the left pontoon of the Cessna 185.

Ninety minutes later, we landed at Manchester Lake to refuel from fuel drums that had been cached there. The wind had increased to 25 knots, and our pilot Gary now looked a bit worried. I didn't know why, but Gary explained.

"The lake might not be long enough to take off into this wind. If we don't lift off by the time we come even with that point down there, I'll have to shut 'er down. Then we can float through the channel to the next lake and see if that lake is long enough to take off into the wind."

Apparently Gary really was worried. Even so, we lifted off easily just before reaching the point and continued east for 45 minutes to where we looked down on Lynx Lake. The outlet bay to the Thelon River seethed in crashing waves, and breakers rolled across the lake's surface, running before the wind.

Gary's voice cracked through the head set: "We gotta get out of here, and look for somewhere else to land. The wind is at 55 knots!"

For those of you who don't know, a knot is equal to one nautical mile, or 1.151 miles/hour (1.852 km/hour). This puts the wind blowing toward us from the northwest at 63.3 miles/hour (101.9 km/hour). I didn't know those conversions myself until I looked them up just now, nearly 13 years later. I think Gary knew all along what 55 knots meant, as he now looked very worried. I don't know how much wind a Cessna 185 can tolerate, but as Gary said, "We gotta get out of here!"

And out of there we got. We banked left, to the port side, and swung back towards the west. We flew in silence, our bodies tense, as the plane tossed and heaved against the wind. We stared downward, looking for safety. You might ask, "Just where do you think you're actually going to find safety? Isn't it windy everywhere? Isn't it windy all the way back to Fort Smith?"

I'm glad you weren't there to ask those questions. You would have been right, of course. Realizing that, I might have been more worried. As it was, I still wasn't too worried. Things always seem to work out for me.

Gary announced his plan through the head set. "We have to find calmer water in the lee of an island, any island big enough to break the wind even just a little. Then we just might be able to land."

Sounded like a good plan to me. I certainly didn't have any better plan. Only problem was, though, there didn't seem to be a lot of big islands in sight. Actually, there weren't any big islands in sight. Just low, small pieces of land surrounded by crashing waves. I now began to worry. I looked at Gary, whose face showed resolve. We flew and searched, and I truly began to appreciate the old phrase, "Any port in a storm."

"I'm gonna try to take the plane down here," Gary said. "The waves look a bit smaller by that island."

We began our slow descent. "Oh my, oh my," Gary said. "Those swells must be four feet [1.2 m]." Kathleen and I didn't say anything. Gary was in charge. Our fate was in his hands. I trusted him.

Suddenly we pulled out of our descent and rose again, and circled around. Gary said, "I gotta check for rocks. We don't want to hit any rocks."

Again, a good plan. We circled around until Gary was satisfied that there were no rocks blocking our intended path to the shore. We began our descent for the second time.

"Oh my, oh my, those swells must be eight feet [2.4 m]."

I'm not making this up. That's what Gary said. I expected that we would now lift up again, like before, and look for somewhere else to land. Eight-foot swells certainly sounded worse than four-foot swells. In fact, they sounded twice as bad. Gary might have been exaggerating during the excitement of our predicament, but the breaking waves did look darn big.

But no, we continued slowly downward. Float planes are supposed to land softly on the water. That's what pontoons are for. On previous canoe trips, we had landed softly every time. This time, though, we hit the water very hard and bounced back up into the air, like a stone skipping across the water. We hit the water again, and bounced a second time. Again, we hit the water, and bounced a third time. The Cessna 185 now veered sharply to port side, and Gary gunned the throttle. This time, when we hit the water, we didn't bounce but rammed forward onto a beach at the foot of an esker, maybe 3 m high. Gary turned to me, reached across the cockpit, shook my hand, and said, "Boy, am I glad to be on the ground."

"You know, Gary, I thought the waves were worse the second time we started to descend. I thought you were going to pull up."

"I wanted to, but we had already lost too much speed. We were committed to whatever was going to happen." I'm glad Gary didn't tell me that at the time.

We set up camp at 5:00 p.m. as the wind intensified even more. We fed our highway food, two gorp snacks and some of our supper soup to Gary, who had brought no supplies with him, not even a jacket. "If I can't fly out of here by 10:00 this evening, I'll have to stay overnight."

We loaned Gary one of our sleeping bags while he rested, waited and shivered in the cockpit. I guess he felt more comfortable in his plane than by our fire. At 9:45 the wind slackened and Gary escaped to the southwest, leaving only a few minutes before it became too dark to fly legally.

We were now alone, as we wanted to be, but we felt a little bit uneasy. We didn't really know where we were, although Gary and I both independently picked the same small island on the map. I don't know why I didn't just ask

Gary to refer to his GPS on the plane. Kathleen and I carry only maps and compass, which are useful only if you know approximately where you are. What had we done? The myriad of bays, channels and low islands would be quite difficult to navigate if we were very wrong about our location.

July 3. We slept late and woke to a calm morning. Best of all, there were almost no bugs. We enjoyed a slow, relaxing morning of bannock. During breakfast, I studied the shoreline west of our camp. According to the map, the island I believed we were on showed a sharp bend to the north around an obvious point. This shoreline, however, seemed to extend more or less straight, with only a slight curve to the north.

We strolled west down the beach and soon confirmed that there was no sharp point bending north. Just a small bay nestled into the shore, which then continued stretching west. We were definitely not where we thought we were. This was bad news. We climbed to the top of a beautiful east/west trending esker that extended for 4 to 5 km. Where could we be? We studied the map, which indicated that only one long esker existed in the immediate area. So, we must be on that esker. If so, we were on a peninsula of the mainland and were only a few kilometres west of the island that we thought we were on last night. Not so bad.

We hiked across to the north side of the peninsula, checking landmarks, curves and bays in all four directions. We became pretty confident that we knew where we were, a very comforting feeling. I wasn't absolutely, completely certain, though. The landscape was low and flat, and many islands and narrow peninsulas share similar physical features. And it was possible that we were just trying to make ourselves feel better by claiming to know where we were. After all, last night we also "knew" where we were.

Nevertheless, we enjoyed the rest of the afternoon strolling across the tundra to greet old botanical friends: Alpine-Azalea, Bog Laurel, Bog Rosemary, Prickly Saxifrage and Labrador Tea. We lay down and immersed ourselves in a close-up view of the tundra's floral elegance. A Lapland Longspur burst out of a beautiful carpet of Red Bearberry and Crowberry that spread downhill

A beautiful carpet of Red Bearberry and Crowberry
spread downhill below our feet.

below our feet. Crowberry, the only member of its botanical family, produces a profusion of black berries eaten by birds, voles, lemmings and bears. Crowberry also makes fantastic kindling for starting campfires. This trailing, ground-hugging plant often grows near the water's edge and is commonly crushed by ice thrust up onto the shore by high water and strong winds during spring breakup. Its fragile, reddened, dead stems and leaves become tinder dry and burst into flames at the touch of a match.

After hiking north, east and south on the peninsula for about 10 km, we arrived back at camp, tired but satisfied. We were now even more convinced that we knew where we were. I felt immensely happy. I love this Barren Grounds landscape—its openness, its emptiness, its vistas, its freedom, and its fragrances, especially that of Labrador Tea. We dozed on the beach in the afternoon warmth. Still almost no bugs. Lynx Lake lapped gently against the shore. Tomorrow we would paddle.

July 4. Our 20th wedding anniversary. Kathleen surprised me with a very cute "Bunnies in Love" card. I laughed right out loud when I saw it. It was so darn cute! Did I give Kathleen anything? I don't remember. Nothing was written in my journal about any gifts. Anyway, there was no time for romance. We had paddling to do. We were already one day and several kilometres behind schedule.

We put on the water at 10:15. So beautiful to paddle through the Barren Grounds. Quiet and inviting. A mosaic of water, tundra, sand and eskers. We paddled 10 km through a maze of islands to reach the north shore of Lynx Lake. We then turned west, closely studying landmarks. I checked our map and compass frequently. At lunch we hiked over a low ridge to confirm that a small river drained into Lynx Lake at this point. We were becoming positive that we knew for certain where we were on the map.

We stopped at 4:30 on a 2-m ridge of Red Bearberry growing in the cracks of the hard Canadian Shield. Bog Laurel proliferated along the shore. We camped in a narrow channel studded with islands. This further confirmed our location, as only one such channel was indicated on our 1:250,000 topographic map. It was time to stop worrying about where we were.

A diving Red-breasted Merganser entertained us during supper, which we prepared using our small Coleman backpacking stove, as no wood was available. We had 10 more days of fuel, which I hoped was enough for the 12 days that I estimated it would take us to reach more or less consistent stands of trees west of Whitefish Lake. What, you say? Ten days of fuel for 12 days to reach trees? Well, we're bound to find little bits of wood along the way. No need to carry more fuel than necessary.

In celebration of our anniversary, we enjoyed fruitcake for dessert, followed by a bedtime brandy. A heavy haze crept into the evening sky as the wind shifted to the southwest, bringing in smoke from the many fires reported to be burning in northern Saskatchewan and Manitoba. Unfortunately, the wind was picking up again, which makes paddling impossible.

As we lay in the tent that evening, we reflected on our paddling day, during which we saw one caribou, and many small groups of flightless Canada Geese noisily running along the shore, away from our approaching canoe.

Early in the paddling day, we had likely passed within 2 km of the outlet to the Thelon River, which had been our planned starting point for this trip. The outlet remained obscured, however, behind low ridges. It would have been nice to visit our camp of 1993, but 2 km was close enough. Close enough to say that we had begun this trip at the same place as our 1993 Thelon River trip. Instead of heading east to Hudson Bay, however, we were now heading west, over the height of land, to reach the Mackenzie River drainage system. Damned exciting.

July 5/6. Thunder, lightning and rain overnight. We decided that the weather was too gloomy and windy to paddle, so we spent a lazy morning and afternoon hiking along an esker ridge. Saw a lone muskox and a lone Arctic fox. Both eyed us cautiously, looking back often as they ran away. Also saw one White-crowned Sparrow. The spruce trees were covered with vibrant cones, which revealed the promise of a new Arctic spring. Just as Kathleen was photographing the cones, her brand new crown fell out. For no reason at all. You might remember my crown came out on the Anderson River while I was eating very sticky, dried pineapple rings. There was a reason why my crown came out. Kathleen's crown came out for no reason at all. It just decided to jump out.

Kathleen said she felt no pain. Not yet, anyway. But we were both worried. Still 25 days to go before our scheduled pickup at Austin Lake. We wandered back to camp somewhat dejected. Long-tailed Jaegers and Herring Gulls soared overhead.

After a soup supper, we crawled into the shelter of our tent, serenaded briefly by Harris's Sparrows, until the thunder, lightning and rain once again bombarded our very exposed, rocky campsite. We both wanted to leave this spot. We lay on our sleeping bags, hoping for an opportunity to paddle. It would be great to paddle in a late evening calm. It would be fantastic to float on a placid lake into a low-angle sun. We were ready.

At around 8:30 p.m., we received our wish, as the storm just suddenly and completely disappeared. We quickly packed up and shoved our canoe out onto the lake just before 10:00 p.m. For the next couple of hours we paddled beneath the intoxicating, restful calm of "midnight" twilight, navigating through a jumble of islands and bays. The flat, somewhat featureless landscape required constant attention to my maps and compass.

After leaving the maze of islands, we paddled 2 km through a clear channel and then swung north around a cape projecting into Lynx Lake. We then paddled 2 km up the cape until we were more or less opposite a large island (2 km x 2 km) situated about two-thirds of the way across an open body of water between us and the southwest shore of Lynx Lake. We wanted to be on that southwest shore, which provided the shortest, safest route to the river flowing into Lynx Lake from Whitefish Lake. Staying on the northeast shore would force us to cross several very large, deep bays. We don't like crossing large, deep bays because of the potential for strong winds and high waves.

Well, I should say that we believed we were opposite the large island. We should be, according to my understanding of where we were. Despite a full moon, though, the night was dark, and we could only faintly make out the general features of this presumed large island.

Trusting our judgement, we began the approximate 2.5-km open crossing at 1:00 a.m., heading for the presumed middle of the large island at a bearing of 250°. Kathleen and I paddled hard, worried that the wind might return. Fortunately, though, we paddled across in calm conditions and reached the island in about 35 minutes.

We beached our canoe and hopped out on shore, hoping to find a suitable campsite. No luck. Just boggy and wet. Despite shivering with cold, we paddled north along the island's eastern shore and finally stopped to set up camp at 2:45 a.m. At 3:30 the sun rose in the northeast horizon, instantly warming us.

We slept until 10:00 a.m., waking to a hot, calm morning. We scrounged some firewood from a small thicket of spruce, and cooked a delicious breakfast bannock. Having firewood was now even more important to us, as one of the fuel bottle's lid had come loose, completely draining three days' supply of white gas. I don't know how this could have happened. Such accidents can be serious, or at least uncomfortable. We now had only seven days of fuel left and approximately 11 days remaining on the Barren Grounds.

During breakfast, a canoe, far out on the lake, passed by, heading east. We were a little disappointed that it did not stop. It would have been nice to chat to people, even strangers. It would have been nice to share stories, yarns and adventures. Thirty minutes later, a second canoe appeared far out on the lake, heading to shore, likely because of an imminent thunderstorm. Out on the lake is a dangerous place to be during a lightning and thunderstorm. We just happened to be camped where the two paddlers landed.

"Where are you headed?" I asked.

"We started at Sandy Lake, and we're heading down the Thelon River to Baker Lake."

"It's a great trip. We did the Thelon in 1993."

"Did you write a book about your trip?"

"Yes, I did." I wondered why he asked that question.

"Well, last week in Yellowknife I bought your book." *[Note. He was referring to our book* Three Seasons in the Wind: 950 km by Canoe Down Northern Canada's Thelon River.*]*

I kid you not—it really happened just like that. There's almost zero chance that we would see anybody else out here. So what's the probability that this chance encounter would be with someone who had read (or at least bought) our book. Apparently, the probability was greater than zero.

[Note: When I was a kid, about 12 years old, I enjoyed watching the Tonight Show *with Jack Paar. Jack hosted the show, before Johnny Carson, from 1957 to 1962. Whenever Jack said something that he thought might be a little or a lot unbelievable, he would hold up his hand, as though taking an oath, stare directly into the camera, and say, "I kid you not." I am holding my hand up right now and staring directly at this page. Those two paddlers who just happened to come ashore at our camp had bought our book in Yellowknife. I kid you not.]*

We chatted for only a few minutes before our two visitors, from Germany, wandered down the shore about 100 m to prepare their breakfast. They didn't seem to want company. Besides, one of them spoke no English at all. The thunderstorm arrived, rain enveloped our low shoreline, and we retired to our tent.

The Germans had been paddling with a GPS. They almost certainly knew exactly where they were. They had been paddling from Sandy Lake, a lake that Kathleen and I would pass through just after we crossed over the height of land to the Snowdrift River. The Germans were likely following the same route that we wished to follow, only in reverse. It was, after all, the safest and shortest route. We must, therefore, be on the large island that we were aiming for in the early morning darkness. Good for us. Just to make sure, though, we spent the afternoon hiking across our tundra island. A long inlet confirmed our exact position on the east side of the large island. This time I quasi promised myself that I might quit worrying about where we were.

Kathleen and I love tundra plants, and are always very careful not to step too heavily on them. You have to put your feet down somewhere, though, and we enjoyed the very earthy fragrance released by Labrador Tea, a member of the heather family, as we returned to camp. We intended to go to bed early and put on the water by 5:00 a.m., hoping to reach the esker at Lynx Creek tomorrow, approximately 27 km to the west.

July 7. We lay in the tent for most of the morning, listening to the wind and rain. At 11:00 a.m. we rose to a cloud-filled sky. We boiled water for tea, ate a bumbleberry granola bar for breakfast, and put on the water at 12:30 p.m. Not exactly 5:00 a.m., but we were on the water, and on our way.

A perfect day for paddling. A slight tailwind. Not too hot. Not too cold. Not too sunny. Almost no bugs. We paddled easily, nearly due west (280°) toward the Lynx Creek esker, behind which we would find the narrow opening leading to Whitefish Lake.

We stopped in the late afternoon for a paddling break and for a snack of hot soup and peanut butter on graham crackers. While Kathleen photographed the pinkish-red blooms of Bog Rosemary, I took a compass bearing down Lynx Lake to confirm our position and direction. I didn't like it that I could see all the way down Lynx Lake, without any visual obstruction. There seemed to be no end to Lynx Lake.

"We better get going, Kathleen. We still have a long way to go."

Around 6:30 in the evening we crossed the last large bay before we would reach the narrow notch leading toward Whitefish Lake. We crossed over to the north shore and headed 240° down the peninsula pointing toward the Lynx Creek esker, expecting to reach the notch leading to Whitefish Lake in a few minutes.

After 20 minutes we hadn't found the notch but instead found ourselves in a bay with cabins at the far end of Lynx Creek. Somehow we had missed the notch. How could that be? Kathleen and I don't go that fast in our canoe. How could we have sped right on by the notch without seeing it? We beached the canoe and climbed to the top of the esker for a better vantage point. The topographical features before us matched those indicated for the bay at the western end of the Lynx Creek esker. We pointed them out to ourselves.

"There's the anvil-shaped peninsula on the south shore."

"There's that little island about a kilometre west of the narrow opening to Whitefish Lake."

Yep, we had indeed been paddling along the Lynx Creek esker but somehow had missed the channel leading to Whitefish Lake. We paddled back east along the esker and set up camp in a very beautiful spot below a tundra bluff. A sandy beach with plenty of sheltering trees and abundant firewood. We cooked and leisurely dined on a wonderfully tasty shepherd's pie. We sipped our tea and retired to the tent at 10:30 p.m. We planned to stroll east along the esker tomorrow to confirm that we actually did know where the opening to Whitefish Lake was.

July 8. We rose at 8:00, fully refreshed, and gazed out upon a warm, sun-soaked beach with virtually no bugs despite the calm conditions. We lingered over the best of our bannocks on the trip thus far—and that's saying something because all bannocks are very good. We then bathed and washed clothes.

Around noon we sauntered east along the esker, and within 30 minutes confirmed our position. We had crossed to the north shore a smidge too late last night and had already gone by the notch, which had been obscured by our poor angle of vision. Our compass now pointed 70° to where a small river led to the rapid coming out of Whitefish Lake, approximately 5 km to the north.

We then sauntered west to the end of the esker, about 3 km, to the little cluster of buildings that we saw last evening. We actually did saunter. We were in a sauntering mood. In addition to the main cabin, there was a smaller cabin, a weather station, two komatiks on plastic runners, an aluminum boat, and approximately 40 cords of wood. The cabin windows were boarded over. Steel spikes on wooden platforms had been placed beneath each window to deter bears from breaking in. The surrounding area was quite scenic, and we agreed that it would be a fantastic spot to spend another northern winter. It would be interesting to find out who owns this place and whether or not we could rent it. If we come across Tundra Tom at Whitefish Lake, he might be able to tell us. *[Note: In case you were wondering, komatik is an Inuit word for their traditional sled designed to travel on snow and ice.]*

Last night we had missed the notch by about 100 m because we didn't know, at that very moment, precisely where we were. This was just an example, however, of how being "lost" provides opportunity. If we had paddled directly from camp to the notch, we would never have discovered the community at the end of Lynx Creek. It's not always necessary, or even best, to know, in minute detail, exactly where you are every second. And this applies not to just wilderness canoe trips. For example, on more than one road trip, I have discovered interesting towns or coffee shops because I had taken the wrong road. I like to live life a little serendipitously.

We then wandered back along the esker toward camp, stopping often to photograph plants. Well, actually, we were still sauntering, but I don't want to overuse that word. Bog Laurel, another member of the heather family, was covered in red and pink blooms. We came across fresh bear scat filled with Rock Cranberry seeds. Rock Cranberry fruits overwinter and are still on the plant as this year's flowers first emerge. Rock Cranberry, therefore, forms an

We sauntered back to camp on an esker,
and stopped often to photograph plants.

important source of early food for animals. Seeing fresh bear scat, however, always worries us just a little bit.

We enjoyed a late afternoon light supper of chicken pasta soup, followed by fruitcake for dessert. We then retired early to the tent to read, to rest, and to enjoy a glass of brandy to celebrate the end of a very successful first week on our Snowdrift River adventure. We had reached the end of Lynx Lake. Tomorrow we would head toward Whitefish Lake.

July 9. Up early, almost with the sun, at 5:00 a.m.—warm, calm and clear. After the 3rd award-winning bannock in successive mornings, we put on the water at 8:00 a.m. Off to meet the rapid flowing out of Whitefish Lake, which we fully expected to portage. We were navigating with a 1:250,000 topographic map. Any rapid marked on such a small-scale map must be a "real" rapid. On the other hand, Whitefish Lake was only 3 m higher in elevation than Lynx Lake, spread out over several kilometres between the two lakes. That's not too much of a gradient. Maybe we would be able to paddle up the rapid.

A little less than 2 km from the rapid, we encountered current and paddled hard, ferrying from inside bend to inside bend, slowly making our way upstream. In a few minutes, we approached the rapid itself, which was nothing more than a shallow, wide, Class I riffle with strong current. Too strong to paddle against. While Kathleen walked along the shore, taking pictures, I dragged the loaded boat about 150 m around the inside bend in knee-deep water. Little more than a jaunt. Just a saunter compared to the overland portion of our Coppermine River trip in 1995.

I have come to believe that one of the greatest thrills of wilderness canoeing is to beat a potential portage. A drag upstream was not a portage. This first potential portage had been easily defeated. Kathleen and I had now left Lynx Lake behind, and we prepared to head north, deep into the vast tundra surrounding Whitefish Lake.

We prepared to head north, deep into the vast tundra
surrounding Whitefish Lake.

A few kilometres later, we encountered a solo paddler, on the right bank, cooking his breakfast. Jeff, about 22 years old, had originally planned to ascend the Yellowknife River with a friend and eventually work his way overland to the Coppermine River. They intended to paddle all the way down the Coppermine River to Kugluktuk. If you have been reading these chapters in order, then you know that going overland to the Coppermine River is physically challenging. Often times, though, physical challenges demand mental more than physical strength. Jeff didn't explain why, but his friend quit on the second day out.

Undaunted, Jeff returned to Yellowknife, found a two-week job, and chartered a flight with Tundra Tom. Jeff worked for one week at Tom's Whitefish Lake lodge in lieu of the $500.00 charter fare, and was now heading down Whitefish Lake, Lynx Lake, and Howard Lake to the Elk River. He then planned to descend the Elk River to the Thelon River, from where he would work his way back up the Thelon to Lynx Lake. I don't remember what Jeff planned to do once he arrived back at Lynx Lake. I do know, though, that Jeff was in for a helluva trip, made even more difficult by paddling on his own. I hope he made it. Such a strong spirit, with grand visions, needed to succeed.

After wishing Jeff good luck, Kathleen and I paddled away easily beneath the sun-filled, blue sky into a slight headwind. We stopped for lunch and for our mid-afternoon snack on a narrow, white sand beach. Sipping our tea quietly, we listened to the water lapping up gently onto shore. No bugs. Four Arctic Terns twirled and dove into the water. Truly an Arctic paradise, except for the defenceless family of Lapland Longspurs being plundered, just then, by a Parasitic Jaeger.

After 23 km we camped on a small island north of LaRoque Bay, on the north side of the first peninsula. Very calm. Very quiet. American Tree Sparrows hunted for bugs. Bumblebees foraged among the Bog Rosemary blooms. Loons cried plaintively and softly. We were surrounded by calm water and glowing tundra. We had enjoyed a truly beautiful day, and are very fortunate to share this truly beautiful life with each other. The only downside, in an otherwise perfect memory, was a powerboat that passed by twice. We were surprised and disappointed to hear that noise penetrating and overpowering our quiet solitude. On the other hand, the boat likely belonged to Tundra Tom, who, we now knew from Jeff, was indeed at the west end of Whitefish Lake. We looked forward to meeting him, and seeing his camp.

July 10. We woke late, 8:00 a.m., to a beautiful morning—just a slight breeze. We cooked our breakfast bannock on the stove, as there was no wood on our island. We packed up leisurely and set off for the mainland, 1 km away, at 10:15, in a brisk breeze.

A few minutes later, Kathleen noted that, "The wind sure seems to be picking up."

By mid-crossing, the white caps appeared, and the rolling swells exceeded our comfort threshold. We turned and ran with the wind to the nearest shore, squeezed our canoe between large rocks in the breaking surf, and stood on shore at 10:30.

For the next several hours, we hiked and relaxed on shore, dozing beneath the intermittent sun. We lay in the fragrance of Labrador Tea and lunched on soup and crackers. At 3:00 p.m., we thought the lake looked a little calmer, and we thrust our canoe out into the surf.

"It does seem calmer, don't you think?"

"Maybe just a little."

It turned out, though, that we were wrong. We rounded the next point into deep rolling, breaking waves. Our canoe surfed backward down a trough as we lurched and tossed toward the safety of a small, sheltered cove.

Again, we stood on the beach. Only 2 km travelled by 3:30 after more than five hours "on the water." We strolled down the beach with our plant identification books and photographed Alpine-Azalea, in full bloom, cascading down an igneous rock face. According to Page Burt, in her book *Barrenland Beauties*, the tender twigs of Alpine-Azalea are protected from the wind during winter by snow sifting down into the intertwined leaves and twigs, which forms a protective drift over the entire plant. In summer, the leathery waxy surface of the leaves reduces water loss.

We then spotted a plant, Least Willow, that we had never seen before. Again, according to Burt, Least Willow is the most northern of willows and is the only willow that occurs north of the 80th parallel. This species is less than 15 cm (6 inches) tall, and occurs in moist areas where the snow persists until late in the season. It must flower and produce seed very quickly because it has sunlight for such a short time after the snow melts. Now that Kathleen and I had seen Least Willow, it seemed to be growing everywhere. Perhaps we had just been overlooking it all the time.

At 6:30 the weather again seemed calmer. We repacked the canoe and paddled across the cove. The waves still rolled off the point but not nearly as intimidating as three hours ago. The shoreline gradually turned north, and then west, and with each turn we gained more shelter from the southeast wind. By 8:00 p.m. we were paddling in the beauty of a wind-free evening beneath a low-angle sun. At 8:30 we glided into a calm bay and set up camp on a welcome sandbar. Tea, cheese and gorp completed our day. Only about 31 km to go to the end of Whitefish Lake, and Tundra Tom's camp.

July 11. We woke to a grey, off-and-on drizzle, but relative calm. We put on the water at 11:00 a.m., after a bumbleberry granola bar and tea. Good paddling conditions. Better to be paddling in the rain than spending a morose day on the shore in the rain.

The wind soon quickened, producing whitecaps and rolling troughs from the southeast.

"You know, Kathleen, the map shows a large island only about 6 km ahead. If we could get there, we should be sheltered from the wind."

We paddled hard, but the wind gusted even harder. The day was fast becoming work rather than joy. We gained the point, and the island, and nestled into a small cove for lunch about 2:30.

"We're nearly off this lake, Kathleen. The wind can't get us now unless it reverses direction."

We turned slightly west, still sheltered from the wind, to begin a 2-km open crossing of a deep bay. Kathleen spotted three muskox on the left bank, and we veered off course to scoot down the shoreline to see if we could get closer. They were already on the move, however, and we could not close the distance to less than 200 m.

We then turned toward the opposite shore, into a strong headwind. How can this be? Had the wind shifted 180° to blow from the northwest? Seemingly it had. It was my fault, though. I should have known better. I should never have been so rash as to say something like, "The wind can't get us now." At least I should have kept those thoughts to myself. By now, I should have known better than to challenge the wind when paddling on a tundra lake. It was just plain foolishness.

Also, I had recently read a quote from someone, I can't remember who, that went something like, "On a wilderness canoe trip on the Barren Grounds, you don't need a compass. All you have to do is head directly into the wind and eventually you get to where you want to go."

We were paddling into a headwind. So we were probably going in the right direction. That was good to know.

Anyway, we struggled to reach the opposite shore, and then sailed back out of the bay, toward open water, to round the next point. We repeated this process two more times. Let me explain this process more carefully. We didn't want to paddle directly across the mouth of the bay. The waves were too high, and the canoe would be broadside to the strong wind. So we paddled into the bay, into the headwind. We continued paddling toward the foot of the bay, reducing the length of fetch, until the waves seemed small enough to safely cross over to the opposite shore. We then sailed back out of the bay, powered forward by what was now a strong tailwind.

I don't like strong tailwinds, which produce a following sea. I couldn't see the waves chasing me from behind. I just knew they were getting larger the closer I got to the mouth of the bay. I used my paddle like a rudder to hold our position as we picked up speed all the way and then zipped around the point at the mouth of the bay, like a skier performing a telemark turn. As we reached the point of our second bay, we sent a frightened family of Greater

White-fronted Geese scurrying across the tundra. They had probably never before seen canoeists performing telemarking turns.

When we rounded the point of that second bay, we stared into a very deep bay, which veered sharply left into what seemed an even stronger head-wind. We paddled pretty much as hard as we were capable of paddling to reach a narrow spit of land about halfway into the bay. We beached the canoe in the relative shelter of the spit, and stood on shore to rest and to assess our situation.

We agreed that it was still too far to cross the bay in this wind. We decided to continue straight into the wind, battling shallow water and rocky shoals all the way to the foot of the bay.

We paddled across to the opposite shore and then sailed, a little more comfortably this time, back out of the bay. We rounded the point and made one final push to a sandy inlet about 200 m into the next bay. I say "one final push" because we were by now getting pretty tired. Also, it didn't make much sense to work so hard and still not make much progress. We should just wait for calmer weather when we could simply paddle directly across the mouths of these bays.

As we began setting up camp, a powerboat started away from an esker across the channel from us. The boat initially seemed to be heading toward us before turning west. We thought they were coming to visit. We would have liked to have chatted to them. Maybe they didn't see us. Perhaps we should have waved.

Oh well. We needed to get our camp ready for the night, anyway. No time for unannounced guests. We found enough firewood for tea, supper, burning garbage, and boiling water for shaving and washing our faces. We lay in the tent at 9:30 p.m., surrounded by swirling winds, rain and thunderstorms. It felt good to rest. Around midnight, the storm seemed to blow itself out. I crawled out of the tent to stand in the calm. The esker across the channel sat bathed in sunlight filtered through the passing storm. We should reach the end of Whitefish Lake and the ecotourism camp of Tundra Tom tomorrow, now only about 5 to 6 km away.

July 12. We were on the beach, loading the canoe at 8:30 a.m. The wind had resumed several hours ago, and swells rolled across the bay. Only small whitecaps, though. The conditions appeared paddle-able, but just barely. We thrust our canoe through the waves breaking on the beach and paddled away at 9:30. Very strong gusts immediately drove stinging rain directly at us. We struggled to round the end of the spit to head deeper into the bay. Minutes later we were back on the beach, to rest and to discuss our situation.

"What do you think? Do you want to continue on?"

"We've just started. Let's not give up yet."

We paddled hard and stopped again very near the foot of the bay. We sat in the canoe for a few minutes and then paddled across to the opposite shore of the bay.

The wind now blew even stronger, and the wide bay frothed with deep rollers. Only 5 to 6 km to the end of Whitefish Lake, though. Maybe we could make it. We headed down the shore toward the mouth of the bay. After two more stops on the beach during gale-like squalls, we finally reached the mouth of the bay. We landed on shore and hiked up the ridge—against wind that nearly knocked us over—to get a look at Whitefish Lake before heading around the point. Before us lay a seething ocean.

"We can't paddle in this."

"Nope."

It was the end of our paddling day. Two hours of struggle to gain only 1 km.

We trudged back to the canoe and set up our tent in a low, exposed position. We crawled in to wait for calm weather. Still 5 km to the end of Whitefish Lake and Tundra Tom's camp. If this wind wouldn't stop, we might never get there. We lay in the tent all afternoon—listening to the wind—listening to our tent fly flapping in the gusts.

"You know, Kathleen, all I want out of life right now is to look up and not see or hear the zipper pulls on our tent door clanging in the wind."

We lay on top of our sleeping bags hour after hour, waiting for the wind to stop. Kathleen and I will be going to Paris in August, assuming that this wind stops before then. I wondered how many Parisian men, sipping wine on sidewalk cafés at this very moment, were wishing they could trade places with me. A rhetorical question, certainly. But I'm guessing that there were no Parisian men sipping wine on sidewalk cafes at that very moment, wishing they were camped out on Whitefish Lake, enduring a storm that seemingly had no end. Watching well-dressed Parisian women promenade on by in the summer sun likely had much more appeal.

By 9:00 p.m. Kathleen and I gave up all hope of paddling again today, as the wind remained as strong as ever. Even so, we didn't even unpack our gear that night. We slept in our clothes, with our PFDs as pillows. We wanted to be ready to paddle away whenever the wind decided to leave us alone. I fell asleep around midnight.

July 13. I woke at 3:00 a.m. Breezy (the wind, not me), but certainly calmer (both me and the wind).

"Are you awake, Kathleen?"

"Yes."

"Let's go then."

We were on the water only 30 minutes later. Easy paddling. The sun appeared over the northeast horizon at 3:45 and threw our shadow up onto the tundra ridge. Beautiful paddling. Finally, we're truly off to Tundra Tom's.

We approached the quiet community of Tundra Tom's at 4:45 a.m. For some reason, everyone seemed to be sleeping. Don't know why. The day was getting on. Not wanting to disturb the sleepers, Kathleen and I paddled on by, a little way down the beach, to cook our breakfast bannock in the morning sun and warmth. We sipped our tea and lay snuggled in the sand. A tremendous morning. The Barren Grounds were again beautiful and alluring.

We paddled back to the compound, where Tundra Tom himself strolled down the beach to greet us. He was quite hospitable and offered us hot coffee and warm showers. We gladly accepted. Refreshed and clean after our shower, we sat down with Tundra Tom's ecotourism guests during their breakfast.

"So, two days ago, Kathleen and I had been camped across from an esker about 6 km from here. We saw a boat with a motor leave the esker and head west. Was it your boat?"

"Yes it was," replied a lady. "We were visiting Gordon's esker. Lots of artifacts there."

"I didn't know that. Why is it called Gordon's esker?"

"It was named for Bryan Gordon," Tom said. "Gordon did a lot of archeological work there. About 10,000 Inuit artifacts have been found on that esker."

Tom further explained that the Whitefish Lake corridor was very important for hunting, as the caribou always crossed Whitefish Lake at Gordon's Esker because the water is only 4 ft. (1.3 m) deep.

"The caribou were easy to hunt in the shallow water."

"Interesting. Too bad Kathleen and I didn't know that. Would have been great to camp on that esker. I have another question for you, Tom. About a week ago, Kathleen and I paddled up Lynx Creek and came across a couple of cabins and a lot of stacked firewood. Do you know who owns that place?"

"It belongs to a trapper. But it hasn't been used now for about 12 years."

That surprised me a little. There was lots of stuff there (40 cords of wood, an aluminum boat, two komatiks) for a place that had been vacant for 12 years. Maybe Tom wanted to keep its status a secret.

Kathleen and I were now on the 12th day of our journey and had reached the end of the large, tundra lakes. We would likely no longer be so affected and trapped by wind. The trip had been pretty easy so far, just like I promised Kathleen. While sipping coffee, I reviewed our topographic maps for the next part of our journey, particularly the marked rapids. One of these waited for us before the height of land, four more within about 10 km below Sandy Lake, one at Ingstad Creek, and one more about 10 km below Ingstad Creek. You might remember that Ed Struzik's report said that this last rapid is actually a waterfall. Ed also wrote that many more rapids existed in addition to the few marked on the topographic maps.

I asked Tundra if any other canoeists happened to be on the Snowdrift River.

"Yep. I flew a group in a few days ago. I'll be picking them up at Siltaza Lake on July 24."

"That's the same day we plan to be at Siltaza Lake. Maybe we'll see you there."

"I doubt it. I'll be flying over you on the 24th. You might as well call that stretch below Sandy Lake a 10-km portage. I would never put any of my clients into there. You should let me fly you and your gear into a lake below that stretch. You'll be saving yourself a lot of work."

Kathleen was standing right there when Tundra offered his opinion. She didn't look worried, though. She knew that the Snowdrift River was going to be the easiest trip of all time. I had told her it would be, and she believed me. Why should she not believe me?

I don't know if Tundra was just trying to scare Kathleen and me into chartering his plane or if he was truly worried about our comfort. I had the impression, though, that he thought we weren't up to the challenge. If you had been there, I'm sure that you, like me, would definitely have heard the sound of Tundra's gauntlet being dropped.

"Thanks for the offer, Tom. But we're committed to going over the height of land."

"OK."

A few minutes later, I chatted with two young men who were working for Tom during the summer.

"Have you guys ever been into the area below Sandy Lake? What's it like?"

"It's pretty shallow. Lot of rocks. You're going to have to do a lot of lining and dragging. You could slip and hurt yourself. You might sprain or break an ankle."

Again about the ankles. Why is everyone so worried about my ankles? I told them about the time Kathleen and I spent 11 days dragging, portaging, tracking, lining and occasionally paddling our canoes 110 km overland from Winter Lake to reach the Coppermine River. They seemed reassured.

"You shouldn't have any trouble."

We left Tundra Tom's camp at 9:30 a.m. and soon reached the little river flowing into the west end of Whitefish Lake. No water in the "river," though. Just rocks. Just like going overland to the Coppermine River. We portaged about 500 m to a small lake up the drainage. We hadn't even reached the first marked rapid and already we were portaging.

The tributary coming from the next small lake contained enough water to paddle all the way except for a 5-m drag. As I mentioned before, a drag is not a portage. Things were going well, now. Back in the canoe, 30 minutes later, we reached the "rapid" marked on the 1:250,000 map. No rapid, though. Just a trickle of water. Not enough water to even drag upstream. I doubt this section is ever a rapid, based on what appears to be more or less permanent grass and shrubs interspersed on low islands throughout the "rapid." Kathleen and I portaged our canoe and gear about 200 m to the next small lake. *[Note: I just checked the Water Survey of Canada reports to confirm the water flows during our trip. Unfortunately, the monitoring station at the outlet of Siltaza Lake had data only for 1976–1991.]*

We eventually again ran out of water and ended our paddling day with a 200-m carry to camp. Note that we carried to camp. As I explained to Kathleen, this 200 m was not really a portage. Canoeists must always carry their gear to camp. Such a routine activity cannot technically be considered a portage. A portage is when you actually have to unpack the canoe, and then pack it again, and then immediately paddle away. As you can plainly see, by this logic, Kathleen and I had avoided another potential portage.

We had also enjoyed a highly successful day, which began cold and windy on Whitefish Lake, but which ended very warm (27°) and calm. We were camped in a taiga landscape of open, scattered stands of spruce. We overlooked a narrow (1.5 canoe widths) channel that leads approximately 1 km south to a small lake near the height of land. Best of all, we were now

Carrying our canoe 200 m from the water to camp, and then another 200 m to the water the next day, could not really be considered a portage.

only about 4 km east of Sandy Lake. Yep. Just like I told Kathleen. This is going to be a very easy trip.

July 14. We lazed over a leisurely bannock breakfast in the morning sun and then spent an hour or so photographing plants. We then carried to the water. We had camped "overlooking" the narrow channel, which was still a fair distance away. Far enough away that many people, such as Kathleen, would have considered this *carry to the water* as a portage. But, as I reminded Kathleen, this could not be called a portage because we didn't actually un-pack the canoe immediately before the carry. Unpacking and repacking the canoe in one session is required to be an official portage. We paddled off toward Sandy Lake shortly after 11:00 a.m.

We easily reached the next lake via the narrow channel, which was deep enough that we never had to get out of the boat to drag. This was very encour-aging, as the last approximately 2 km to Sandy Lake was via a small, twisty river. Such streams with so many bends usually occur in deltas or flat areas with very little gradient. I had been worried about this section, concerned that we wouldn't be able to paddle much of it. Based on our success in this narrow channel, however, the last 2 km to Sandy Lake might also be very navigable.

This lake at the end of the narrow channel lay only a few hundred metres east of the height of land. We paddled to its west end and climbed a knoll to gain perspective. Looking into the Mackenzie River watershed, we could see six small lakes and ponds laid out in a chain to the northwest, just as indicated on our 1:50,000 topographic map. The first and last of these lakes were only about 200 m across. In between these two lakes lay four ponds connected by creeks, down which we should be able to drag our canoe. It didn't appear that the water would be deep enough to paddle. The outlet of the last, or sixth, lake led to the small, twisty river taking us to Sandy Lake.

"All right, Kathleen. This is it."

We easily portaged 200 m up and out of the Hudson Bay drainage into the Mackenzie River watershed leading to the Arctic coast.

We sat down at the edge of the first lake draining to the northwest. "This is going very well, Kathleen. We're over the height of land. The hardest part of this section of the trip is over. Maybe even the hardest part of the whole trip is over." I was pretty happy with the day's progress.

Kathleen asked me if we had just completed a real portage. I wouldn't say that there was sarcasm in her voice. Indeed, there would be no need for sarcasm. Of course we had just completed a real portage. After all, we unpacked and repacked the canoe in one session. Definitely a real portage.

"You know what, Kathleen? This doesn't look quite right. This lake seems to be completely surrounded by a low bank. It doesn't look like it drains to the northwest."

"What do you mean? Are you saying that we're not over the height of land yet?"

"Maybe not. This is very confusing."

I once heard a quote attributed to Daniel Boone, the 18th century frontiersman who blazed the "Wilderness Road" through the wilds of Kentucky.

Someone asked Daniel if he had ever been lost. He thought about the question for a while and shook his head no.

"Nope. I can't say that I have ever been lost. There was that one time, though, for three days, that I was a might bewildered."

Kathleen and I were a might bewildered. We certainly weren't lost, as we had known exactly where we were only 200 m ago. But the drainage system before us didn't seem to match the map. This lake was supposed to drain to the four ponds connected by creeks. I don't like uncertainty when going over the height of land. I prefer to know exactly where I am. We again hiked to the highest knoll and confirmed that another small river flowing toward us from the southwest had flattened out in this marshy area, which created ambiguous, intermittent lake shorelines. The little lakes and ponds on the map didn't actually exist so distinctly in real life. At least not on that particular day.

In fact, there wasn't enough water in any of these lakes to bother with trying to paddle our canoe. We bit the bullet and portaged our gear another 400 to 500 m to launch our canoe on the twisty river leading to Sandy Lake. At 4:15 p.m. we were finally on water flowing to the west—water flowing in the direction we wanted to go.

"You see, Kathleen. I told you this was going to be a gentle journey. We've been on the trip only two weeks and already we've reached moving water. If we're right about where we think we are, we should arrive at Sandy Lake between 5:15 and 5:45."

We headed downstream on the barely discernible current. I didn't count, but maybe 15 times we were frustrated by shallow, rocky sections and mud-flats that required dragging and pushing the canoe. At 5:35, though, we finally reached Sandy Lake. We paddled 2.5 km west and camped on a ridge on the south shore. A beautiful spot with spruce trees now denser and larger than even last night. We had made it over the height of land. We had successfully navigated from the outlet of Lynx Lake, through Whitefish Lake, and along a very circuitous route to Sandy Lake. We were pleased with ourselves that night. We hoped to reach the Snowdrift River tomorrow, about 20 km away. We worried only a little about the rapids below Sandy Lake—the rapids that

Tundra Tom said we might as well consider to be a 10-km portage. We would see what happens when we get there.

July 15. We rose late, cooked a bannock breakfast, and put on the lake at 11:45. Instantly, a strong tailwind rose, blowing nearly due west down the lake. We surfed and sailed, feeling very uncomfortable in the following sea, before we beached in the shelter of a small cove at 12:30. Whitecaps filled Sandy Lake. We rested a bit and then hiked onto the ridge.

"Kathleen, I know we've had a lot of wind, canoe drags, carries to and from camp, and even some real portages. But this is going to be a real easy trip pretty darn soon. Believe me."

She looked skeptical.

We returned to the beach for gorp and soup, and then dozed on the sand, soaking in the warmth of the sun. At 5:30 we made camp, boiled water for tea, and retired about 7:30 for reading, map reviewing and Sunday brandy.

It had been a good day, despite so little progress. We were well rested, only about 14 km behind schedule, and ready to deal with the rapids and possibly low water below Sandy Lake; hopefully, we would be able to get there tomorrow.

We were at about the northernmost point of the trip—62.5°. From now on, we would be travelling south—into denser forest.

July 16. We woke at 3:00 a.m. The wind had been blowing all night. The lake looked paddle-able but was nearing the whitecap stage. "Let's get out of here. Let's go."

We ate a quick breakfast of beef jerky and peanut butter on graham crackers, and put on the water at 4:00 a.m. We crossed over to the north shore, which gave a slight but very welcome lee position to the northeast wind.

With each stroke toward the west end of Sandy Lake, we distanced ourselves a few metres farther from the wind chasing us from the Barren Grounds. With each stroke, the wind seemed to slacken. Sun beckoned to us from the west end of Sandy Lake. Black clouds threatened us from behind. We passed by the tributary leading to the Lake of Woe but decided not to take the 4-km hike to possibly see how the lake might have gotten its name. We were already feeling woeful enough. We needed to get off Sandy Lake and away from this wind.

We arrived at the outlet at 7:00 a.m. and photographed ourselves at a stone pillar. I don't know why the pillar was there. It was not in the shape of an Inukshuk. It just stood straight up, pretty much exactly Kathleen's height. Back on the water, a few minutes later, we approached the first rapid marked on the 1:250,000 map. Very little water filtered through the rocks. We ran it, though. So far, so good.

From then on, each time the river narrowed, which was frequently, rocks replaced the vanished water. Kathleen and I would hop out to guide, push, pull and coax the canoe through the labyrinth. Still no portage, though. Canoeists were still winning.

By 10:00 a.m. we reached the second marked rapid and got out to scout. We walked down the left bank all the way to the end of the third marked rapid and reluctantly concluded that we would need to portage nearly 1 km past both rapids, over very rocky and hummocky terrain. Quite disagreeable. We stopped for lunch to fortify ourselves and then climbed a small ridge to get a better view of our task. Pretty much just a boulder field with virtually no water.

"You know, Kathleen, I think I can get the boat through this and save ourselves a portage."

"But there's no way through. You can't drag through this."

"Oh yeah, Cupcake. There's a dozen ways through here. Just stand back and watch. I'll be slicing our canoe through those rocks so fast you'll be able to hear the vinyl on our canoe hull rip and peel."

[Note: Pretty much everything in this book is exactly like it actually happened. The previous four sentences represent the first obvious deviation from the truth. For example, I didn't actually refer to Kathleen as "Cupcake."

Tundra Tom had told us, "You might as well consider that stretch below Sandy Lake a 10-km portage."

Sometimes a man just writes spicy stuff like that when he tries to embellish a story or when he wants to give the impression that he is fearless.

On the other hand, exaggeration often has a way of becoming truth. When we first gave a slide show of the Snowdrift River to our canoe club in 2002, I used the Cupcake line. The crowd liked it. I liked it. Kathleen even seemed to like it. Ever since then, my affectionate name for Kathleen has been Cupcake.

Finally, if the truth be known, I wasn't slicing our canoe through those rocks fast enough for peeling vinyl to be heard at any great distance.]

An hour later I was nearly through. Not too bad. One time Kathleen lent great support by helping me drag the fully loaded canoe over a 2-m wide, mid-channel island to reach more "open" water on the other side. There isn't much else to say. Just a lot of pushing, pulling, yanking, guiding, and a few choice words at the appropriate time. Just like Janice said on the Coppermine River trip when Carey and I were dragging upstream, "They're guys. They love it."

I was indeed enjoying myself, standing in the water, struggling to get my canoe to the bottom of this nearly dry riverbed. The last 300 m, however, proved impassable, so we carried to camp approximately 100 m. Once again we had experienced the sheer joy of avoiding a likely portage.

We had stopped for the day at 12:30 in the afternoon, content with our progress. We had escaped the wind of Sandy Lake and had passed through the first three of four marked rapids without any real portaging.

After bannock supper we climbed a ridge high above the right bank and gazed downstream. There seemed to be mostly water. I estimated a maximum of eight more kilometres to reach permanently moving water. The worst case scenario, I told Kathleen, is only three more kilometres of portaging on the whole trip.

"So far we've had no real portaging in this section, although we will have a carry to the water tomorrow morning. Pretty good, wouldn't you say?"

"Don't forget the so-called carry to camp today. Maybe it wasn't an official portage, but we still had to carry all our gear and the canoe. Today was hard work."

I had to agree. I was a little tired myself. Into the tent to rest for the night at 6:00 p.m.

July 17. We rose at 6:00 a.m. to a gentle mist resting on the surrounding tundra ridges. Very comforting. After bannock breakfast and tea, we carried to the water 200 m over some difficult, rocky terrain to the end of the third rapid marked on the 1:250,000 map. We began our paddling day at 9:00 by heading south, down a small lake with a rocky protrusion on the east shore.

The end of that small lake drained into a very narrow channel that I expected we would be forced to drag or portage. Surprisingly, however, we half ran/half lined down this channel and then paddled nearly another 1 km through a couple of rapids until forced to portage 200 m to a very small lake that ran out of water only minutes later.

Kathleen and I now faced our longest portage on the Snowdrift River—a real portage of about 400 m to the beginning of a 3-km string of larger lakes.

The first of these lakes drained into the second through a 100-m chute, which we dragged. The last of these lakes ended in a thin arm on the east side, from which we lined and dragged, quite easily, about 150 m to a small hourglass-shaped lake. I say quite easily because there was almost enough water to run. At the lake's outlet, however, the water completely disappeared into rocks. We began our carry to camp of about 200 m at 2:30 p.m. Not a real portage, though. Just a carry to camp.

We were camped on the right bank, in a lovely, open, boreal forest. Dry and quiet. We had enjoyed transitioning into the boreal forest and seeing again some of its common plants, such as Twinflower and Fireweed. The scientific name of Twinflower is *Linnaea borealis*. *Borealis* because it is so common in the circumpolar boreal forest. And *Linnaea* in honour of Carl Linnaeus, who created the binomial taxonomic system for naming plants and animals. Twinflower was apparently Linnaeus' favourite plant. Interesting, wouldn't you say?

Toward the end of today's paddle, we approached a moose feeding along the shore, and minutes later a pair of Greater Yellowlegs chased us, very noisily, from their nesting territory. We were camped only 2 km away from permanent water. Only 2 km remained in Tundra Tom's 10-km portage. Looking at the topographic map, I expected, at most, there was only one more kilometre of portaging. Maybe we would get lucky and wouldn't have to portage at all. I doubted it, though. I expected we would be on the true portage trail tomorrow. About the same difficulty as today. But after that, the most demanding portion of our journey would be over. Should be a gentle journey then.

July 18. Up at 7:00 a.m. in a low, grey drizzle. On the water at 9:30. We paddled down a small lake and ran the 300-m chute leading to the first of two very small lakes. The short chute to the second of the small lakes, just above the fourth rapid marked on the 1:250,000 map, was completely clogged with rocks. We beached on river right to scout. Un-runnable. Un-draggable. We scouted on the right bank all the way to what appeared on the topographic map to be "permanently flowing water." We eventually found a pretty nice trail through open forest. Our route cut off most of the slight bend and avoided the large boulders and rocks near the river.

We began our 1-km portage at 10:45 and finished at 12:30 just below the last "wide" section above the anticipated "permanently flowing water." We leapfrogged our gear along the trail, which went reasonably well for two reasons. First, we didn't lose any gear, and secondly because Kathleen never once uttered those dreaded words, "I thought you said this was going to be an easy trip."

From the look on her face, though, I assumed she was thinking it much of the time.

After lunch, just past the end of the fourth marked rapid, we lowered our boat and gear down a 2-m cliff, which was the easiest and shortest access back to the river. That launching spot, however, was too shallow to paddle or line down to the beginning of a short gravel bar, beyond which lay runnable water.

"If only just a few of those rocks weren't in the way, Michael. We might have deep enough water to drag down to that gravel bar."

"That's a great idea. Why didn't I think of that?" I eagerly jumped into the shallow water and tossed aside seven or eight rocks.

We then dragged our loaded canoe 50 m to the gravel bar, lifted over a few canoe lengths, and ran, what I believed, was the final 75 m of Tundra Tom's dreaded 10-km portage.

Note that we *lifted over*. As I explained to Kathleen, a lift over is not really a portage, which requires that you actually carry your canoe and gear a significant distance. Kathleen looked skeptical. Her argument went something like this: "But I thought you said a portage is when you unload the canoe, carry all your stuff, load the canoe and then paddle away."

Hey. I don't make the rules. I just explain them. For example, if you drove your van to the water's edge and then carried your canoe and gear a few metres to the river, would you call that a portage? Of course not. I wouldn't either. It therefore follows that what Kathleen and I had just done was not a portage. It was a lift over.

By 2:00 p.m we had spent 4.5 hours on the water. Since leaving Sandy Lake, we had spent a total of about 15.5 hours "on the water," including lunches, breaks, scouting, paddling, dragging, carrying to and from camp, lifting over and portaging. Tom didn't point out or mention where his portage ended, but we had gone about 10 km, maybe a little bit more, since leaving Sandy Lake. Also, based on the topographic map, I believed that the hardest portion of our journey was now over. We certainly didn't endure a full 10 km of portaging, but quite of bit of work, nevertheless.

We then easily paddled 3 to 4 km to a very pretty lake and set up camp at 3:00 p.m. on a gentle slope clothed with open forest. After a chili supper, Kathleen and I lay in our tent, relaxing and sipping tea. We were definitely back in the boreal forest now. Today we saw American Robins, Gray Jays (also known as Canada Jays and Whiskey Jacks), four moose (1 male and 1 female with two calves), and one Tundra Swan. Red squirrels scolded us from treetops.

We were only about 10 km behind schedule, and we intended to take a layover day tomorrow—laundry, fishing and strolling. Let the gentle journey truly begin.

July 19. We slept very well and rose at 8:00 a.m., already feeling much refreshed and renewed. I set up a clothesline, made breakfast, and hauled water and wood while Kathleen did the laundry.

The day remained grey, misty and windy. We returned to the tent at noon to doze and relax. Up at 3:30 for a brief, unsuccessful fishing attempt in the very shallow water next to shore. No bites except from scores of frenzied mosquitoes. A Least Sandpiper wandered up to within 2 m.

After a quick supper, we organized gear for our descent down the Snowdrift River tomorrow. We hoped to reach Ed Struzik's "Waterfall Rapid," about 27 km away. But we'll see what we feel like. Maybe we wouldn't go that far.

Our laundry never completely dried, despite hanging on the line for five hours. Today's strong northeast wind carried a great deal of mist. To the tent at 7:00 p.m. We anticipated an early start. We were ready to resume paddling.

One of the most enjoyable parts of the day occurred during supper, when two Common Loons performed their mating dance. They repeatedly rose up, flapped their wings, plunged downward, and then glided with their heads along the surface of the water, like Northern Shovelers.

July 20. I woke at 4:30 a.m., ready to get up, but very reluctant to do so. Another cool, grey, dreary, windy day. We forced ourselves out of the tent at 6:00 a.m., boiled tea water on the stove, ate a granola bar, and headed west, down the lake at 7:00. We felt cold in the brisk wind and the 10° temperature.

We ran a fairly long rapid about 1 km below the lake, where the river constricted as it bent south and then north again. Another fairly long rapid 2 km downstream of the next lake required some dragging to push our way through. A few more Class I riffles and we arrived at the marked rapid just upstream from Ingstad Creek. Ed Struzik's guide reported that "this is actually a cascade and waterfall, turbulent enough to make lining out of the question." *[Note: This is not what I call Ed's Waterfall Rapid, which still waited for us downriver.]*

As Ed suggested, though, Kathleen and I portaged. We found a very pleasant and easy route on the north, or right, bank, through open stands of spruce with a park-like understory of lichen and Crowberry. The portage was only 150 m. We barely breathed heavily, and I actually enjoyed the exertion to warm up a bit.

"You know, Kathleen, it's not really a portage if you enjoy the activity. Portages happen only if you're not having fun."

She didn't say anything. I think Kathleen might have been growing a bit disenchanted with the "it's not a portage if…" game.

We lunched on a 6-m cliff, down which we lowered the boats and gear, and launched across a swath of alder and willow. In case you are a bit skeptical that we lowered our stuff down a 6-m cliff, I didn't say the cliff was vertical. You might be right to be skeptical, though. It was, perhaps, more like a steep bank. We did use rope, however. We loaded the canoe and ran the outlet rapid below the falls.

We then paddled through the next lake and ran a somewhat rocky and lengthy rapid just after the lake's outlet, again where the river narrowed, bending south and then north. A nice, swift chute greeted us in the narrow "breakout" through the esker in the next lake. If you weren't paying attention, you could pass right on by the outlet without noticing it.

A few more chutes and riffles put us at Ed's Waterfall Rapid, which, as he promised, was a must portage. Following Ed's advice, we beached on the north shore and found a very pleasant route—a stroll actually—of about 500 m through open stands of spruce. We set up camp halfway, meaning that the portage had become merely a carry to camp. Nice work on our part. Ed recommended that we "might want to camp here, as it is one of the prettiest spots along the river route." We agreed completely.

It was a very good day. Lots of wildlife. Greater Yellowlegs incessantly chased us down the river. An Arctic Tern dive-bombed repeatedly within a metre of Kathleen's head. Bald Eagles soared above in nearly every viewpoint. Five more moose—two lone bulls and a cow with two calves—stared intently at us, even after we had already paddled by more than 150 m.

The weather had also been kind to us. No rain despite never seeing the sun. A day-long tailwind. Cool weather that made portaging so much easier.

We had pushed noticeably deeper into the boreal forest. We had seen Water Birch, Paper Birch and Northern Comandra. Firewood became increasingly more plentiful. We had completed virtually all of the likely portages, had paddled 27 km, and were dead on with our tentative itinerary. Things were going very well. Because the rest of the trip should be easy, we would likely reach Austin Lake, our end point, with several days to spare.

July 21. Up at 6:00 a.m., with the sky still very grey but improving. Calm and quiet. By the time we finished our breakfast bannock, the sky was mostly blue.

We again scouted the rest of the portage, or rather the carry to the water. We confirmed that yesterday's first impression of the best route was correct, and we returned to camp, photographing along the river in warm, bright sunshine. We easily completed the carry to the water and began paddling downstream at 10:00 a.m., with Bank Swallows darting and swooping overhead.

"You know, Kathleen, this is our 20th day on the trip. Not even three weeks and already we have reached water flowing permanently in the direction we want to go, with likely no more real portages. I told you this was going to be an easy trip."

There was no response from Kathleen in the bow. She probably couldn't hear me over the sound of the river.

We glided along, so very much enjoying the scenery and warmth, so very unlike the two previous cold days. A beautifully varied and wooded river. Approximately 500 m downstream of today's first lake, we ran a rocky rapid. Interesting, but not Class II as purported. Another 500 m later, where the river bent left (west), split by an island, we entered a second, more challenging rapid. We eventually ended up on river left, against the shore, above a narrow chute falling over a low ledge. We easily lined the remaining 50 m and set off again.

Near the end of the next lake we rested for lunch. Beautiful gravel beach, open forest, medium-sized boulders for chairs, and a cow moose with calf browsing and foraging on the opposite shore. We lingered and savoured.

Off again, we encountered a third, marginally challenging Class II rapid below the lake's outlet, in the narrow bend left and then right. We moved easily back and forth, and eventually scooted over the ledge at the bottom of the drop.

We then drifted through a very long, straight section, with much of the forest on river left recovering from a recent fire. Two Ospreys scolded us as we neared their enormous nest on the top of a tall, shoreside snag. Greater Yellowlegs, perhaps the world's most annoying bird, badgered us constantly, in relays, down the river.

Three large sandy bends, where the banks were caving in from the force of spring floods, provided variety to our vistas. We then paddled up the delta of the Eileen River to admire this trip's most spectacular waterfall/cascade. A Belted Kingfisher plunged headfirst into the swirling pools at the bottom of the rapid.

At 3:30 p.m. we paddled over to the right bank and set up camp with a great view of the Eileen River. We immediately heated several pots of water, and stripped and bathed for the first time since July 13—eight days ago at Tundra Tom's camp. We basked in warm afternoon heat—hot water poured over our heads and hair—and no bugs. A perfect end to a perfect day.

July 22. Another glorious, sunny, calm morning. A relatively uneventful, mesmerizing sedative paddle across golden-green water broken occasionally by black depths.

During one somnambulant period, when we were more asleep than awake, we were stunned to see a muskox foraging on the north shore. Surprised to

We were surprised to see this muskox so far from the tundra.

see a muskox so far from the tundra. Maybe we shouldn't have been surprised, but we were. In case you're wondering, we sighted this muskox at approximately 62°25' N, 108°45' W. These coordinates were only my approximation from the 1:250,000 map, as I didn't have a GPS. If you have information that this sighting at this location was unlikely, please let me know. Anyway, we were downwind, and easily drifted with the current to within 15 m of the solitary muskox before he noticed us. He stared, twitched, then quickly walked up the ridge, looked back once, and then disappeared.

Moments later, we frightened a Common Merganser family, which included five or six young. The mother flopped and flapped toward river centre, luring us away from her brood, which scooted along right up against the shoreline, where they soon hid themselves, cheeping all the while. The mother continued to feign injury, noisily thrashing in the water for another 500 m, when she easily took flight, flew inland over river right, and circled back to her family. I was confident that a happy reunion ensued.

Much of the journey today occurred along and beneath nearly vertical, 10-m banks of pure sand. Amazing that the dense forest is able to exist and prosper on such poor, deficient ground. All the banks on the outside bends were badly eroded and slumping from the short, intense power of spring floods. Carpets of moss, lichen, Rock Cranberry and Crowberry festooned the edges and hung, draped over the precipice, like bunting at ceremonial parades. Black Spruce, White Spruce and Tamarack stood in long lines along the edge, seemingly to gain the best view of canoeists parading past. Some had stood too close, and now hung headfirst over the precipice, barely hanging on by the very tips of their roots. The Snowdrift River is actually named for these high banks of white sand, which from a distance look like snow.

Black Spruce and White Spruce have nearly identical distributions in North America, predominantly north of the 49th parallel. Both species can be found all the way to treeline. Yet it seems that most people travelling in northern Canada tend to call all spruce Black Spruce. There seems to be an assumption that northern spruce must be Black Spruce. This assumption is incorrect, however. Black Spruce tends to occur on poorly drained, boggy, nutrient-poor sites, whereas White Spruce tends to occur on well-drained, moist sites. Next time you're wondering about distinguishing between these two species, have a look at the cones. Those of Black Spruce are generally less than 3 cm (1 inch) long and are ovoid or egg shaped. The cones of White Spruce tend to be somewhat longer and more cylindrically shaped. If nothing else, just don't assume that all northern spruce are Black Spruce. This has always bothered me.

We had advanced today about 27 to 30 km to the bends toward the west, when we stopped at 5:00 p.m. Eight hours for 30 km. We probably paddled closer to 40 km, though, as we continually zigzagged from outside bend to outside bend, seeking water deep enough to float the canoe. Very interesting and scenic country with varied vistas and landscapes. Seemingly endless and empty. Only us, the boreal forest, a few birds, and even fewer mammals. We often saw tracks of moose, and occasionally of bear. In general, though, the land belonged to us. We were alone. The weather had become quite hot, nearing 30° by mid-morning, and we sought shade for our camp.

July 23. A few sprinkles of rain in the morning but clearing by the time we put on the river at 9:15 a.m. We seemed to have more current today, and covered 15 km by noon. Blue sky, and again hot, reaching 30° by lunch. Kathleen and I paddled quietly, with few words, as we drifted through our serene, gentle forest.

At approximately longitude 109°08' W, just beyond an island, in a sandy area, we entered an area where a large wildfire had burned. Although this is not really a guidebook, I thought you might like to know where the burned area began. If so, just find the above longitude at the bottom of your map and trace up until you reach the river. That will necessarily also be the appropriate latitude. We felt a little depressed to see blackened stems where park-like stands of spruce once dominated.

Historically, though, the boreal forest burns every 50 to 100 years, and rarely does a stand exceed 150 years. We learned later that this wildfire on the Snowdrift River occurred in 1994.

About 30 minutes later, as we approached a narrow constriction, at approximately 109°14' W, we heard the sound of a large rapid. We could see no rapid, though. As we neared, the sound grew louder, but we could still not see whitewater above or below the apparent, but invisible rapid. We floated on.

"This doesn't seem to be much of a rapid. Shall we just slam that puppy down the middle, Kathleen?"

[Note: I have plagiarized that last phrase from Dave Kilpatrick, a fearless member of our Beaver Canoe Club. Whenever Dave was asked about the best way to run a rapid, he would always say, "Just slam that puppy down the middle."]

Surprisingly, Kathleen said, "OK."

I say surprisingly because we are very cautious. We normally don't slam puppies or rapids down the middle.

We drifted closer to the sound. "How can there be so much noise when there's no rapid below and no rapid above?"

"It must be a ledge. Let's go to shore and have a look."

That sounds more like us.

Sure enough. A ledge. Slamming that puppy down the middle would have put us into a diagonal, recirculating hole. Glad we stopped. A safer route presented itself on river left—a green tongue, between two rocks, that extended into a train of haystacks only 70 cm (2 feet) high. We ran easily, and again congratulated ourselves for having stopped to look first.

Once again we drifted beneath a warm sun, gliding above a rippled, sandy riverbed bathed in green, yellow and golden hues. Once again we were surprised to see a muskox on river right, at approximately 109°18' W. This one galloped off into the bush almost immediately. When I say "this one" galloped off into the bush, I mean the muskox, not me.

We drifted on, ready to camp, but found nowhere in the burned remnants of a forest that yesterday had been so inviting and soothing. Finally, at 5:30 p.m., about 10 km upriver from Siltaza Lake, on a hard bend to the left (south), an unburned patch beckoned. A small stand of red-barked Water Birch and white-barked Paper Birch invited us to set up camp in a small oasis of park-like forest surrounded by blackened stems at approximately 109°24' W.

We pitched our tent on a point above the river, which slid silently by. Jack Pine and Common Juniper, two more plant species common to the boreal forest, adorned our sandy site. Kathleen and I lingered by the fire, enjoying a relaxed supper cooked over a bed of glowing coals. In the tent at 9:15. Late for us. We felt comfortable and content. Likely only two more paddling days, approximately 48 km to the cabin on the topographic map, our pickup point on the north shore, halfway down Austin Lake.

July 24. Up at 7:15 a.m. Sore and tired but driven by the excitement of only two more paddling days to our pickup halfway down Austin Lake.

On the water at 9:45. A beaver briefly swam in front of our canoe, with only its head above water, and then disappeared beneath the surface.

Very hot again—26° by late morning. We paddled silently from outside bend to outside bend, seeking the deepest water and trying to avoid sand bars and flats. Crossing over as soon as possible and then running with the current right up against the bank worked best.

We landed for a break and clambered up the bank into the burned forest. Willow, Birch, Green Alder, Common Horsetail, Bluejoint, Fireweed and scattered spruce seedlings already grew luxuriantly only seven years after the 1994 fire.

We reached Siltaza Lake at 12:30, struggling slightly against a persistent headwind. We hadn't seen another potential campsite since we left camp this morning. We headed down the north shore, crowded with thick, unburned forest. Dense, with no camping spots; 31° heat. At 3:30 we rested at the base of a point about 8 km down the lake. We sat on the shady side of the point, wishing that the beach had been wide and sandy instead of narrow and rocky. If so, we would have gladly stopped to camp.

"It's a scenic spot here. Maybe there's good camping up on top of this point. Let's go have a look."

A quasi trail led up the 10-m ridge, which was only 15 m wide. Even so, we found a very camp-able site that was open and flat. In fact, others had camped here before us, but not likely for 10 years or more. There were two fire pits, and rustic tables and chairs that were now crumbling and decaying. Rock Cranberry and Crowberry trailed over a neatly stacked pile of sawn firewood. We gladly set up camp in our new home.

Although this camp had obviously been well used at one time, there was not any garbage. Not even a single can. Quite unusual for semi-permanent bush camps. Exactly like the well-used site at our camp opposite the Eileen River. It would be nice to know who used these camps at one time. Perhaps trappers, as the Eileen River camp had stakes for tying dogs.

Only one paddling day, approximately 25 km, to the cabin at Austin Lake. We should arrive at our pickup spot two days early. It would be nice if somehow we could contact Big River Air to let them know that we would be ready sooner than expected. I guess that's one reason people bring satellite phones on wilderness canoe trips.

July 25. Up early. Another glorious day. On the water at 8:15. Already 24°. Excitement building about reaching Austin Lake today. As we entered the narrow portion of Siltaza Lake, on the north shore, we finally caught up with Tundra Tom's clients. They had been dropped off July 11 at the same lake Kathleen and I had reached on July 18. Eric, his wife Sandy, and their 13-year-old daughter Brittany were in their last camp, waiting for pickup tomorrow afternoon. They were very much looking forward to being picked up, as last night a bear had ransacked their camp. No one was hurt or threatened, but the bear had absconded with the pack containing their toilet paper. Apparently the bear didn't need toilet paper, as a 15-minute search that morning produced the missing pack and all of its very valuable contents.

This family from Florida was quite hospitable and invited us into their large, bug-free tent for morning coffee. We chatted a bit and learned that Eric carried a satellite phone because of his heart condition.

"Would it be possible for us to make a phone call? We can pay for it.

We'd like to call Big River Air in Fort Smith to see if they can pick us up early."

"Sure. Do you know the number?"

"Actually, we don't. I never thought about bringing their number. Too bad. It would have been nice to call."

"Well, you can call information."

That hadn't occurred to me. I'm not really accustomed to making phone calls from the wilderness. This was my first time.

Anyway, I called information and got the number for Big River Air. Doug answered the phone, and said he would pick Kathleen and me up two days early, around noon on the 27th. The technology was amazing, but it certainly diminished and shrank the feeling of wilderness.

After about an hour-and-a-half of conversation and coffee, we all wished each other luck and said our goodbyes.

"Be sure to say hello to Tundra Tom for us. Tell him we're sorry we didn't have time to wait for him."

I couldn't help myself. It's too bad Tundra wasn't coming today, though. It would have been great to see the look on Tom's face as we helped him down out of the plane's cockpit. Ten kilometre portage indeed. "Hah," I say to that.

Kathleen and I paddled down to the outlet of Siltaza Lake for lunch. Back on the water, we soon encountered a rapid—quick, shallow, and rock strewn, but mostly fun.

Then, two more rapids in quick succession, a little more difficult, where there were two "button" bays on river left, about 1 km below the outlet. Both rapids had granitic, shield outcroppings that created ledges and deep, reversing troughs. We lined the first and escaped the second by running down a side channel on river right.

The rest of the river to Austin Lake was quite pleasant. A few drops and pools, interspersed with quiet sections. Still a lot of burned forest, particularly on the left bank.

We approached Austin Lake around 4:00 p.m. As we scooted down the last chute, a Bald Eagle flew across our bow. When we entered the lake, a Common Loon yodelled its welcome. A tailwind sped us along the north shore, which offered many excellent camping spots.

We reached the cabin at our pickup spot less than an hour later but were very disappointed with the garbage and debris spread over what seemed like a hectare (2 acres) or more. We paddled east, back up the lake about 15 minutes, to set up camp in an open forest. Sandy beach. Beautiful evening light. We had arrived. To the tent for celebratory brandy.

July 26. We woke feeling relaxed at 7:00 a.m., and crawled out of the tent into yet another hot, sunny morning. Another bannock, over a very slow fire, followed by a bath on our sandy beach. We then dozed in the shade until noon, when we hiked up the ridge and then west, down to the site of the cabin, which we learned later had been a fire suppression camp. Such a horrible mess. If they can bring all that stuff in, why can't they take all that stuff out? Anyway, I put some of this debris to good use. I set three, 4-litre (1 gallon) white-gas cans on stumps to practice with my .308 rifle. Three, quick dead-centre shots at about 50 m, the distance at which I envision shooting at a charging bear. I was very satisfied and pleased.

On our return to camp, through the bush, we overshot by about 150 m and discovered a teepee site. Virtually no garbage. We saw another teepee site on the opposite shore, in the narrows to the east. Three "communities" within 1 km of each other. We were certainly close to civilization now.

Back at camp for lunch and more resting. Still so very hot at 33°. We amused ourselves with activities that people normally do while waiting to be picked up. Kathleen played solitaire in the shade to get away from the heat. For a diversion, she sometimes fed mosquitoes to ants. I scratched in the sand with a small stick. I studied the contents of our repair kit, and for some reason, seemed particularly interested in my roll of electrician's tape.

Later in the afternoon, I restrung the day pack with spare rope, of which we always bring a very plentiful supply. As you know from the Anderson River story, I am fond of saying that you can never have too much rope

on a wilderness canoe trip. Kathleen photographed Lesser Fritillary butter-
flies feeding on Spike-like Goldenrod. According to E. C. Pielou, the Lesser
Fritillary settles on plants in a way that maximizes the warmth it can absorb
from the sun. It settles with its wings spread, and then, if the sun is shining,
it will turn itself until its head points away from the sun, which orients the
spread wings at the best angle to be warmed.

During our soup supper, a proud family of four Common Loons promen-
aded along our shore, yodelling confidently in their joyous freedom. It was as
though they were saying farewell and inviting us to come back again. I always
wonder, at the end of each trip, if this will indeed be the last time. Twenty-
four hours from now, we should be back in Fort Smith, with our month-long
adventure already a memory. I miss the tundra even now. I already miss the
Snowdrift River, which indeed had eventually become a gentle journey.

July 27. Yet again, another hot, sunny morning. Also, yet again, we relaxed
over a slow fire and a bannock cooked even more slowly to the proverbial
golden brown. We then started to pack, for the final time, and to load the canoe for the 15-minute paddle down Austin Lake to our pickup spot. I folded
the tent and fly, rolled them up, and crammed them into the stuff-sack. We
carried the canoe and all the smaller parcels and hand-held items down to the
beach. I leaned my .308 rifle up against the canoe. We then returned for the
three large canoe packs.

"Michael. There's a bear!"

I turned. Sure enough. A large (aren't approaching bears always large?)
black bear was ambling toward the packs, striding right through the patch
of Kinnikinnick where our tent had stood only moments ago. Together,
Kathleen and I backed off slowly toward the beach and my .308 rifle leaning
up against the canoe. The bear kept advancing, but not toward us. Kathleen
and I stopped, stood together to appear larger and more formidable, and
yelled out things that bears probably wouldn't like to hear, such as "Hey,
bear."

The bear didn't seem to mind these harsh words too much, though, as he kept advancing and was now only 5 m from the canoe packs.

Kathleen and I have seen a lot of bears during our wilderness experiences. Well, it seems like a lot to us, anyway. I estimate about 200 black bears, 40 grizzly bears and five polar bears. Other than the polar bears, this is the first bear that appeared unafraid and undeterred by our presence.

What to do? I preferred not to turn my back on the bear to walk about 30 m to get my .308 rifle leaning, somewhat inconveniently, up against the canoe on the beach. So we yelled some more. Probably said, "Hey bear," again, with no visible effect whatsoever.

"Why don't you try your bear banger, Kathleen. Do you have it?"

"Yes. I almost packed it away, but I thought no, we're still in the wilderness. I better keep it with me."

My foresightful adventuring partner reached into her shirt pocket and pulled out the pen-sized launcher on which the explosive was screwed. She fumbled only slightly with the release mechanism and held the banger overhead.

The first small bang when the explosive launched produced no impact on the bear at all, who was now within sniffing distance of our three large packs of gear, clothing, food (and toilet paper). Seconds later, the loud "bang" overhead caught the bear's attention. He looked over at us, and seemingly for the first time, noticed that we stood in the clearing.

He appeared confused, uncertain about his course of action. He looked at us again and then turned to walk away. After a few steps, he broke into a run and disappeared into the willows and spruce, heading along the shore, west, down the lake. It was good to know that the bear banger does actually work. At least sometimes.

We resumed packing, checking the periphery of our forest clearing with furtive inspections every few seconds. Minutes later, we paddled away onto a lake of glass beneath a warm, blue sky.

We glided up to the sand spit at our prearranged pickup site and spread our gear on the sand so that the pilot could more easily see us from the air. The morning grew hotter, and we talked of our first meal back in Fort Smith.

"I don't know whether to have beer and burgers, or beer and pizza. All I know is that I really want a cold beer."

"Me too," Kathleen agreed. "Maybe Doug the pilot will bring us a cold beer."

"That would be great. Not likely, though. But that sure would be great."

Around noon, just as arranged by satellite phone at Siltaza Lake, we heard, and then saw, the Cessna 185 flying in low from the southwest. Our pickup was coming. Pretty darned exciting.

The float plane taxied up to the spit, and Doug stepped out holding a small box. "Are you guys thirsty? Would you like a cold beer?"

As I write these words, I'm staring directly into the page and holding my right hand up, just like Jack Paar, as though taking an oath. It really happened. Just like that. I kid you not.

We sucked in the beautiful liquid, as we stood in the hot sun on an isolated sandy spit on the north shore of Austin Lake. After Doug lashed our canoe onto the pilot-side pontoon, I helped him load our gear into the plane. I then climbed into the back, with our gear, while Kathleen stepped into the co-pilot's seat. We taxied east up the lake and lifted off the water. Our adventure was now truly over.

It seemed like three adventures in one trip. The challenge of finding our way, with compass and maps, from the outlet of Lynx Lake to the upper end of Whitefish Lake. The joy of heading over the height of land and then down the disappearing water below Sandy Lake. When I stood strong and still young—running rapids, portaging through the boreal forest, dragging and pushing our canoe through an unending labyrinth of impenetrable rock gardens. Then, to drift easily down the Snowdrift River, camping in a park-like setting every night. Alone in the wild isolation of northern Canada. Just me, the loons, the moose, the muskox, and my willing, supportive, necessary, and much appreciated adventuring partner, otherwise and forever after, known as Cupcake.

PROPOSED SNOWDRIFT RIVER ITINERARY (2001)

Date	Activity	Kilometres		Miles	
		Daily	Total	Daily	Total
July 2	Fly to Lynx Lake	0	0	0	0
July 3	Revisit beginning of Thelon River	0	0	0	0
July 4	NE entry to island-studded channel	13	13	8	8
July 5	Near tip of peninsula on north shore	14	27	9	17
July 6	Entering channel in west arm of Lynx Lake	14	41	9	26
July 7	Esker at Lynx Creek	20	61	12	38
July 8	Hiking, resting & fishing at Lynx Creek	0	61	0	38
July 9	North end of LaRogue Bay	15	76	9	47
July 10	North side of western promontory of Whitefish Lake	20	96	12	60
July 11	Narrows in outlet of Whitefish Lake	18	114	11	71
July 12	Rapid leaving Whitefish Lake	13	127	8	79
July 13	Over height of land to Sandy Lake	7	134	4	83
July 14	Hiking & resting at Sandy Lake	0	134	0	83
July 15	Outlet rapid below Sandy Lake	24	158	15	98
July 16	Hiking & resting at outlet rapid below Sandy Lake	0	158	0	98
July 17	End of 4th rapid below Sandy Lake	12	170	7	105
July 18	Ingstad Creek rapid	20	190	12	117
July 19	Hiking on esker at Ingstad Creek	0	190	0	117
July 20	Ed's "Waterfall Rapid"	13	203	9	126
July 21	Double bend on river	12	215	7	133
July 22	Bend toward west	30	245	19	152
July 23	Bend toward south	27	272	17	169
July 24	Siltaza Lake	20	292	12	181
July 25	Outlet of Siltaza Lake	17	309	11	192
July 26	East end of Austin Lake	15	324	9	201
July 27	Cabins half way down Austin Lake	6	330	4	205
July 28	Hiking & resting at Austin Lake	0	330	7	205
July 29	Fly back to Fort Smith				

MAPS FROM THE
CANADIAN NATIONAL TOPOGRAPHIC SYSTEM

1:50,000

    75 J/14 Lake of Woe

    75 J/13 Fabien Lake

    75 J/12 Triangular Lake

    75 K/9 White Quartz Lake

1:250,000

    75 I Beaverhill Lake

    75 J Lynx Lake

    75 K Reliance

    75 L Snowdrift

1:1,000,000

    NP-12/13 Lockhart River

CHAPTER 6

REFLECTIONS

A s I read my journals of these four river trips, I was often quite surprised at how much of the information and stories I had forgotten after nearly two decades: Coppermine River (1995), Seal River (1997), Anderson River (1999) and Snowdrift River (2001). That's a lot of time gone by. Time gone by scary fast. For me, these stories that occurred so long ago are almost historical. And, in fact, our book about the Thelon River trip in 1993 is shelved in the History section of the Vancouver Public Library. How humbling is that, I ask you?

As I wrote in my journal at the end of the Snowdrift River trip, "I always wonder, at the end of each trip, if this will indeed be the last time." Well, it wasn't quite the last time. But almost. In 2003, Kathleen and I paddled the Dease River in northern British Columbia with two other couples plus some friends of mine from childhood. Then, in 2004, with one other couple, Kathleen and I paddled the Arctic Red River in the Northwest Territories. But nothing since then. That's been 10 years. Way too long.

There's a good reason for this, though. Kathleen and I moved to Pender Island in 2003 after we retired from the University of British Columbia. Pender Island is one of the Gulf Islands, about halfway between Vancouver and Victoria. Summer was certainly the best time to enjoy Pender Island, and we spent a lot of time ocean canoeing, which was interesting but not nearly as interesting for me as paddling for a month or more down a northern Canadian wilderness river.

Winters on Pender Island were cool, rainy, soggy and grey. Kathleen and I needed the sun. Pender Island offered rural amenities, but Kathleen and I needed more isolation. So, near the end of winter in 2006, we drove to Dawson City in the Yukon. From there we travelled by snowmobile 12 km down the Yukon River to a cabin, where we stayed two months, caring for 29 sled dogs and waiting for the tumultuous moment when we would see the Yukon River burst free from its immense load of ice. Certainly quite exciting, but not nearly as exciting for me as paddling for a month or more down a northern Canadian wilderness river.

In September of 2007, Kathleen and I drove to Inuvik in the Northwest Territories to house and dog sit for our friends Alan and Marilyn Fehr, who were away in Ottawa until February 2008. This is when we met five beautiful sled dogs named Brownie, Grey, Patsy, Sailor and Slick. We quickly fell in love with those dogs. As you probably know, it's very easy to fall in love with a dog. In 2008, Alan and Marilyn moved to Prince Albert, Saskatchewan. Somewhat by coincidence, Kathleen and I also moved to Saskatchewan, on a secluded property of 230 ha (565 acres). Brownie, Grey, Sailor and Slick joined us there, as did Patsy, four years later.

Since then, Kathleen and I have devoted ourselves to caring for our sled dogs. Our priority has been their health, comfort and happiness. We wanted them, and they needed us. There was no time for me and Kathleen to be paddling for a month or more down a northern Canadian wilderness river. But oh, how I missed venturing out onto the Barren Grounds. And the calendar pages kept turning.

In 2008, three of our sled dogs were nine years old, and two were 11. We lost Brownie in 2011 and Grey in 2012. Sailor passed away on Boxing Day in 2013. Patsy died in June of 2014, leaving behind her brother Slick, who is 15 years old. He now goes for only short walks and spends lots of time lying around and contemplating life. Sometimes he chases Robins off his property. Sometimes he becomes annoyed with squirrels. But mostly he just lies around, dozing and waiting for his next meal. Sort of like me.

My point is, we now have only one dog, and he is easy to care for. Our friend Marilyn Fehr has volunteered to come house and dog sit for us for two weeks this summer so that Kathleen and I can go on a canoe trip. It will be a short trip of only 105 km—on the Paull River in Saskatchewan. This short trip is perhaps best for us. The other day I was going through some slides of my 1990 trip down the South Nahanni River. There were several images of me and Kathleen taken a quarter of a century ago. We definitely looked much more fit and oh so much younger. Last week I accidentally caught a glimpse of myself as I walked by a full-length mirror. Not a pretty sight—I looked like a 66-year-old man. A geezer, if you will.

The Paull River, according to Laurel Archer's guidebook *Northern Saskatchewan Canoe Trips: A Guide to Fifteen Wilderness Rivers*, flows through Precambrian Shield country, and has many drops and pools. Laurel lists 17 potential portages, with two of them approximately 1 km long. So, the Paull River offers an excellent test of whether or not Kathleen and I still have the physical ability to paddle for a month or more down a northern Canadian wilderness river. And by northern, I mean out onto the Barren Grounds.

I hope that we pass this test. I gotta go back to the Barren Grounds. I have to return to that Arctic oasis where I felt so much contentment just being alone with Kathleen on the river. I crave that unbroken silence, and the simplicity of standing, as people were meant to stand, surrounded by wild, nurturing isolation—forever adventuring—forever strong—and dare we hope, no matter what our age, forever young.

We crave that unbroken silence,
and the simplicity of standing,
as people were meant to stand,
surrounded by wild, nurturing isolation.

REFERENCES

Archer, Laurel. *Northern Saskatchewan Canoe Trips: A Guide to Fifteen Wilderness Rivers.* Boston Mills Press. 2003.

Back, Admiral Sir George. *Arctic Artist: The Journals and Paintings of George Back, Midshipman with Franklin, 1819–1822.* Edited by C. Stuart Houston. McGill-Queen's University Press. 1994.

Burt, Page. *Barrenland Beauties – Showy Plants of the Arctic Coast.* Outcrop Ltd. 1991.

Canadian Heritage Rivers System. *Seal River: Manitoba.* Manitoba Department of Natural Resources Parks Branch. Undated.

Franklin, John Sir. *Journey to the Polar Sea.* Conway Maritimes Press. 2000.

Gahlinger, Paul M. *Northern Manitoba: From Forest to Tundra – A Canoeing Guide and Wilderness Companion.* G. B. Communications. 1995.

Hohn, E. O. *Roderick MacFarlane of Anderson River and Fort.* The Beaver. Winter 1963.

Hood, Robert. *To the Arctic by Canoe, 1819–1821: The Journal and Paintings of Robert Hood, Midshipman with Franklin.* Edited by C. Stuart Houston. McGill-Queen's University Press. 1974.

Jason, Victoria. *Kabloona in the Yellow Kayak: One Woman's Journey through the Northwest Passage.* Turnstone Press. 1995.

Johnson, Derek, Linda Kershaw, Andy MacKinnon and Jim Pojar. *Plants of the Western Boreal Forest & Aspen Parkland.* Lone Pine Publishing. 1995.

Johnson, Karen L. *Wildflowers of Churchill and the Hudson Bay Region. Manitoba Museum of Man and Nature.* 1987.

MacFarlane, R. *On an Expedition down the Begh-Ula or Anderson River.* Canadian Record of Science. 1890.

MacKinnon, Andy, Jim Pojar and Ray Coupé. *Plants of Northern British Columbia.* Lone Pine Publishing. 1992.

Mackay, J. Ross. *The Valley of the Lower Anderson River, N.W.T.* Geographical Bulletin 11. The Queen's Printer. 1959.

McCreadie, Mary (ed.). *Canoeing Canada's Northwest Territories: A Paddler's Guide.* Canadian Recreational Canoeing Association. 1995.

Madsen, Ken and Graham Wilson. *Rivers of the Yukon: A Paddling Guide.* Primrose Publishing. 1989.

Mason, Bill. *Path of the Paddle: An Illustrated Guide to the Art of Canoeing.* Key Porter Books. 1984.

Mason, Bill. *Song of the Paddle: An Illustrated Guide to Wilderness Canoeing.* Key Porter Books. 1988.

Mowat, Farley. *Tundra.* McClelland & Stewart Inc. 1973.

Pielou, E. C. *A Naturalists' Guide to the Arctic.* University of Chicago Press. 1994.

Pitt, Kathleen and Michael Pitt. *Three Seasons in the Wind: 950 Kilometres by Canoe down Northern Canada's Thelon River.* Second Edition. Hornby House Publications. 2000.

Pitt, Michael D. *Beyond the End of the Road: A Winter of Contentment North of the Arctic Circle.* Agio Publishing House. 2009.

Richardson, John, Sir. *Arctic Ordeal: The Journal of John Richardson Surgeon-Naturalist with Franklin, 1820–1822.* (Edited by C. Stuart Houston.) McGill-Queen's University Press. 1984.

Stager, John K. *Fort Anderson: The First Post for Trade in the Western Arctic.* Geographical Bulletin. 1967.

Struzik, Ed. *Explorers' Guide: Snowdrift River.* Northwest Territories River Profiles. Undated.

Travel Manitoba. *Land of Little Sticks Routes.* Manitoba Department of Natural Resources Parks Branch. Undated.

Wilson, Hap. *River of Fire in the Land of the Sayisi Dene.* Canadian Recreational Canoeing Association, Kanawa Magazine. Winter 1995.

Wilson, Hap and Stephanie Aykroyd. *Wilderness Rivers of Manitoba: Journey by Canoe through the Land Where the Spirit Lives.* Boston Mills Press. 2004.

APPENDIX 1

KILOMETRE AND MILE EQUIVALENCIES

Kilometres	Miles
1	0.6
3	1.8
5	3.1
10	6.2
15	9.3
20	12.4
30	18.6
40	24.8
50	31.0
100	62.0
200	124.0
300	186.0
400	248.0
500	310.0

APPENDIX 2

CELSIUS AND FAHRENHEIT EQUIVALENCIES

Celsius	Fahrenheit
0	32
5	41
10	50
15	59
20	68
25	77
30	86
35	95
40	104

APPENDIX 3

COMMON AND SCIENTIFIC NAMES
OF PLANTS MENTIONED IN THIS BOOK

The plants mentioned in this book have been listed below, in alphabetical order by common name rather than according to botanical groupings. Common names for plants often differ among regions and botanical references. I have provided the scientific names in parentheses so that you will know to what plant I am referring. My editor, Tracey Hooper, has pointed out that the current official list of common and scientific names for North American plants is presented by the organization NatureServe on their website explorer. natureserve.org. The names presented by NatureServe often differed from the names presented in my somewhat outdated botanical references. Where appropriate, I have included my best interpretation of the common and/or scientific name now preferred by NatureServe.

I have not included a similar appendix for bird species mentioned in this book, as common names for birds are essentially the "official" names. There should be virtually no variation in the common names of birds across regions or among more recent bird identification references.

> Alpine-Azalea (*Loiseleuria procumbens*)
>
> Bear Root (*Hedysarum alpinum*); Alpine Sweet-vetch at NatureServe
>
> Black Spruce (*Picea mariana*)
>
> Black-tipped Groundsel (*Senecio lugens*)
>
> Bluejoint (*Calamagrostis canadensis*)
>
> Bog Birch (*Betula glandulosa*); likely *Betula pumula* var. *glandulifera* at NatureServe

Bog Laurel (*Kalmia microphylla*); considered synonymous with *K. polifolia* by some

Bog Rosemary (*Andromeda polifolia*)

Bunchberry (*Cornus canadensis*); Dwarf Dogwood at NatureServe

Cloudberry (*Rubus chamaemorus*)

Common Butterwort (*Pinguicula vulgaris*)

Common Horsetail (*Equisetum arvense*); Field Horsetail at NatureServe

Common Juniper (*Juniperus communis*); likely *Juniperus communis* var. *montana* at NatureServe

Crowberry (*Empetrum nigrum*); Black Crowberry at NatureServe

Mouse-ear Chickweed (*Cerastium arvense*)

Fireweed (*Epilobium angustifolium*); *Chamerion epilobium* at NatureServe

Green Alder (*Alnus crispa*); *Alnus viridis* at NatureServe

Jack Pine (*Pinus banksiana*)

Kinnnikinnick (*Arctostaphylos uva-ursi*)

Least Willow (*Salix herbacea*); New England Dwarf Willow at NatureServe

Lapland Lousewort (*Pedicularis lapponica*); Northern Lousewort at NatureServe

Lapland Rosebay (*Rhododendron lapponicum*); Lapland Azalea at NatureServe

Large-flowered Wintergreen (*Pyrola grandiflora*); Arctic Wintergreen at NatureServe

Labrador Tea (*Ledum groenlandicum*); Common Labrador Tea at NatureServe

Marsh Ragwort (*Senecio congestus*)

Moss Campion (*Silene acaulis*)

Mountain Avens (*Dryas integrifolia*); Entireleaf Mountain-avens at NatureServe

Northern Bog Violet (*Viola nephrophylla*)

Northern Comandra (*Geocalum lividum*)

Northern Sweet-vetch (*Hedysarum mackenzeii*); Boreal Sweet-vetch (*Hedysarum* boreale ssp. *mackenziei*) at NatureServe

Paper Birch (*Betula papyrifera*)

Pink Corydalis (*Corydalis sempervirens*); Pale Corydalis at NatureServe

Prickly Saxifrage (*Saxifraga tricuspidata*)

Purple Paintbrush (*Castilleja raupii*); Raup's Indian-paintbrush at NatureServe

Red Bearberry (*Arctostaphylos rubra*); Red Manzanita at NatureServe

Rock Cranberry (*Vaccinium vitis-idaea*); Mountain Cranberry at NatureServe

Sea-shore Chamomile (*Matricaria ambigua*); False Chamomile (*Tripleurospermum maritima*) at NatureServe

Shrubby Cinquefoil (*Potentilla fruiticosa*); *Dasiphora fruiticosa* at NatureServe

Spike-like Goldenrod (*Solidago spathulata*); Likely Mt. Albert Goldenrod (*Solidago simplex* var. *spathulata*) at NatureServe

Tall Jacob's-Ladder (*Polemonium acutiflorum*)

Tamarack (*Larix laricina*); American Larch at NatureServe

Twinflower (*Linnaea borealis*)

Water Birch (*Betula occidentalis*); Spring Birch at NatureServe

White Spruce (*Picea glauca*)

Wild Chives (*Allium schoenoprasum*); likely Chives at NatureServe

Willow (*Salix spp.*)